Uncle John's
BATHROOM READER.

GOLDEN PLUNGER AWARDS

AWARDS

Uncle John's
BATHROOM
READER
GOLDEN
PLUNGER
AWARDS

By the
Bathroom Readers' Institute

Ashland, Oregon, and San Diego, California

Uncle John's Bathroom Reader
Golden Plunger Awards

For information, write The Bathroom Readers' Institute
10350 Barnes Canyon Road, Suite 100, San Diego, CA 92121
e-mail: unclejohn@btol.com

ISBN 13: 978-1-59223-853-8
ISBN 10: 1-59223-853-X

Library of Congress Cataloging-in-Publication Data
Uncle John's bathroom reader golden plunger awards.
p. cm.
ISBN-13: 978-1-59223-853-8 (pbk.)
1. Popular culture—United States—Miscellanea. 2. United
States—Social life and customs—Miscellanea. 3. United States—
Intellectual life—Miscellanea. 4. Popular culture—Miscellanea.
5. Manners and customs—Miscellanea. 6. Intellectual life—
Miscellanea.
E169.1.U525 2008
306.0973—dc22
                                        2008004559

Printed in the United States
First printing: June 2008

08 09 10 11 12   10 9 8 7 6 5 4 3 2 1

THANK YOU!

*The Bathroom Readers' Institute sincerely thanks
the following people whose advice, assistance,
and hard work made this book possible.*

Gordon Javna

JoAnn Padgett

Melinda Allman

Amy Miller

Julia Papps

John Hogan

Bethanne Kelly Patrick

Michael Brunsfeld

Thom Little

Brian Boone

Jay Newman

Jeff Altemus

Angela Kern

Dan Mansfield

Bonnie Vandewater

Sydney Stanley

Laurel Graziano

Monica Maestas

Lisa Meyers

Ginger Winters

David Calder

vi

CONTENTS

LET US ENTERTAIN YOU

WORDS TO THE WISE

INTRODUCTION

Here's just what the world needs . . . more awards. But these aren't your typical Oscars, Emmys, Peabodys, or even Espys—they're the Golden Plunger Awards! Bestowed upon the world's unsung heroes, we celebrate enduring, odd, and obscure marvels from ancient history all the way to today. Without this book, these people, places, and things would probably never win anything. Okay, maybe a few have been honored, but they've never gotten the Golden Plunger treatment. For example:

- The golf tee, little black dress, and other things so simple and effective that they haven't changed in decades

- Feats of the weird: the woman who turned herself into a cat, the corniest palace, the stinkiest cheese, and the hungry "athlete" who excels at gurgitating plenty without regurgitating any

- Timeless toys, such as Play-Doh, Donkey Kong, and Hot Wheels (and Matchbox, too)

- The biggest accomplishments from the smallest room, such as a wedding dress made out of TP, enviro-toilets, and how the rubber duck floated its way into the sea of scientific knowledge

- Enduring icons—from the martini to Marilyn Monroe to the Chrysler Building—and why they're still as popular as ever

Warning: the Golden Plunger Awards are not controversy-free. Based on some of the "lively" debates we've had around the office (like whether or not vanilla is better than chocolate, or mayonnaise is better than ketchup), we can only imagine what kind of reactions may be coming our way. But while you may not agree with every award, we guarantee you'll emerge from this book somewhat wiser . . . and definitely more opinionated. And for that, you deserve your own Golden Plunger Award!

—Uncle John and the GPA Committee
(and Porter the Wonderdog)

THE GURGITATOR AWARD

Competitive Eating

Some people don't need to be told to finish their plates.

LET THE GAMES BEGIN

New Yorkers know how to make a hot dog. They know how to stuff one down, too. The first Nathan's Fourth of July International Hot Dog Eating Contest was held in 1916 at New York's Coney Island. The contest not only endured but also went on to become the most famous match in the sport of competitive eating. In 2007, an estimated 40,000 spectators journeyed to Coney Island to watch.

Did we say sport? You bet we did. Nathan's hot dog–eating contest is broadcast on ESPN, and the competition is overseen by the International Federation of Competitive Eating (IFOCE), whose contests are supervised and have strict rules:

- Any vomiting during the match results in immediate disqualification.

- Liquid can be used only as a dip to help the food go down more easily.

- Competitors can eat items individually—in other words, eat the hot dog and then the bun—or together.

In the 2007 contest, Joey "Jaws" Chestnut, of San Jose, California, scored a major upset against six-time champion Takeru Kobayashi of Japan. Chestnut, a relative newcomer to the competitive eating field, has managed to become a major player in just a few years. Not only did he win in 2007, but he also set a new world record: 66 hot dogs in 12 minutes. In 2008, he claimed top honors in two other contests: 78 matzo balls in 8 minutes in Houston, Texas, and 241 chicken wings in the Wing Bowl (held before

---

Bless you! In Italian, "ah-choo" is spelled *ecci ecci.*

the Super Bowl) in Philadelphia. In all, he holds 16 world records in competitive eating, from waffles to pulled pork to asparagus, and is currently the top-ranked gurgitator—that's what contest participants are called in the field.

THE REIGNING QUEEN

Chestnut isn't the only hungry champion to make a name for himself. Sonya "the Black Widow" Thomas of Virginia is currently ranked fifth in the world and holds the record for women in the Nathan's Famous hot dog-eating contest (37 hot dogs in 12 minutes). At 5'5" and weighing just 100 pounds, Sonya holds several world records:

- 48 soft chicken tacos in 11 minutes

- 46 crab cakes in 10 minutes

- 44 Maine lobsters in 12 minute

- 65 hard-boiled eggs in under 7 minutes

- 11 pounds of cheesecake in 9 minutes

- 552 Acme oysters in 10 minutes. (This is the record she says she's most proud of.)

That's a lot of food for such a small person. The United States Department of Agriculture estimates that physically active women between 31 and 50 years of age should have from 2,000 to 2,200 calories a day. A Nathan's Famous hot dog has 309 calories, meaning Thomas had 11,433 calories on the day she ate 37 of them (or nearly a week's worth of calories in one meal). Thomas says that she thinks she can handle up to 18 pounds of food and liquid overall and that her body digests her large feasts in 8 to 12 hours. She maintains that she doesn't get sick after a contest.

THE STAKES (AND STEAKS) GET BIGGER

In the sport of competitive eating, as moderated by IFOCE, timing is key. Events are monitored, and the battle is over in a set amount of time. But amateur eating contests go on all over the world, usually sponsored by restaurants, and they often don't limit contestants on time. For their troubles, the eaters usually get the meal free—and sometimes a T-shirt. Consider these (there are thousands more):

- **AJ's Steakhouse in Grinnell, Iowa:** The restaurant regularly offers an 80-ounce (five-pound) steak challenge, but to celebrate its one-year anniversary in 2001, AJ's served up a 205-ounce sirloin. No one was able to finish it, but one man, Denny McNurlen, got down 155 ounces.

- **The Kestrel Inn, Staffordshire, England:** The Kestrel Inn offers a record-setting 220-ounce steak. (That's almost 14 pounds!) A sign warns people who order it to "Bring a doctor."

- **Roma's Pizza, Augusta, Georgia:** Anyone who can eat a 28-inch cheese-only pizza in 90 minutes or less gets $200.

- **Charlie Parker's, Springfield, Illinois:** The restaurant serves pancakes in a 16-inch pizza pan, but the contest is to eat a big stack: four of them. Do it and the pancakes are free.

- **Mr. Bill's, Las Cruces, New Mexico:** A six-pound burger with all the fixin's is the challenge here, and it must be finished in 30 minutes or less.

- **Swingbelly's Beach Side BBQ, Long Beach, New York:** This challenge is big. It includes not one but five barbecue items: a slab of ribs, a quarter pound of pulled pork, a quarter pound beef brisket, four chicken wings, and three rib tips. But wait, there's more: contestants also have to eat two side dishes and a piece of cornbread.

- **Bubi's Awesome Eats, Windsor, Ontario, Canada:** A big challenge and a big prize—anyone who can eat an eight-pound burger with four toppings in 90 minutes or less wins $1,000.

A note from Uncle John: Anyone thinking of trying one of these contests would do well to remember that health professionals also recommend against it. Consuming so many calories isn't healthy, they say; plus choking and damaging the stomach by overfilling it are risks.

THAT WAS DELICIOUS! WHAT'S NEXT?

Food-eating records range from some delicious foods to some truly questionable choices. Ukrainian gurgitator Oleg Zhornitskiy once ate 128 ounces of mayonnaise in eight minutes. Don Lerman indulged in seven quarter-pound sticks of butter; he also ate 120 jalapeño peppers in 15 minutes and seven pounds of cow brains (in a different contest, which he didn't win). Yum.

THE TOO GOOD TO BE TRUE AWARD

Diet Scams

If you're ready to lose weight, put down that brownie and hit the gym. But if you're ready to lose weight while eating everything you want and not exercising at all, read on.

FAT AND PROUD OF IT

In 1866, the Fat Man's Club of Connecticut was formed for tubby guys to show off. If you could afford to gain weight, you must be doing something right. But by 1903, the club had to close. In just 37 years, American eating habits had changed so much that weight gain was no longer seen as a status symbol of the wealthy. That opened the door for the diet scam industry to gain prominence in the nation.

THIS DIET IS KILLING ME

A rush on diet products ensued at the turn of the century, and pills were particularly popular. Pills promising rapid weight loss hit the market, and even though they were largely viewed as "snake-oil" treatments, they were popular with overweight Americans for decades. It was easier to market fad pills and drinks in the early part of the 20th century because there was no effective Food and Drug Administration oversight until 1930. Prior to that, there was an agency that would become the FDA (it had been established by Theodore Roosevelt in 1906), but it was severely hampered by poorly written laws.

In the 1930s, dinitrophenol—previously used to make dyes and explosives, and also an ingredient in weed killers—was introduced in pill form as a diet aid. Approximately 100,000 people tried it out. So many deaths and injuries were attributed to the drug that it was banned in 1933 by the FDA. Even so, the drug found a

---

Studies show: English speakers say "uh" before a short pause and "um" before a long pause.

home on the black market—particularly in image-conscious Los Angeles—despite the fact that it had been linked to blindness, cataracts, nerve damage, heart disease, and death.

THE WORM TURNS
Probably the most famous rumor associated with diet pills is that they had tapeworms inside them. It especially gained popularity in the 1950s, but there is no evidence that tapeworms were used in a pill available then. However, there is some evidence that between 1900 and 1920, tapeworms were included in diet pills and that those early ads resurfaced in the 1950s, giving credence to the rumor. (Web sites that debunk rumors also note that verifying whether or not tapeworms were actually included in these early pills is still difficult because ads for early medical miracle cures often contained false claims.)

THE SKINNY
In America alone, 50 million people go on a diet every year. More than 15 percent of those people—about 8 million—try to do it in a structured program with supervision. The only real solution is simple: eat fewer calories, exercise more, and lose weight. Nevertheless, if someone offers a way to avoid a sacrifice that dieters don't want to make, people have a tendency to believe less-than-logical explanations. As one person said, "I think it's enticing. It's the microwave effect—you want to have instant results." And it's just that attitude that fuels the diet industry, which rakes in about $40 billion per year from Americans alone.

THE SCAMS
The following are typical diet scams:

- **Calorie-burning or metabolism-boosting pills:** The pills typically contain herbal ingredients, which are not regulated by the FDA. They claim to speed up your metabolism so that you burn fat faster, but doctors say they may increase your chances for a heart attack because the pills often raise blood pressure.

- **Carbohydrate- and fat-blocking pills:** These pills interfere with the body's ability to process important nutrients, and bloating, gas, and diarrhea are all side effects.

King Henry III of France liked to walk the streets with a basket of puppies around his neck.

- **Herbal weight-loss teas:** Caffeine is a main ingredient in many teas, not just weight-loss teas, and it is a diuretic. Losing water may result in a temporary weight loss, but it is not the same as losing fat.

- **Diet patch:** While patches have helped people quit smoking, no effective weight-loss drugs can be delivered through the skin.

STAYING SCAM-FREE

The Federal Trade Commission monitors weight-loss scams and false claims. Its Web site lists several warning signs of diet scams:

1. Claims of losing two or more pounds per week.

2. Products that promise you can eat whatever you want and still lose weight.

3. Permanent weight loss.

4. The ability to block fat or calorie absorption.

5. Weight loss of more than three pounds a week for more than four weeks in a row.

6. Claims that the product works the same for everyone.

7. Creams, patches, wraps, earrings, and things to be worn or applied to the body to lose weight.

Despite this, ads for weight-loss scams regularly appear on TV and in magazines, with most promising at least one of these results. Let's back up a second here. Weight-loss earrings? Say that again?

It's true. Companies sell magnetic earrings that supposedly work on pressure points around the ear to stimulate weight loss. Eyeglasses and other products that hang on the ear are also available. Not surprisingly, no measurable weight-loss results have ever been recorded from these in any scientific tests.

Thousands of years ago, our ancestors ate a very different diet. Grains, fruits, vegetables, and meats, for the most part, along with nuts and other legumes, were the norm. They didn't need to be put on a diet. But if someone had tried to sell them magnetic earrings . . . well, they probably might have fallen for it, too.

The ostrich is the only bird with eyelashes.

THE THREE LITTLE PIGS AWARD, #1

South Dakota's Corn Palace

*The buildings of Frank Gehry and Frank Lloyd Wright
shouldn't get all the glory, so Uncle John has singled out
three unique buildings for recognition. Here's
the first one. A-maize-ing!*

IF YOU BUILD IT, THEY WILL COME

The town fathers of Mitchell, South Dakota, wanted to showcase the agricultural richness of their region to attract more settlers. Their idea: "corn palace"—a large building decorated with corn and other locally grown grains. The Corn Palace *has* succeeded in bringing tourists to South Dakota—as many as half a million annually—but there aren't any statistics on how many people stayed because of the building's grainy glory.

The original Palace was built in 1892, but it took two more attempts to get the right-sized structure. The third and current building was built in 1921 and is located right on Main Street. The actual structure isn't made of corn; its foundation and walls are reinforced concrete. In the 1930s, architects added back the Moorish-inspired minarets and columns of the early palaces, making the whole thing look like something out of *The Arabian Nights*. Every June the corn, rye, and dock are torn off and the walls redecorated with locally grown corn. And it's those fresh corn murals that draw the crowds.

GETTING GRAIN-ULAR

Farmers in Mitchell grow tons of maize every year, and the crop, often called "Prairie Gold," rules the town. The local radio station's call letters are KORN, and the town's high-school team is the Kernels. And plus, the locals are so serious about their

---

The first draft of John Steinbeck's classic novel *Of Mice and Men* was eaten by his dog.

corny Palace that they've failed to decorate it only twice in 116 years:

- In 1943, when building materials like nails were needed for the war effort.
- In 2006, when a drought decimated the crops. The citizens of Mitchell decided to leave the 2006 murals and decorations up through 2007, but after awhile, the effects of wind, sun, moisture, and critters had the Corn Palace looking faded and fragmented. Fortunately, the 2007 crop was normal, meaning a new 2008 set of ear-tastic art could be created.

CORN-BY-NUMBERS ART

The 2008 Corn Palace mural designer, Cherie Ramsdell, an Assistant Professor of Art at Dakota Wesleyan University, has been choosing themes and sketching "corn by numbers" art since 2003. Themes have included "Everyday Heroes," "Lewis and Clark," "Youth in Action," "South Dakota Birds," and "Space Exploration."

Once the murals' sketches are done, transferred to tar paper, and tacked to the concrete, construction begins. The initial design work starts in the spring, and installation begins in the summer. Common colors or shades of corn used in the designs: red, brown, black, blue, white, orange, calico, yellow, and even green. The assembly is a precision job: each corncob is carefully sliced in half with a power saw, the two halves are trimmed with hand axes as necessary for detail work, and finally, they are nailed in place.

IT'S FOR THE BIRDS

While corn is king, other grains are also used: wheat, rye, and sorghum. All this material doesn't come cheap: it costs $130,000 each year for the thousands of bushels of grain and 100,000 corncobs. But the decoration costs are made back during August's Corn Palace Week, which celebrates the end of the harvest. Once Corn Palace Week is over, local fauna are allowed to feast on the building, giving the Corn Palace the unusual designation of being the world's largest birdfeeder.

The other Three Little Pigs Awards can be found on pages 52 and 208.

Harpo Marx once tried to adopt Shirley Temple.

THE OLDEST TRICK IN THE BOOK AWARD

The Nigerian Scam

Well known as the bane of e-mail users everywhere, the old "Nigerian trick" has actually been scamming people long before the Internet age. This award is your warning to beware of this con.

PSST!
You know the con—here's how it goes: Someone is in trouble, usually in Nigeria, hence the name, but other countries are also used. The person, allegedly a wealthy refugee, is blindly contacting someone outside the country to ask for help. The subject line of his e-mail usually reads something like "Urgent Business Transaction." The writer is very polite, but he sounds desperate. He has a lot of money, though it's tied up in a bank. The authorities are after him—sometimes because of a political uprising in his home country; other times because of the actions of a dictator—so he must be discreet. If you will only help, through a kind donation, you will receive a large sum of money for your trouble as soon as he's free. Just send a few thousand dollars, and later, you'll be rewarded with much more.

HEY, SUCKER!

For many, the Nigerian scam sounds too good to pass up. Some people lose a few hundred dollars, but some fall hard. Victims have been lured to Nigeria or elsewhere to collect their imaginary winnings and have wound up in lots of trouble. The U.S. State Department has issued warnings about people who travel to meet the people behind the e-mails and end up "beaten, subjected to threats and extortion, and in some cases murdered." This crime is serious business.

Apollo 11 had only 30 seconds of fuel left when it landed safely on Earth.

BEWARE THE SPANISH PRISONER

The Nigerian scam has been around for decades—before e-mail, it was perpetrated through letters. But it seems to be based on an even older con: the Spanish Prisoner. This scheme involves a poor soul who's been imprisoned in Spain. But, as luck would have it, the prisoner is wealthy. He just can't access his money to extricate himself from his dilemma. If you could help out by loaning him some of your money, once he gets out of prison, you'll be rewarded for your efforts.

The Spanish Prisoner typically targeted wealthy businessmen who were conned into paying for one expensive escape attempt after another until they ran out of money or started asking too many questions.

WHO DEALS WITH IT?

According to the FBI's Internet Crime Complaint Center (IC3), the average amount of money lost in 2006 by someone falling for the Nigerian scam was $5,100. The number of people who actually respond to the Nigerian scam e-mail is estimated to be about 1 percent—about half the response rate for the average direct-mail piece. Although 1 percent sounds small, if you multiply that by the millions of e-mails sent out, it comes to a lot of money.

If you report a Nigerian scam to the FBI, you'll be referred to the Secret Service. Established in 1865 to deal with counterfeiting, the Secret Service protects a lot of America's financial interests, in addition to protecting the president.

According to scambusters.org, the Secret Service fields about 100 calls and from 300 to 500 letters daily from victims or potential victims of the Nigerian e-mail con, which is also called a "419" plan (because that's the number of the Nigerian penal code that covers such fraud).

One of the provisions of the Patriot Act, passed in 2001, ordered the Secret Service to create "a nationwide network of Electronic Crimes Task Forces." A local Secret Service office will handle the case, but these crimes are notoriously difficult to solve. First, the authorities have to find the perpetrator and then transport him to the victim's country for prosecution. (The U.S. government can't prosecute people that are out of its jurisdiction.)

Soldiers from every country in the world salute with their right hands.

In an effort to help, Nigeria established the Economic and Financial Crimes Commission (EFCC) in 2003 to combat the problem and to improve its country's image in the global community. In 2006, the EFCC announced that it would start punishing Internet service providers in Nigeria if they helped the scammers complete their cons. The penalty for not taking proper security measures: up to 20 years in prison.

Still, some scammers find a way to circumspect the laws. Con artists have been able to target people who have contacted the EFCC to report being scammed. Posing as EFCC representatives, they have been able to get personal information out of past victims and use that to access bank accounts. So the scamming continues.

Nigerians would love to put this scandal and its name behind them. But until then, beware the e-mail that begs for help and promises huge rewards in return.

*　　*　　*

I'LL DRINK TO THAT AWARD

- Oldest brewery in the world: The Weihenstephan Brewery in Freising, Germany, founded in 1040.

- Highest alcohol content: Between 1918 and 1940, the Estonian Liquor Monopoly made a potato-based alcohol that was 196 proof, or 98 percent alcohol.

- Highest alcohol content (beer): The Vetter Brauhaus in Heidelberg, Germany, makes a beer that is 33 percent alcohol. Most beer is usually about 8 percent.

- Highest alcohol content (person): An unconscious Latvian man was picked up by the authorities in 2003 with a blood alcohol level of 0.7%. The average person would stop breathing at 0.4%.

- Most expensive wine ever sold: A bottle of 1787 Château Lafite sold at Christie's in December 1985 for $160,000.

- Biggest drinker: A Dutch man known only as Vanhorn drank four bottles of port every day from 1888 until his death in 1911. That amounts to nearly 34,000 bottles of fortified wine.

The *Oxford English Dictionary* lists 49 words that can be used to describe buttocks.

THE GOOD GUY AWARD

Superman

Sure . . . he can fly, leap tall buildings in a single bound, and lift cars over his head, but when it comes right down to it, Superman's just a regular guy—with a dash of super-humanity thrown in for good measure.

NOT JUST ONE OF THE GUYS

Superman is probably the world's most famous superhero. He's endeared himself to fans and become an important part of the American culture. He's classically "good," choosing to help people, even though he could do or have anything he wants. He's not influenced by money or corruption and he intervenes only to right wrongs. Superman also maintains a strict code of conduct: no killing, no matter what. He puts the world's needs ahead of his own, and he never lies.

Superman's costume is not his cape and uniform—those are actually his "real" clothes, sewn from the blankets he was wrapped in inside the rocket ship that brought him to Earth. He disguises himself as the mild-mannered Clark Kent. Even though most superheroes put on a mask to disguise their identities, Superman puts on a business suit and glasses and becomes human.

BIG BLUE BOY SCOUT

His disguise is just one way Superman doesn't match his super-peers. His powers also set him apart. Most superheroes gained their powers through accidents, struggles, or medical experiments:

- Batman trained both his body and mind to become the world's greatest athlete and detective.
- Captain America endured medical experiments to become strong.

At least one UFO abduction is reported in California every day.

- Wonder Woman won a contest against her fellow Amazons.
- The Hulk got zapped by gamma rays.
- Spider-Man got bitten by a radioactive spider.

But not Superman. He got his powers by doing absolutely nothing. And that's a "gift" not appreciated by some of his fellow superheroes—who have been known to mock him by calling him the "big blue Boy Scout."

A REAL MENSCH

Superman was the brainchild of Jerry Seigel and Joe Shuster, who were both living in Ohio during the Great Depression. Seigel, the writer, and Shuster, the artist, spent years creating the character and several more trying to convince someone to publish their story. They contacted several publishers as early as 1932, but it wasn't until Detective Comics, Inc., saw potential in the story and published it in June 1938 that Superman found a home. (A pristine copy of that comic book would sell today for more than $1 million.)

Seigel and Shuster played off various religious motifs in their creation of Superman. His birth name was Kal-El—"El" in Yiddish means "God." Like Moses, little Kal-El was sent off to be raised by others to fulfill a destiny. The concept of the "super man" was also inspired by Friedrich Nietzsche's "übermensch" from his book *Thus Spoke Zarathustra*. Early on, Seigel and Shuster's superhero had tremendous mental abilities like the übermensch, who transcended the laws of humanity to achieve a higher mental state. Later, they settled on a muscle-bound, colorful hero who ultimately didn't share many characteristics with Nietzsche's superman, who didn't follow society's definition of morality but set it for himself. Superman, on the other hand, follows society's (specifically, American society's) definitions almost universally.

Seigel and Shuster developed Superman's powers slowly. First, he merely leaped tall buildings. Later, he flew over them. Super speed, X-ray and heat vision, super breath, super ventriloquism, and the ability to travel through time were added over the years. As his legend grew, so did Superman's abilities.

Sixteen percent of truck drivers say they think of "nothing at all" while driving.

THE AMERICAN WAY

Few heroes, real or fictional, embody the American dream the way Superman does. Like the immigrants of old, Superman arrived in the United States with nothing but was able to succeed both as mild-mannered reporter Clark Kent and as the Man of Steel. His abilities come naturally to him, but Superman does have three vulnerabilities: kryptonite, magic, and a red sun. When exposed to one of his vulnerabilities, Superman loses his superpowers and becomes just a mortal man.

Most of the time, though, Superman has few fears and he always approaches problems with a determination to do what's right. The essence of Superman is not in his bravery—which he has, to be sure—but in his altruism. The ability to look good in tights doesn't hurt either.

*　　*　　*

A BRIEF HISTORY OF KRYPTONITE

Kryptonite first appeared in *Superman #61*, dated December 1949, more than a decade after the hero's debut. The kryptonite was red, not green. Superman, with no idea what the substance was, took a quick trip through time and space to learn of its origins—and his own. After this, normal kryptonite was colored the traditional green.

But other kinds of kryptonite, with various effects on Superman and other beings, were introduced in almost every color of the rainbow. Red kryptonite had unpredictable effects on Superman, often turning him into a monster; gold kryptonite permanently removed any Kryptonian superpowers; blue kryptonite was harmful only to the Bizarro version of Superman; and white kryptonite killed plant life. Other forms of kryptonite came in silver, yellow, black, purple, jewel, and even pink. (With the power to turn Kryptonians gay, pink kryptonite appeared once in a 2003 issue of *Supergirl* as a joke and was never mentioned again.)

Then there were the synthetic kinds and assorted others: anti-kryptonite (deadly to humans), X-kryptonite, kryptonite X (yes, those last two are different), mango-kryptonite, and slow kryptonite.

"Advertising is legalized lying." —H. G. Wells

THE CHEESEY DOES IT AWARD

Cheez Whiz

The next time you're doing the wash, grab the detergent, the fabric softener, and the Cheez Whiz if you want to get out those really tough stains.

DUE PROCESS

In *Clean Your Clothes with Cheez Whiz,* Joey Green revealed alternative uses for a variety of household products, like toothpaste and shaving cream. One of the oddest discoveries was that Cheez Whiz was great at getting out grease stains in clothes.

Cheez Whiz's laundry power comes from its enzymes, which can't gobble up enough grease. Dab some of the spread on a grease-based stain and let it sit for 10 minutes. Then throw the laundry in the washing machine. Enjoy some crackers and Cheez Whiz while you wait for the wash to be done.

HOME ON THE PHILLY

The Philadelphia cheesesteak was invented in 1930 in South Philadelphia, so Cheez Whiz, which didn't make it to market until 1952, couldn't have been part of the original recipe. No matter. Many tried and true Philly cheesesteak lovers swear by it now and consider Cheez Whiz to be the authentic cheesesteak cheese.

Make that three authentic cheeses. No matter what you've heard, there is real cheese in Cheez Whiz: mozzarella, Swiss, and cheddar. Kraft, the maker of Cheez Whiz, combines those cheeses with water and milk products and adds preservatives, emulsifiers, and other additives to make the Whiz nice and yellow and spread-able at room temperature.

Originally created as a topping for crackers, Cheez Whiz soon found a home in lots of foods: in macaroni and cheese, on hot

When Saigon fell, the radio alert for Americans to evacuate was Bing Crosby's "White Christmas."

dogs and nachos, and in dips and sauces. With this much history, it's no wonder Cheez Whiz stands out. It started as a by-product of the 1950s' push to market ease and convenience to housewives across America. Now, though, it's an American food icon. Spread the word.

THE FATHER OF INVENTION

Sadly, on June 5, 2007, the inventor of Cheez Whiz passed away. Edwin Traisman lived a long, robust life, though—he was 91. A Chicago native, he earned a degree in chemistry from the University of Illinois in 1936 and worked for Kraft Foods from 1949 to 1957. It was his food science skills that combined all the right things to make Cheez Whiz—a spreadable processed cheese and a counterpart to Kraft's nonspreadable processed cheese, Velveeta.

Cheez Whiz wasn't Traisman's only contribution to America's popular dining habits. After he left Kraft, Traisman bought into the McDonald's franchise, eventually owning four stores. His food science expertise came into play when McDonald's founder Ray Kroc needed a way to keep all the potatoes used for French fries fresh, so he could have a consistent brand at all his stores. Traisman was up to the challenge. He came up with a flash-cooking process: one minute or so at 300°F to get rid of the potatoes' moisture and then freeze them. The uniform frozen French fry was born.

*   *   *

THE ORIGIN OF ANOTHER CHEESEY PRODUCT

Kraft first marketed Velveeta in 1927. Its main ingredient is whey, a liquid by-product of cheese making (it's the liquid left over when milk hardens to cheese). Cheese manufacturers used to just throw it away, but now it's made into Velveeta, which is officially labeled by the Food and Drug Administration as a "pasteurized processed cheese product." That means it's a cheeselike thing that tastes like cheese but is actually made up of less than 50 percent cheese. Kraft says Velveeta gets its unique flavor from the whey left over from making cheddar, colby, and Swiss cheeses. It gets its unique spongy texture from an added stabilizing agent called carrageenin —a derivative of Irish moss.

THE STAND AND DELIVER AWARD

Richard Pryor

This legendary performer changed the world of stand-up forever and raised the bar for what comedy could be.

R EMEMBERED
When asked about their most profound influences, countless comedic greats—from Sam Kinison to Dave Chappelle—have answered without hesitation: Richard Pryor.

"Richard Pryor is to comedy what Gretzky is to hockey, what Ali is to boxing. He is the Beatles of comedy."
—Paul Rodriguez

"To fully appreciate the power of Richard Pryor as a stand-up comedian, you had to follow him at the Comedy Store. I did once, and I'm lucky to be alive."
—David Letterman

"Richard Pryor is an alchemist who can turn the darkest pain into the deepest comedy. [He] doesn't go for the jugular—he goes straight for the aorta."
—Robin Williams

Pryor introduced a new style of comedy that gave people of all races permission to laugh at themselves and at each other. Though often controversial, vulgar, and brash, his performances empowered other comedians and actors to look inside, to find truth in their art, and to embrace what comes naturally—being honest and being themselves.

A ROCKY ROAD TO STARDOM
Richard Franklin Lennox Thomas Pryor III was born in Peoria,

Illinois, on December 1, 1940. After his mother deserted him when he was 10, Pryor was raised by his grandmother, Madam Marie Carter, in her brothel. His early childhood was a test of emotional endurance, characterized by sexual assault, poverty, and a desperate determination to rise above it all. Expelled from school at age 14, Pryor earned a living by working various odd jobs before joining the army in 1958. Two years later, he was discharged for assaulting another G.I.

THAT'S ENTERTAINMENT

Through it all, Pryor found refuge in the one thing that consistently brought him happiness: performing. Starting with a role in a local production of *Rumpelstiltskin* at age 12, Pryor showcased his comedic gift at every opportunity. But it wasn't until 1963 that his career as a stand-up comedian really started to take shape.

Initially, he was influenced heavily by Bill Cosby, whose performances revolved around clean, funny, family-oriented stories. Pryor performed his Cosby-esque comedy routine to receptive audiences in New York City and quickly made a name for himself. Ed Sullivan, Johnny Carson, and Merv Griffin all invited him to appear on their shows.

Despite his success, Pryor found his family-style comedy to be predictable, repetitive, and unauthentic. He reached his breaking point in the middle of a sold-out performance at the Aladdin Hotel in Las Vegas, when he walked off the stage, feeling restricted by the conventional atmosphere of the upscale Las Vegas hotels of the time. From then on, he became the Richard Pryor the world knows now: a bold, risk-taking performer who would forge new paths for all comedians who followed.

DIAMOND IN THE ROUGH

Pryor moved to Berkeley, California, in 1969 to regroup. During the next few years, the company he kept—people like African American writer Ishmael Reed and the cofounder of the Black Panthers, Huey P. Newton—and the counterculture he observed helped him to grow both as a person and a comic.

Pryor no longer just delivered jokes. Instead, he acted out life as he saw it, bringing real and often taboo topics to the public for the first time: race, sex, drugs, poverty, discrimination, and violence. Mixed-race audiences howled as he paced the stage spewing profanities while slipping in and out of his many personas, including crowd favorite Mudbone, the drunken philosopher. Pryor talked about the ugliness inside people and brought it out for examination; then he'd defuse the animosity and ill will with laughter. His humor was color-blind, and through exaggerated characters and animated, often sexually explicit monologues, Pryor softened the edges of hard truths so that no topic was off limits, not even his private life.

ROUGH STUFF

Pryor wasn't afraid to spotlight his personal demons, of which he had many. From cocaine addiction, tax evasion, and repeated domestic violence charges to serious health issues, his willingness to make himself the object of laughs made it possible for people whose lives bore no resemblance to his to relate to him. After he shot his car full of holes, he joked about how bad drugs were if they could make you do that. After he set himself on fire while freebasing cocaine, he joked about what he had learned: "When you run down the street on fire, people will move out of your way."

His raw, raunchy style of stand-up was clearly not for everyone, but it left many wanting more. His three offensive words (beginning with "M," "N," and "P") included a racial slur and two profanities. Pryor had to be himself and that meant using the honest, foul language of his life to make his experiences universal and funny.

Later, he explained in his autobiography how he'd renounced the use of the "N" word after visiting Africa and noting the people's self-respect. But he also joked, "I went through all the phone books in Africa, and I didn't find one goddamned Pryor."

THE MORE THE MERRIER

Starting in the late 1960s, audiences began getting more Pryor, and in more places. He landed roles in more than 30 films during his career. Among them was his role as Gus Gorman in 1983's *Superman III*, for which he earned rave reviews and a hefty fee of $4 million—$1 million more than Christopher Reeve, Superman himself. In 1974, when the western spoof *Blazing Saddles* was

The Dutch national anthem, "Het Wilhelmus," is the oldest national anthem in the world (1574).

released to critical acclaim, movie audiences experienced a new side of Pryor: screenwriter.

Pryor's television career was equally robust. He proved himself to be extremely versatile, able to capture the hearts of a wide spectrum of audiences, even children, as a host, an actor, and a comedian. Few will forget his 1975 *Saturday Night Live* appearance, where he and Chevy Chase left audiences' mouths agape as they exchanged racial slurs in a skit called "Racist Word Association." And as a writer for hits like *Sanford and Son*, *The Flip Wilson Show*, and two Lily Tomlin specials, Pryor earned recognition and continued to gain respect.

A LIFE WORTH LIVING

Throughout his career, and even posthumously, Pryor has been honored repeatedly for his accomplishments: comedian, actor, director, screenwriter, author, host, animal-rights activist, husband, and father. He earned two platinum albums, five gold albums, five Grammys (for his recorded performances), an Emmy, a Writer's Guild Award, and the first annual Mark Twain Humor Prize, to name a few. For his devotion to animal rights, particularly the protection of baby elephants from circus life, he was honored by the People for the Ethical Treatment of Animals.

Pryor turned every obstacle into a springboard. Through severe drug addiction, a suicide attempt (the freebasing incident, according to his interview with Barbara Walters), seven marriages to five different women, six children, repeated run-ins with the law, and living with multiple sclerosis for nearly 20 years, he still managed to become one of the most beloved characters in show business. His contributions to the art of comedy continue to be celebrated long after his death at age 65 on December 5, 2005.

*　　*　　*

"I went to Zimbabwe. I know how white people feel in America now: relaxed. Cause when I heard the police car, I knew they weren't coming after me!"

—**Richard Pryor**

 # THE LET YOUR FINGERS DO THE TALKING AWARD

Rudest Hand Gestures

A picture is worth a thousand words, but a hand can say so much more.

IN YO' FACE

People have many ways to show their displeasure with someone else: a withering look, a frown, a choice word or two. Then there are the hand gestures. Nothing is worse in terms of rudeness than an in-your-face flick of the hand that says what the lips haven't. Here are our least favorite hand gestures.

DIGITUS INFAMIS

There was a time, not too long ago, when the "F" word was one of the rudest things one could ever utter in the English language. Very few words topped it for effect and impact. Nowadays it's commonplace (though not quite to the point where we can print it here). The correlating hand gesture has similarly become increasingly used in public. That doesn't stop it from being rude, though. For a long time, people have been rightly offended by it, and that's not going to change anytime soon.

Who was first offended by it, though, is up for debate:

- Some accounts of the gesture's origin trace it back to 423 BC, when a Greek playwright named Aristophanes included it in one of his works. A modern translation of his play *The Clouds* features a character giving the finger to Socrates, who calls him a crude buffoon in reply. But scholars debate whether it was actually included as a stage direction.

- Other sources trace it back to the ancient Romans, who are said to have called it the *digitus infamis*—the infamous finger. They may have used that term, but there's no way to know which finger they were talking about.

A third, persistent story is based on the fact that British soldiers in the 1415 Battle of Agincourt during the Hundred Years War used longbows made of yew. When they were captured, the French would cut off their middle fingers, making the English unable to use the bow. English soldiers who were not captured supposedly began showing their middle fingers to the French to show they could still pull the bow.

That story goes to an even further extreme by claiming that the soldiers bragged they could still "pluck yew." Hogwash, linguistic historians say. The longbow-using soldiers at Agincourt were mostly Welsh mercenaries, and it's unlikely that any of them would ever utter the phrase "pluck yew." It's also unlikely that the French had a plan to cut off the fingers of captured soldiers. It's a fun story, though.

However, none of the bird's origin stories offer a realistic explanation for why the gesture is primarily one used by Americans. The obscenity is universal. Many cultures use a finger as a phallic symbol: in Iran, an American "thumbs up" is equivalent to flipping the bird, and Sri Lankans use their index finger. But the middle finger is uniquely American. Movies, television, the Web, and global travel have helped to spread the American version, but for the most part, foreign countries already have their own rude hand gestures and are sticking with them.

Whatever its beginnings, and regardless of how common the "F" word has become in popular culture, flipping the bird remains a top insult . . . and a good reason to keep your hands at your sides before they get you into trouble.

TALK TO THE HAND

This way of saying "Don't bother speaking" gained popularity in the early 1990s, when it was a staple on daytime talk shows. It quickly exploded in common usage. At first, it required the actor not only to extend the arm and put the hand facing up, palm toward the recipient, but also to say the words "Talk to the hand." (The expanded verbal version included "because the face isn't lis-

---

Technically, a drizzle is 14 drops per square feet per second; a light rain is 26 drops.

tening" or "because the face does not understand.") Nowadays, the hand motion alone is sufficient, but a scowl or a head tilt can always be added for extra emphasis.

The palm-outraised hand has been used for decades to signify "stop." There's a notion that "Talk to the hand" originated on *The Jerry Springer Show*, but there's no proof of that. Certainly, guests on that show, which was one of the most popular daytime talk shows during the 1990s, used the phrase a lot and helped to popularize it.

Wherever it began, "Talk to the hand" has earned a distinction as one of the rudest hand gestures. Author Lynne Truss even wrote a book about rudeness in popular culture and titled it *Talk to the Hand*. She wrote in the book:

> I chose it for the title because it's the way I've started to see the world. Nearly 60 years ago, George Orwell wrote in *Nineteen Eighty-Four* that the future was a boot stamping on a human face forever. I see it as a forest of belligerent and dismissive palms held up to the human face instead.

FLICKING THE "V"

When you raise your index and middle fingers and face your palm out, you're either making a peace sign or a "V" for victory sign. If that palm is facing back at you, you're doing the British equivalent of flipping the bird.

The origin of the rude "V" sign is unknown, but it, too, is often thought to have originated at the Battle of Agincourt. Not true, say scholars. Its first recorded use is somewhere around 80 years after that battle. It probably began along with the bird and evolved separately. At least that's the current theory.

More than a few Americans don't know about this little cultural difference or that it extends beyond England to Ireland, Australia, and New Zealand. President George H. W. Bush didn't know when he traveled to Canberra, Australia, in January 1992. From his limo, he gave people on the street the "V" sign, but he faced his palm the wrong way. Oops!

He's not the only one. The rude "V" sign's close relationship to the positive peace and victory signs has spelled trouble for quite a few politicians several times. During World War II, Winston

---

The Amazon River basin could hold the country of France 13 times over.

Churchill made the incorrect gesture at cheering crowds. Rumor has it that aides told him that he was doing the victory sign wrong and he corrected himself from then on. A picture of Margaret Thatcher flicking the "V" circulated back in the 1980s as well.

So there you have it. There are more than a few ways to say something rude with your hands, and they are usually different from culture to culture. So when in doubt, keep your hands to yourself.

*   *   *

"PROFANE" WORDS

"All hockey players are bilingual. They know English and profanity."
—Gordie Howe

"Profanity is the common crutch of the conversational cripple."
—David Keuck

"If profanity had an influence on the flight of the ball, the game of golf would be played far better than it is."
—Horace G. Hutchinson

"In certain trying circumstances, urgent circumstances, desperate circumstances, profanity furnishes a relief denied even to prayer."
—Mark Twain

"Take not God's name in vain. Select a time when it will have effect."
—Ambrose Bierce

"Grant me some wild expressions, heavens, or I shall burst."
—George Farquhar

"Many a man's profanity has saved him from a nervous breakdown."
—Henry S. Haskins

"Swearing relieves the feelings—that is what swearing does. I explained this to my aunt on one occasion, but it didn't answer with her. She said I had no business to have such feelings."
—Jerome K. Jerome

There has never been a left-handed pope.

THE YELLOW TIDE AWARD

Science's Ducky Helpers

They're not just for the bathroom anymore.

THE SCENE

In January 1992, a storm tossed a cargo ship in the middle of the Pacific Ocean. On its deck, a crate of children's bath toys was journeying from China, where they were manufactured, to the United States, home of the company that sells them—plastic turtles, frogs, but mostly rubber ducks.

The cargo ship survived the storm not too much the worse for wear, bit it lost about 29,000 passengers. The storm tossed the giant steel containers holding the plastic toys overboard, smashing open their doors on the high seas. The ducks and fellow fauna survived the fall and made their way into the ocean, where they began a long journey around the globe.

The amazing thing about their trip is how many of them ended up in so many different places. If so many items of like weight, shape, and size were set adrift in one spot in the ocean, why didn't they all wind up in the same place?

THE TRAVELING TOYS

By October 1992, the first ducks had washed up on the shores of Alaska. Within years, others appeared as far away as Hawaii and Massachusetts. Some of the ducks traveled along the Bering Strait, got ensconced in ice, and wound up in Iceland. And in the summer of 2007, more than 15 years after they first hit the waves, more plastic ducks came ashore in Great Britain. They had lost their distinctive yellow coloring, but otherwise were in perfect working order.

Forty percent of all mammal species are rodents.

DRIFTING AWAY

More than just a fun story, the ducks proved invaluable to science thanks to Curtis Ebbesmeyer, a former oceanographer for Mobil Oil (tracking icebergs so tankers could avoid accidents). In 1991, just a year before the ducks were set adrift, Ebbesmeyer read a news story about shoes washing ashore from Oregon up to the Canadian coast. The shoes came from 21 containers that had fallen off of a ship during a storm in the Alaskan peninsula a year earlier; some 61,000 had gone overboard. When he read about their reemergence, Ebbesmeyer was intrigued. When the ducks went overboard in 1992, he knew he was on to something with great potential for scientific study.

In 1996, Ebbesmeyer formed the Beachcombers' and Oceanographers' International Association and set up a Web site called beachcombersalert.org to ask for help from people worldwide in tracking the movements of the rubber ducks and other objects lost at sea. With the help of his global team and other scientists, Ebbesmeyer made many discoveries about the oceans and the way they move, which led to even more information about shipping and transportation, our understanding of weather and climate, and biology.

SEPARATE WAYS

Cargo getting washed overboard from ships is not a rare occurrence. It's estimated that about 10,000 containers are lost each year. As of 2007, only about 1,000 of the 29,000 ducks, turtles, and other plastic toys from the 1992 spill had been recovered. Many of the ones that are unaccounted for probably disintegrated over the years, but the ones that have been found have appeared all over the world: on both coasts of North America, Japan, Scotland, Hawaii's Lanai Island, and many other places. Based on the data he's collected, Ebbesmeyer has been able to predict the toys' journeys with remarkable accuracy, but he says there's still much to be learned from them about ocean currents and movements. For now, though, we're proud of how much our rubber duck friends have helped with scientific discovery.

The *Oxford English Dictionary* lists 39 euphemisms for "bathroom."

THE SOLDIER OF FASHION AWARD

Military-Inspired Fashions

*Here's our 21-flush salute to the military for giving us
so many fashion staples.*

FUNCTIONAL FASHION

The "military look" in fashion comes and goes—epaulets, braid, and gold buttons adorn everything from evening dresses to T-shirts. And khakis are always in style. But people sporting military-inspired attire may not be aware of the practical military and battlefield origins of some of their favorite fashions. For example, thick loops of fancy braid weren't put on coats to make them look pretty—the braids were there to protect a soldier's shoulders from sword thrusts. And rows of silver buttons might be stylish today, but their original purpose was to act as spare ammunition.

Even though military style comes and goes, there are quite a few items of clothing with military origins that have become standard issue . . . er, attire.

BUTTONED UP

Cardigans—sweaters that typically button down the front—are a fashion staple and wardrobe basic for men and women. For this legacy, we can thank 19th-century British military officer James Brudenell, who was famous (or infamous) for leading the bloody Charge of the Light Brigade at the Battle of Balaclava during the Crimean War. During the battle, Cardigan and his men charged their Russian adversaries, made some headway, but took many casualties and eventually had to retreat. For his efforts, Brudenell was named "the Hero of Balaclava" (despite some allegations that he hadn't properly supplied his troops) and was celebrated throughout England. The knit-

---

Marijuana was prescribed by Chinese herbalists as a cure for forgetfulness.

ted waistcoat he wore became a fashion staple called the "cardigan," because he was also the 7th Earl of Cardigan.

SEA CHANGE

Look around any college campus and you'll see a lot of "peacoats": short, double-breasted navy blue woolen jackets with slash pockets and large, simple lapels. They're warm, flatter a variety of figures, easy to get on and off, and long lasting.

The British Navy originally developed this jacket for its sailors in the early 1700s. The coat's length allowed sailors to move quickly and easily around decks, and the double-button closure kept the coats from flying open in a gale or while climbing a mast. The pockets made it easy to quickly warm frozen hands, and the lapels could be flipped up for extra warmth. The U.S. Navy officially adopted peacoats in the early 1900s.

But why are they called "peacoats"? (They're also sometimes known as "pea jackets" and "reefer coats.") The name comes from a Dutch–West Frisian word for the heavy woolen cloth used to make them: *pij*. But have no fear—they're heavy no longer. Originally 30 ounces in weight, today's peacoat can be anywhere from 22 to 32 ounces.

IN THE TRENCHES

One of most enduring fashions for both men and women is the trench coat. The traditional trench, a rather severe shade of olive brown called khaki, usually comes to the mid-calf. It had fringed shoulder decorations (called epaulets), a buckled belt with several metal loops along the bottom, straps at both wrists, and a button-in liner.

High-end designer Burberry makes coveted trench coats, and with good reason—Thomas Burberry invented the coat. He invented a fabric called gabardine, which is tightly woven wool. In 1901, he submitted a gabardine coat design to the British War Office. The Brits latched onto it immediately: Burberry's fabric was lighter and more serviceable than the heavy wool typically used for officers' greatcoats. By World War I, gabardine coats were common among British (and French) officers. The coat's D rings were handy for hanging canteens, utility knives, and more, and

---

Most popular cat names in Britain: Lucy and Charlie.

the epaulets allowed everyone to see an officer's rank while he remained dry and warm. (Too bad for the lower ranks, who weren't allowed to wear—or even purchase—them.) The coats got their name from their appearance in this war, too: officers wore them in the trenches all over Europe.

BLENDING IN TO STAND OUT

Camouflage has been around for millions of years . . . if you count all of the animal species whose coats and coverings blend in with different surroundings. But the idea of soldiers in Western societies blending into their surroundings didn't take hold until the 19th century. British, French, and even some American armies usually wore brightly colored uniforms, probably to distinguish themselves from their enemies.

The first move toward making military uniforms less visible came during the mid-1800s when British soldiers in India started dyeing their red coats brown. Other armies picked up the trend, making their uniforms brown, green, khaki, gray, or some combination (grigio-verde, or gray-green, worked well in the Italian Alps). Widespread use of camouflage began during World War I, when the French created a "Camouflage Division" of 20,000 *camoufleurs* (largely made up of former theater stage designers and artists) whose job was to alter or disguise equipment and locations with painted canvases so the Germans couldn't find them. (*Camoufler* means "to disguise" or "to veil.")

The camouflage worked, but back then, mass-producing printed fabrics was expensive. So the painted uniforms were first restricted to snipers and other exposed soldiers. During World War II, when mass-produced printed fabrics were more widely available, armies of several nations began producing battle fatigues in the splotchy pattern we now call camouflage.

Perhaps because of its connection to battlefield action, wearing camouflage took a long time to catch on among most civilians (though hunters have worn it for years). However, in the past decade "camo" has become a popular fashion style and is available in shades from greens and browns to fluorescent pinks and purples—and in garments from baggy combat-inspired trousers to skintight tank tops and cargo skirts.

In Japanese, the verb *tsujigiri* means "testing a sword on a chance passerby."

THE CLASSIC RIVALRY AWARD

Army–Navy Football

The annual Army–Navy matchup remains one of the few major football games played for the sheer love of the sport . . . or perhaps for sheer love of rivalry. Uncle John thinks both are award worthy.

BIRTH OF A TRADITION

The first intercollegiate football game took place in 1869 between Rutgers and Princeton universities, but in 1890 a historic sports rivalry began:

Army (the United States Military Academy at West Point)

vs.

Navy (the United States Naval Academy at Annapolis)

The matchup takes place every first Saturday in December (it used to be played on the Saturday after Thanksgiving). Most of the players aren't thinking of playing in the NFL, since they have a five-year minimum military commitment after graduation. Instead, they play for the love of the game . . . and to beat Army or Navy, as the case may be.

THE LINEUP

On November 29, 1890, two squads of football players faced off in New York on the Great Plain, the field at West Point. The Navy team, which had been playing organized football since 1879, had challenged Army Cadet Dennis Mahan Michie (for whom Army's Michie Stadium was named) to the game, and he accepted. West Point didn't even have a team, so Michie had to organize and coach the players in a matter of weeks. As might be expected, that first meeting was a rout. Navy shut out Army 24–0. The next year, Army came back to beat Navy. And so began a passionate rivalry.

Lyndon Johnson was the first president to wear contact lenses.

TIME-OUT

The football game between America's two biggest military academies has been played ever since with only four interruptions:

- **1894–1898:** After the 1893 Navy victory, a Navy rear admiral and an Army brigadier general had an argument that nearly ended in a duel. To keep things peaceful, President Grover Cleveland decreed that for a period of five years, the Army and Navy football teams be confined to their home turf (other schools could visit them). Thus, they couldn't compete against each other. In 1899, with tempers no longer hot, the Army–Navy game resumed, but this time neither team had the home advantage: they played in Philadelphia, "neutral territory" because it was about halfway between the schools.

- **1909:** Army canceled its entire schedule because one of its players was killed during a game against Harvard.

- **1917–1918:** Called on account of World War I.

- **1928–1929:** Neither academy could agree on player eligibility standards, so they didn't play again until 1930.

The game was canceled again in 1963 because it was scheduled for just eight days after President John F. Kennedy was assassinated. But his widow, Jacqueline Kennedy, insisted that it be rescheduled and played because her husband (a former Navy officer who'd been rejected by the Army) had so enjoyed the contest. That year, Navy won.

A GOAT AND A MULE WALK INTO A STADIUM . . .

The traditions surrounding Army–Navy have grown with the years—from the phrases that each academy chants ("Beat Navy!" and "Beat Army!") to the practical jokes played on the teams' mascots. The Navy goat and the Army mule have both been kidnapped, sometimes repeatedly. In 2007, three Navy goats were nabbed, and a video of the "crime" was posted on YouTube. (The goats were later returned, unharmed.)

At the end of each game, both schools get to hear their fight songs—first the losing team and then the winner. In a show of respect and solidarity, the winning team stands alongside the los-

There are about 140,000 ladybugs to the gallon.

ing team and faces the losing academy's students. Then the losing team accompanies the winning team, facing its students.

INSTANT REPLAY

Here are a few fun facts about the Army–Navy rivalry:

- Navy's team name is the Midshipmen, and its colors are gold and blue.
- Navy's mascot is a goat named Bill; the animal was selected because of its traditional inclusion on ships as a source of fresh food for sailors.
- Army's team name is the Black Knights, and its colors are black, gold, and gray.
- Army's mascot, a mule whose name has changed over the years, was selected for its usefulness in military operations where it hauled supplies, ammunition, and guns, although the first mascot pulled an ice wagon.
- In 1963, the Army–Navy game was the first televised football game to use instant replay during the broadcast.
- The game was the subject of a 1973 M*A*S*H episode in which the Korean War–based soldiers tried to watch the game but thought they'd been bombed by the enemy. The "bomb" that landed in the middle of their camp turned out to be a propaganda shell filled with CIA leaflets.

SUCCESS STORIES

A few Army–Navy players did go on to the NFL:

- **Roger Staubach (Navy 1965)** had a stellar career as a quarterback with the Dallas Cowboys.
- **Phil McConkey (Navy 1979)** was a wide receiver and kickoff/punt returner for the New York Giants in their Super Bowl XXI victory.
- **Napoleon McCallum (Navy 1985)** was allowed to serve in the Navy while playing for the Los Angeles Raiders. He joined the team full-time when his military service was over, but a knee injury ended his football career in 1994.

Olive Oyl's shoe size: 14AAAAAA.

THE LET THE CHIPS FALL WHERE THEY MAY AWARD

The Toll House Cookie

Uncle John can't verify whether or not the chocolate-chip cookie was an accidental or intentional creation, but he can proclaim it the most incredibly delicious cookie ever.

HOME IS WHERE THE COOKIE IS

Apple pies were first baked in England, hot dogs and hamburgers come from Germany, but the chocolate-chip cookie is an all-American creation. In fact, chocolate-chip cookies are such a fixture in American culture that it's hard to believe they've only been around since the 1930s . . . invented by accident (perhaps) in Whitman, Massachusetts.

In 1930, Kenneth and Ruth Graves Wakefield bought an old tollhouse in Whitman. The house had once been a way station for passing travelers—they paid tolls, rested, and could get home-cooked meals. The young couple christened it the Toll House Inn and set about turning the 1709 building into a modern lodge. Ruth decorated with colonial furnishings and started cooking all homemade meals for their guests. She was a good cook, especially of desserts, and soon her creations attracted crowds. One of Ruth's trademarks was sending guests away with a full meal and her homemade Butter Drop Do cookies—plain sugar or a chocolate version she made by adding powdered baker's chocolate to the dough.

THE BATTER THICKENS

Here's where Ruth Wakefield's chocolate-chip cookie story gets tricky. There are two versions of what happened. In Nestlé's

---

How many M&Ms are there in a pound? About 192 peanut or 512 plain.

official account (Nestlé now owns the Toll House Cookie brand), which is also supported by the Wakefield descendants, Ruth ran out of powdered chocolate and substituted a semi-sweet chocolate bar, which she cut into pieces and then added to the batter. The chocolate had come from a friend, Andrew Nestlé—yes, that Nestlé. Ruth assumed that the chocolate would melt during baking and produce chocolate cookies. Instead, the pieces retained their shape and studded the Butter Drop Do cookies with bits of chocolate.

Different though they were, the cookies were a huge hit with visitors to the inn. Andrew Nestlé saw their potential and made a deal: Nestlé would buy the rights to Ruth's cookie recipe and sell its semi-sweet chocolate bars (complete with a small chopper to make chocolate chips) with the recipe printed on the back. In exchange, Ruth would receive a lifetime supply of chocolate to make cookies at her inn. The deal was a success; as word spread about Ruth Wakefield's Toll House Cookies, Nestlé sold a lot of chocolate and eventually developed packages of individual chocolate bits to simplify the cookie-making process. Today, Nestlé still makes chocolate chips, and Ruth Wakefield's recipe is still printed on the bags.

NOT EXACTLY HOW THE COOKIE CRUMBLES

That official tale is all well and good, but George Boucher, the former head chef at the Toll House Inn, and his daughter Carol Cavanaugh tell a slightly different story of the chocolate-chip cookie's birth. Ruth Wakefield was a graduate of what is now Framingham State College and had worked as a dietitian and food lecturer. Cavanaugh claims that Ruth, an accomplished chef and cookbook author, would have known that chocolate chunks wouldn't melt completely into batter and wouldn't have used them as a substitute for chocolate powder.

According to Cavanaugh and Boucher, the chocolate bar in question accidentally fell into Ruth's Butter Drop Do batter and cracked into bits due to the vibrations of the industrial-sized mixer she was using to make the cookies. Ruth was going to throw the batter away; she thought it was ruined. But Boucher convinced her to cook the dough instead. The result was a rich chocolate-chip cookie that was an instant hit with the guests.

Boucher also claims that Wakefield never sold her recipe to Nestlé—only the rights to reproduce it on the chocolate wrapper. According to him, Nestlé's lawyers found loopholes in the initial agreement that let the company take ownership of the recipe.

CHIPS OFF THE OLD BLOCK

Ruth continued to cook and author cookbooks, including a series called *Ruth Wakefield's Recipes: Tried and True* that went through 39 printings. In 1966, the Wakefields sold their inn, and over the years, the property was used as a nightclub and then another bed and breakfast. It burned down in 1984. We may never know whether or not Ruth Wakefield's Toll House Cookie was the result of canny culinary forethought or a happy accident, but at least we'll always have her original recipe.

SOME MORSELS OF INFORMATION

- About two thirds of Americans prefer their chocolate chip cookies without nuts.

- Half the cookies baked in American kitchens are chocolate chip.

- On July 9, 1997, Massachusetts designated the chocolate chip cookie as the Official State Cookie, after a third grade class from Somerset proposed it.

BIGGEST COOKIE EVER

In 2003, the Immaculate Baking Company made the world's biggest chocolate chip cookie: 100 feet wide (about the length of a Boeing 737) and weighed 40,000 pounds. The recipe included the following ingredients:

- 6,000 pounds of semi-sweet chocolate chunks
- 12,200 pounds of unbleached flour
- 6,525 pounds of unsalted butter
- 184 pounds of salt
- 5,000 pounds of granulated sugar; 3,370 pounds of brown sugar
- 79 pounds of baking soda
- 30,000 eggs
- 10 gallons of pure vanilla

. . . consuming an average of 3,774 calories a day.

THE GLOBAL WARMING SOLUTION AWARD

The Tesla Roadster

It's the first eco-friendly vehicle that could appeal equally to conservationists and muscle-car fans, which qualifies it for an award in itself, but it also gets points for helping us save the planet.

ECO ENGINE

Sports cars' speed, style, sass, and power have captivated people for decades. Who cares about fuel economy when you've got prestige and sex appeal? That was before the Tesla Roadster. This first-ever all-electric sports car goes from 0–60 in four seconds and doesn't depend on gas. It's no suburban hybrid car, either. The Tesla is as curvy and appealing as any Italian coupe. And this car gets 135 MPG on the highway.

Let's say that again: 135 MPG. That's almost two and a half times the mileage of some of the most efficient hybrids, including the Toyota Prius (55 MPG) or the Honda Civic (50 MPG). And it's nearly five times the mileage of popular compacts like the Mini Cooper (28 MPG).

The Tesla can be fully charged in three and a half hours on a 240-volt circuit, but it can also be charged overnight using a regular household outlet. Even though that takes longer, it's an amazing step ahead for the electric car world. The Tesla goes about 220 miles on a single charge.

CARS ON CURRENTS

The Roadster is an innovation, but "electric carriages" have been in the works since 1832, when Scotland's Robert Anderson tried

---

Big eaters: Polar bears have been known to kill and eat beluga whales.

to create one. In 1835, Professor Stratingh of the University of Groeningen in the Netherlands made his own attempt. There were various other tries throughout Europe, but the United States didn't have electric vehicles until the late 1890s.

In 1897, a fleet of electric taxicabs was established in Manhattan, and for a decade or so, it seemed that electric cars might be the wave of the future. Electric cars didn't have the smell, vibrations, or noise that gasoline-powered cars had, and they also didn't require cumbersome gear changes.

But Americans wanted cars that traveled long distances, and the early electric cars couldn't provide high mileage. That drawback might have been overcome, but in the early part of the 20th century, there was also no place an electric-car driver could stop en route from New York to Las Vegas to plug in and recharge. This, combined with the discovery of Texas crude, meant that gas-powered cars seemed like the smartest way to motor.

SLEEKER STYLING

From the 1930s until 1990, a few companies fueled by America's growing environmental conscience tried to market boxy little electric cars to alterna-Americans, but they had little success because the cars just didn't look appealing to the mainstream. Finally, by the early 1990s, concern about the environment prompted enough public interest in finding a good electric car solution. Manufacturers made strides, but the cars' heavy battery packs and ignition/acceleration problems plagued them, and people dismissed electric cars as a fad.

PRIME PERFORMANCE

The shortcomings of early electric cars are part of the reason the Tesla Roadster is so noteworthy. It seems to address all of the old problems: it's completely electric, it's easy to recharge, it looks great, and it accelerates as quickly as many lesser sports cars.

That latter quality especially is what the Lotus Company, which makes the Tesla, is banking on as its ace in the hole. The Tesla may be environmentally friendly, but it's not bank-account friendly. A fully loaded Tesla, delivered to your door, will set you back $100,000, although a $30,000 model is suppos-

The first letters of the months July through November spell the name Jason.

edly in the works. Lotus hopes to offset resistance to the price tag with the Tesla's cash savings (in gas) over time. On the other hand, Martin Ebehard, former chairman of Silicon Valley–based Tesla Motors, told the *New York Times* in 2006 that the way to get a new product into the mass market is to sell it to rich people. "Cell phones, refrigerators, color TVs, they didn't start off by making a low-end product for [the] masses," he said. "They were relatively expensive, for people who could afford it." The companies that sold those products at first, Ebehard continued, did so, "not because they were stupid and they thought the real market was at the high end of the market," but because that was how to get production started.

TESLA OR "TOM"?

The car's name is a nod to Nikola Tesla, a onetime employee of Thomas Edison and the man who came up with the idea of alternating electric currents. It was Edison, however, who spent a lot of time trying to create electric batteries for horseless carriages. Maybe we should nickname these sexy new sportscars "Toms."

*   *   *

AN AWARD ORIGIN

MacArthur Genius Grant: John D. MacArthur made millions as the owner of several insurance companies in the 1930s and 1940s. His wife, Catherine, held board member positions at many of her husband's firms. When John MacArthur died in 1978, most of his fortune was used to start the John D. and Catherine T. MacArthur Foundation. The major work of the charity is the awarding of the MacArthur Fellowship, or "Genius Grant." Between 20 and 40 Americans each year—nominated by a small selection committee—receive $500,000 dispensed over five years as an "investment in a person's originality, insight, and potential." Among the more than 700 winners are historians, writers, scientists, artists, musicians, and inventors. Writer Thomas Pynchon, paleontologist Stephen Jay Gould, and critic Henry Louis Gates are all MacArthur fellows.

THE LI'L SPEED RACER AWARD

Toy Cars

*They're fun to run on a track or along a sidewalk. They're
fueled by fantasy or based in reality. Either way, they're
at the top of the heap for childhood memories.*

CAR WARS
Some debates are so classic that they can't be resolved:
The Godfather vs. *The Godfather Part II*. Who's stronger,
Superman or the Incredible Hulk. Or which toy cars are better—
Matchbox or Hot Wheels?

To understand this fight fully, it's essential to understand the
differences between the two lines:

Matchbox: Introduced first in Britain in 1953, and then in the
United States in 1954; manufactured realistic play versions of cars
kids would see on the street.

Hot Wheels: Introduced in 1968; created fantasy-oriented cars
that included racing stripes and flame decals, along with realistic
versions of American muscle cars.

When Hot Wheels were introduced, Matchbox saw its sales
plummet. The public seemed to prefer Hot Wheels' sporty, colorful line. But that's hardly the end of this story.

ROUND AND ROUND

Matchbox began in 1953 when Jack Odell, co-owner of a die-cast-
ing company called Lesney, developed a toy car for his daughter.
She liked to take spiders to school in matchboxes, so he made her
a small toy to take instead. The first car his company produced
was based on a toy steamroller it was already making in a larger
size. A mini dump truck and a cement mixer followed for an ini-

---

A standard umbrella has seven ribs.

tial offering of three different Matchbox vehicles. The model cars were a hit, and other makes and models were soon introduced. For the next 15 years, Matchbox dominated the market, selling more toy cars than any other company. But in 1968, a competitor entered the scene and shook up the race.

MEET THE COMPETITION

A year earlier, one of the founders of Mattel Toys, Elliot Handler, had an idea to design model cars with low-friction wheels that made the toys race at speeds that would have equaled almost 300 miles per hour if they were actual size. Reportedly, Handler remarked, "Wow, those are hot wheels!" after seeing one perform, and a brand name was born. Mattel soon patented the design.

While Matchbox focused on creating exact (sometimes painstakingly so) replicas of real cars, Hot Wheels generated fantasy cars—with some realistic replicas, particularly of racing cars, thrown in. The split between philosophies split buyers as well.

THE FINISH LINE

The Matchbox and Hot Wheels competition raced through the 1970s, with some kids fiercely loyal to one brand. Most, however, mixed and matched sets, collecting both and using the accessories interchangeably. The early 1980s, though, brought economic tough times to Britain and forced Matchbox into bankruptcy. The company was sold to Universal Toys, which a decade later sold the company to Mattel—maker of Hot Wheels. The competition between the two brands would never be the same.

Since then, the toy car market has continued to produce faster and better cars. Now they are made of tough molded plastic instead of cast iron, but they've broken new records in speed, including some models that would exceed 500 mph if they were life sized.

QUITE A COLLECTION

The toy car market is a specialized industry. Its serious collectors are passionate about their hobby and make note of each car's ratio to actual size. The most popular size with collectors is 1:24; other popular sizes include 1:64 and 1:87. Remote-control cars and

---

The year they were introduced, only two Volkswagen Beetles were sold in the United States.

video games have cut into the market somewhat, but toy cars remain a more than $2-billion-a-year business.

In 2008, Hot Wheels celebrated its 40th year, which coincided with the manufacture of its four billionth toy car. In honor of its success, the company created a car covered with $140,000 worth of jewels to be auctioned off for charity. It is cast in white gold and loaded with black, white, and blue diamonds—rubies take the place of headlights.

That's just one of the thousands of collectible cars that have been produced over the decades. Collectors pay top dollar, or tens of thousands of dollars, for the rarest ones, and Web sites and magazines are devoted to the hobby. They help collectors locate the hard-to-find models that have come and gone through the years. From a small idea so many years ago to a giant hallmark of childhood for so many, toy cars have gone around the track and come out a winner.

✳   ✳   ✳

KIDDIE BOOK AWARDS

- **Newberry Award.** John Newberry was an 18th-century publisher who specialized in children's books. It's believed he was the first publisher to specialize in kid lit. Since 1922, the American Library Association has presented the Newberry Award annually to the author of the best novel written for children. Some Newberry winners: Hugh Lofting (*The Voyages of Doctor Dolittle*), Esther Forbes (*Johnny Tremain*), and Katherine Paterson (*Bridge to Terabithia*).

- **Caldecott Medal.** Randolph Caldecott was an English illustrator in the 19th century. He drew pictures for books, including *The Babes in the Wood* and *The House that Jack Built*. Like the Newberry Award, the Caldecott Medal is a prize for children's literature presented by the American Library Association, but this one awards only the illustrators. Caldecott-winning titles include Ezra Jack Keats (*The Snowy Day*), Chris Van Allsburg (*The Polar Express*), and Maurice Sendak (*Where the Wild Things Are*).

THE MR. LONELY AWARD

Fire Lookouts

Incredibly solitary but vitally important, fire spotters live above the fray and keep an eye out for everyone.

MOUNTAIN HIGH
From its 2,571-foot peak high above San Francisco Bay, the Mount Tamalpais Fire Lookout Station in Marin County has a magnificent view over 200 miles, 25 counties, and nine bodies of water. Since 1921, fire lookouts have been surveying this horizon for evidence of destructive wildfires.

Once upon a time, fire control wasn't necessary, because it cleansed and renewed land and vegetation as part of a natural and regular cycle. Fire removed old, dead matter and made room for healthy, new growth. But as humans moved into areas like the thickly forested Marin County and built homes, schools, and stores, a way was needed to control the fires.

SMOKE OF A DISTANT FIRE

Fire lookout stations are not new. The oldest known station dates back about 2,000 years. It was located on Mount Masada, in what is now Israel, and was built by King Herod's army to protect his empire against enemy burning.

By the time the United States Forest Service was founded in 1905, many communities had already recognized the need for fire lookouts. But it was "the Big Blowup" of 1910—still the biggest recorded forest fire in U.S. history—that forced a more regulated approach to forest fires. During that disaster, 3 million acres across Washington, Idaho, and Montana burned, and sent smoke as far east as Washington, D.C.

However, most of the country's lookout stations (about 8,000 in all) were built during the 1930s as part of President Franklin D. Roosevelt's New Deal program. And the golden age of fire lookouts was from 1930 to 1950—before technological advances made them less necessary. (The only state never to have had a fire lookout is Kansas, because its flat landscape makes them unnecessary.) Firefighters, though, have found that in many areas and situations, there is no substitute for the human eye in detecting smoke.

BIRD'S-EYE VIEW

Fire lookouts have to be in high places with clear views on all sides. Sometimes that means a sturdy, one- or two-story windowed building high on a peak—like the Mount Tamalpais Fire Station. Other times, it means a very tall structure on stilts, with several flights of stairs that climb to the top.

The lookouts spend anywhere from a few days to a few months at a time at their stations, which are also usually in the middle of nowhere—getting to them can mean a long hike or even a helicopter ride. Some stations have amenities like electricity and running water, but others are much more primitive. A husband and wife who manned Idaho's Gisborne Station in the 1970s had to haul water every day, so they conserved the use of water for meal preparation and ate foraged greens and berries, which they dried on the station's steps.

THE BEAT GOES UP

Several well-known writers were fire spotters at one time or another, including environmentalist Edward Abbey and Beat poet Gary Snyder. But the most famous fire spotter and the only one who used his experience in his work was Beat novelist Jack Kerouac.

Kerouac spent the summer of 1956 as a fire lookout on Desolation Peak in the North Cascades, between Washington State and British Columbia. His 63 days in the simple 14' x 14' structure provided him with material for *The Dharma Bums* and *Desolation Angels*. He wrote:

> When I get to the top of Desolation Peak and everybody leaves on mules and I'm alone I will come face to face with God or Tathagata [one Buddha's titles] and find once and for all what is the meaning of all this existence and suffering and going to and fro in vain but instead I'd come face to face with myself . . .

Most costume changes in a movie: 85, by Madonna in *Evita*.

Desolation Peak's lookout station is closed to visitors, so Kerouac pilgrims who manage the 4.7-mile, 4,400-foot climb won't be able to sit at the desk where he penned some of his most famous passages, but they can look in through the many windows.

SIGHT LINES

A lot has changed since Kerouac wrote *The Dharma Bums*, but the job of fire lookout hasn't. Lookouts still monitor the weather (lightning strikes can start fires), confirm fires, and help firefighters to determine the extent of a blaze. For example, smoke is generally bluish—when it turns black, the fire is growing.

The lookouts still use the Osborne Fire Finder, a tabletop device developed in the 1920s by William "W. B." Osborne, a National Parks Service employee. The Finder consists of a topographic map of the lookout's area with two sighting apertures a user moves until he can center the crosshairs on the fire.

Their equipment may be simple and from decades ago, but a fire lookout's task remains important. In 2007, 16 countries besides the United States had active fire lookouts. In the United States, there are about 155 fire lookouts, a combination of volunteer and paid positions. Modern techniques, especially the use of planes in fire prevention and spotting, have helped, but when it comes to fighting fires in the wilderness, there's nothing as effective as a pair of human eyes.

*　　*　　*

WANTED: FIRE LOOKOUT

A real ad: "This is a full-time seasonal paid position, which begins as soon as the snow melts . . . and ends when the snows fly in the fall (typically 5 days per week, May–October). Built in 1934, Fence Meadow is a 30' metal tower with a 14x14' wooden live-in cab, powered by electricity and comes furnished with a single bed, stove, refrigerator, lights, heater and a fine-by-any-standards double-head outhouse. The lookout is located off of paved roads . . . The lookout is in the process of being refurbished (already newly painted on the inside and carpeted). Carpentry skills and smoke monitoring experience a plus!"

Alphabetically, the last place on Earth is Zywocice, Poland.

THE UNSOLVED MYSTERY AWARD

D. B. Cooper

This man on the run has been puzzling investigators for nearly 40 years.
The subject of countless books, movies, TV shows, and endless
speculation, he is also now the recipient of our
best unsolved mystery award.

INTO THIN AIR

In today's post-9/11 society, the possibility of an airliner being hijacked by a lone criminal who escapes without ever being caught or positively identified is both deeply disturbing and highly unlikely. But on November 24, 1971, before the days of airport metal detectors and other stringent security regulations, one polite, well-dressed man did exactly that.

What's more, his apolitical and "stick-it-to-the-man" motivations, relaxed threats, and willing release of innocents earned him a community of supporters who deemed him a modern-day Robin Hood. And, at the time, antiestablishment types were in vogue. Thirty-five years later, with no new leads, the FBI is still trying to uncover the true identity of "Dan Cooper," the man behind the only unsolved commercial skyjacking in U.S. history, a man who seemingly vanished into thin air.

FASTEN YOUR SEAT BELTS

On a rainy afternoon at Oregon's Portland International Airport, a middle-aged man wearing a dark suit with a slim tie and mother-of-pearl tie clip purchased a one-way ticket on Northwest Orient Airlines to Seattle, Washington. He paid $18.52. The name on the reservation was Dan Cooper. After taking his seat in the last row of the Boeing 727 aircraft, he ordered a bourbon and Coke from an attractive flight attendant, 23-year-

---

In Turkey, turkeys are called "the American bird."

old Florence Schaffner. Then he lit a Raleigh filter-tip cigarette and settled in for the ride.

According to the flight staff, Cooper was cordial, tipped generously, and had a smooth demeanor. In fact, when he handed Florence a piece of paper to let her know that he was toting a bomb in his briefcase, she slipped it into her pocket unopened, assuming he'd simply passed along his phone number, as many male passengers before him had done. But Cooper urged her to open the note. The note threatened to blow up the plane if Cooper's demands weren't met:

> $200,000 in unmarked $20 bills, four manually operated parachutes (two chest and two back), and a fuel truck waiting in Seattle to refuel the plane.

THE GREAT ESCAPE
Northwest Orient president Donald Nyrop instructed the pilot to cooperate, and the FBI scrambled to meet Cooper's demands, while at the same time preparing to apprehend him. When the plane finally landed in Seattle, Cooper released all 36 passengers and two flight attendants, leaving only himself and four airline employees onboard as the plane was refueled. Bags filled with the cash, weighing a total of 21 pounds, were delivered as promised.

As the plane left the runway, this time in a heavy storm, Cooper gave the pilot specific instructions: Keep the plane under 10,000 feet, wing flaps at 15 degrees, and speed under 200 knots. He then ordered everyone into the cockpit, strapped the money to his waist, put one chute on his chest and one on his back, opened the plane's rear door, and plunged into the darkness somewhere over the dense pine forests and deep canyons of the Cascades in southwestern Washington.

GOING ON A MANHUNT
The search for Dan Cooper, or any shred of his whereabouts, was on. For several weeks, the FBI scoured miles of forest for a body or any evidence of a landing—successful or otherwise. But the case, code named NORJAK, offered investigators precious few clues.

They knew that Dan Cooper was an alias. But police brought a man named D. B. Cooper in for questioning shortly after the hijacking and alerted the media, who confused his name with the name used by the jumper. Although D. B. Cooper was quickly ruled out as a suspect, his name would be forever linked with the crime.

The FBI also worked with a composite sketch and personality profile of the suspect, based on flight crew accounts, and—decades later—a DNA sample from his tie (he took it off before he jumped), obtained in 2001. The number of suspects totaled close to 1,000 over 30 years. Many who couldn't possibly have been Cooper falsely confessed to committing the crime, often just before their final breaths. Of the handful of suspects who were seriously considered, Kenneth Peter Christiansen was a favorite. To many, Christiansen seemed to be an obvious match.

DID HE DO IT?

A former paratrooper in the army, Christiansen had extensive sky-diving experience and was accustomed to no-frills equipment and brutal landings. As a retired flight attendant and purser for Northwest Airlines, he was obviously well-versed in airline procedures—plus, he was living in Washington at the time of the crime. He smoked Raleigh cigarettes and collected bourbon. And he supposedly bore an uncanny resemblance to the composite sketch—at least according to his brother Lyle, who recognized his face while watching *Unsolved Mysteries* on television.

Civilian researchers theorized that Christiansen's motive was retaliation against an airline known at the time for unfair employment practices (mainly against women) and layoffs that led to frequent strikes, which helped to further fuel the Robin Hood syndrome. FBI investigators, however, were not convinced. Deviating from their original assumption that the hijacker was an experienced jumper, they ultimately ruled that only a novice would have jumped under those impossible conditions, and without first checking his chutes. (He jumped with one designed for training, which had a sewed-shut reserve chute.) They also contended that Christiansen, who died in 1994, did not resemble the man in the sketch after all and therefore could not have been Cooper. And so the search continues.

GONE BUT NOT FORGOTTEN

Although they firmly believe that Cooper could not have survived

---

Pope John Paul II created nearly 500 new saints; more than were created in the last 500 years.

the jump, the FBI is still determined to get their man, at least on paper. On December 31, 2007, the Bureau revived the 36-year-old case by releasing to the press and public details and evidence surrounding the case, including photos of the deteriorating $20 bills ($5,800 total was recovered) that were found on the banks of the Columbia River on the Washington-Oregon border in 1980. (The FBI matched the serial numbers on the bills to those delivered to Cooper, but nothing more came of the discovery.)

Immortalized through books, movies, music, airline safety features, and even an annual festival in Cowlitz County, Washington, the man known as Dan Cooper continues to elude capture, if only in spirit.

TRIVIA

- D. B. Cooper jumped out of the plane on the eve of the Thanksgiving holiday.
- Universal Pictures used the robbery as a publicity stunt and offered a $1 million reward to anyone who could produce information leading to the capture of the real Cooper—no one ever got the money.
- D. B. Cooper's necktie was from JC Penney.
- In order to trace the bills, the FBI used bills whose serial numbers all began with the same letter. They also got all of the bills from the same Federal Reserve bank.
- The eight-year-old boy who found the cash got to keep half; the other half was returned to Northwest's insurance carrier, which had paid out the extortion money.

*　　　*　　　*

LONELY AT THE TOP

Q: What do James Baldwin, Graham Greene, Evelyn Waugh, and James Joyce have in common?

A: All were overlooked for the Nobel Prize for Literature.

THE "HE WROTE THAT?" AWARD

Ian McEwan and Roger Ebert

Some famous writers show up in some surprising places at the movies.

THE NAME: Ian McEwan
THE MOVIE: *The Good Son* (1993)
In 1993, Macaulay Culkin was the go-to kid for on-screen cuteness. Moviegoers knew and loved him for his work in *Uncle Buck*, *My Girl*, and the first and second *Home Alone* films. While he may have been the hottest child star of the moment, Culkin's overbearing stage parents were running his career and annoying moviemakers in the process.

Reportedly, his father desperately wanted Culkin to star in *The Good Son* (it would be his first dramatic role) to show the young actor's range and thus ensure his continued success. He threatened to pull Macaulay off *Home Alone 2* if he couldn't also star in *The Good Son*. The movie earned Macaulay $5 million and made about $60 million at the box office. But critics hated it. The *New York Times* remarked, "*The Good Son* has more interesting ambiguity in its title than it does anywhere else" and Roger Ebert asked, "Who in the world would want to see this movie?" It also signaled the end for Macaulay's career. He went on to make *Getting Even with Dad* and *Richie Rich*, but audiences never again took to Macaulay as they once had.

What's most surprising about this movie, though, is the literary pedigree behind it. Screenwriter Ian McEwan was a celebrated novelist with 10 books to his credit before he wrote *The Good Son*, and he'd already won the following prizes:

- Somerset Maugham Award (1976), for *First Love, Last Rites*, his first collection of short stories

- Whitbread Novel Award (1987), for *The Child in Time* (one of the United Kingdom's most prestigious awards, now renamed the Costa Book Award),

- Prix Femina Etranger (1993), for *The Child in Time* and others.

Even more notable, McEwan later won the 1998 Man Booker Prize for Fiction for *Amsterdam*—an international award given every two years for an author's achievements in fiction. And his 2002 novel *Atonement* won numerous awards, including:

- The WH Smith Literary Award (2002)
- The National Book Critics' Circle Fiction Award (2003)
- Los Angeles Times Prize for Fiction (2003)
- Santiago Prize for the European Novel (2004)

The finished version of *The Good Son* was reportedly far different from what McEwan originally wrote—Macaulay Culkin's father is said to have made substantial changes during filming. Although McEwan hasn't commented about the making of the movie, he has talked about writing for movies in general. In 2002, he told the *San Francisco Chronicle*, "Hollywood has a particular demand on writers. Writers can get swept aside . . . Occasionally, some of us are blessed by witnessing bad behavior, but in Hollywood you really see it, people behaving monstrously." Not surprisingly, McEwan's Web site doesn't mention *The Good Son*.

THE NAME: Roger Ebert
THE MOVIE: *Beyond the Valley of the Dolls* (1970)
Jacqueline Susann's best-selling novel *The Valley of the Dolls* was a scandalous smash in 1966. It featured three young actresses who struggle to achieve success and then pay a mighty price for it, falling prey to men, drugs, fame, and fortune. A year later, a movie version opened, and instantly became a campy cult classic.

The story doesn't end there, though. In 1970, legendary sexploitation filmmaker Russ Meyer (whose obsession with breasts fueled a career that included such classics as *Faster Pussycat! Kill! Kill!* and *Mud Honey*) made an even campier, X-rated sequel. It again focused on three young women, but this time they were musicians. They played in a band called the Carrie Nations, and as their musical careers exploded, their personal lives imploded. *Beyond the Valley of the Dolls* ratcheted up the sex, drugs, and rock 'n' roll, earning its "X" rating with a bloody decapitation at the end. It was also hilariously funny from start to finish. Oh! And one of the most famous movie critics of our time, Roger Ebert, cowrote the skin flick.

Ebert was already a respected film critic for the *Chicago Sun-Times* when he got involved with the movie. He was a longtime fan of Meyer's work, and when the two met, they formed a friendship. When Meyer was hired to direct a sequel to *The Valley of the Dolls*, he turned to Ebert for help writing the script. Critics slammed the film, even if one of their own helped to create it. Vincent Canby of the *New York Times* trashed the film, saying, "Meyer's earnestly vulgar sensibility, which once met the audience on its own level by giving it exactly what it wanted, has become patronizing."

Years later, Ebert offered this description of his script: "Pure cinema, combining shameless melodrama, highly charged images of violence, sledge-hammer editing and musical overkill." Ebert has said he and Meyer took six weeks to write the movie, and they laughed the entire time. Audiences seem to have gotten the joke: the movie, which cost under $1 million to make, has grossed $40 million.

Ebert wrote two more movies with Meyer, and he would have worked with Meyer on a third—a 1978 movie for the British punk band the Sex Pistols—but the production company went bankrupt and filming was stopped.

Ebert's association with Meyer didn't hurt his career. In 1975 he won the Pulitzer Prize for criticism, he became a famous critic through his weekly TV show reviewing movies, and he still writes for the *Chicago Sun-Times*.

*　　*　　*

TWO BITS OF OSCAR TRIVIA

- What do Audrey Hepburn, Eva Marie Saint, Julie Andrews, Barbra Streisand, and Marlee Matlin have in common? They all won Academy Awards for their first movie role.

- Only three women have ever been nominated for Best Director at the Academy Awards: Lina Wertmuller (*Seven Beauties*, 1976), Jane Campion (*The Piano*, 1993), and Sofia Coppola (*Lost in Translation*, 2003). None won.

Sir Walter Raleigh was buried with a tin of tobacco and his favorite pipe.

THE THREE LITTLE PIGS AWARD, #2

Book Houses

*The Italians are known for their art, but this Venetian and his
Golden Plunger–winning ideas are in a league all their own.*

BOOKS MAKE THE MAN
Books have long been objects of art. Collectors may specialize in illustrated, paper-engineered, or handmade books.
The 20th century ushered in artist's books—one-of-a-kind, often highly conceptual works of art that range widely in form and usually include a combination of media. But no one has ever taken it quite as far as Italian sculptor Livio De Marchi. Books, not bricks, are the inspiration of this Venetian-born sculptor. His *Casa di Libri* (Book Houses) can be found in Italy, Germany, and Japan.

De Marchi didn't construct his houses with actual printed books, though, which would be vulnerable to weather and vermin. Instead, he sculpted the houses almost entirely from wood. The first Casa di Libri, in the Veneto village of Sant'Anna di Tambre, Italy, was finished in 1992. Its outer walls are designed to look like stacked books of varying thicknesses, some with spines turned out, others with spines turned in. The tin roof resembles a giant green book, opened upside down. Its "pages" are also carved from wood. The smokestack for the wood stove (yes, it's also made of wood) is a large green fountain pen, its point to the sky. The shutters are book jackets; when closed, they look like complete books standing face out, ready to be read. Even the concrete foundation looks like a book.

FULLY BOOKED
Inside, the fantasy continues. Nearly everything is made to look like books: the tables, the chairs, the dining furniture, even the shelves filled with carved wooden volumes. There are other clever wooden

items, too, ranging from the extremely simple bowls and plates on the dining table to elaborately carved hats, jackets, shoes, and even a handbag. Although you can't put on the draped jackets or the wooden suit hanging in the (book-shaped) armoire, everything else in the Casa di Libri is fully functional. The shelves of faux books cleverly conceal modern, working kitchens and bathrooms, and the enormous platform book bed is topped by a comfy mattress.

DRIVING ON WATER

The artist created two other book houses and plans more. Livio De Marchi's fantastical designs aren't limited to houses. He also creates fully functional vehicles out of wood. Some of his best-known creations are waterborne cars that he "drives" around Venice's canals. In 1989 he made a Fiat Topolino; in 1997 a Mercedes Seagull; in 1999 a convertible Volkswagen Beetle. But his masterpiece is 1994's Pumpkin Coach, which accommodates four people and even includes horses "handled" by a coachman. How fitting that a fairy tale inspired this fantastical and bookish artist.

For the other Three Little Pigs Awards,
turn to pages 7 and 208.

* * *

TWO AWARD ORIGINS

- **The Heisman Trophy.** John Heisman was a football coach at Auburn, Clemson, and Georgia Tech in the 1890s and early 1900s. In the 1930s, he moved on to be the athletic director at New York City's Downtown Athletic Club. Since then, the club has issued the Heisman Trophy in his honor. It's voted on by the nation's college football reporters. Past winners include Roger Staubach, Tony Dorsett, Barry Sanders, and Bo Jackson.

- **Tony Awards.** The Tonys are awarded to the best Broadway plays, musicals, and performances of each year. They're named for Antoinette "Tony" Perry, a stage actress and theater director in the early 20th century. In the 1940s, she founded and led the American Theatre Wing, which promotes theater and, today, hands out the Tonys. All-time Tony leader: Julie Harris has been nominated ten times and won five times.

Camels chew in a figure-eight pattern.

THE DON'T CALL IT A COMEBACK AWARD

Gray Wolves

In 1973, gray wolves were on the verge of extinction in the United States when the federal government stepped in to help. The animals made a remarkable recovery. But 35 years later, gray wolves were back in the news—and this time, the government had signed their death warrants.

LONELY WOLF

Once upon a time, gray wolves ranged over the entire Northern Hemisphere. In the United States, they were concentrated in the West and Midwest—states like Idaho, Montana, Wyoming, Wisconsin, and Minnesota. Many lived in Yellowstone, the country's first national park. When Yellowstone was established in 1872, hundreds of gray wolves roamed there and were the area's top predator. But just half a century after the park's formation, the animals were gone.

From the late 1800s until about 1940, ranchers in Yellowstone and throughout the West practiced "predator control." This meant that wolves could be hunted (even inside the park) in an effort to keep them away from local farms and populations. Wolf hunters received bounties of $20 a pelt, a hefty sum at the time. By the mid-1940s, few visitors or ranchers reported seeing wolf packs in Yellowstone, and by the 1970s, scientists could find no evidence that any wolves still lived there at all. In fact, the only U.S. states with wolf populations were Montana and Minnesota, and those were home to just a few hundred each.

So in 1973, via the Endangered Species Act, the U.S. government decided to protect gray wolves. The act imposed a $100,000 fine and up to a year in jail for anyone who deliberately killed a wolf. This put a stop to the widespread killing and helped the gray

---

Misery? Stephen King was once a high-school English teacher.

wolf make a comeback. In particular, efforts in Yellowstone National Park helped America's gray wolves rebound.

GETTING REACQUAINTED

In 1987, the government decided to explore the reintroduction of wolf populations to Yellowstone. Since the animals were indigenous to the region, it seemed logical. Much debate and investigation followed—nearby ranchers, in particular, worried that a wolf population would wreak havoc on their livestock. Finally, by 1995, wildlife biologists were ready to send a group of wolves back to Yellowstone.

Fourteen wolves were captured in Canada and transported to the park. Catching an entire pack is difficult, so the scientists took lone animals from different packs. A year later, 17 additional wolves were brought from Canada and released into Yellowstone.

On arrival, the wolves were placed into one-acre acclimation pens for eight to ten weeks in an effort to confine them to a limited range at first. Three chain-link fence pens were positioned at different locations in northern Yellowstone—at Crystal Creek, Rose Creek, and Soda Butte Creek. Biologists wanted the wolves to form new packs, so the scientists placed a dominant male wolf, a dominant female, and several young subordinate wolves into each acclimation pen to mirror the natural pack structure. Within 24 hours, the wolves began acting like packs in the wild, and in two out of three cases, the newly formed "alpha" pairs eventually had pups.

While in the acclimation pens, the wolves were fed only once every seven to ten days to mimic the waxing and waning eating habits of wild wolves. A typical pack of six in the wild consumes about 800 pounds of meat per month (about two adult elk and a small deer).

FREE AT LAST!

Then it came time to let the wolves go. At first, when scientists opened the front enclosure gates, the wolves wouldn't venture into the park. Instead, they avoided the front gate and spent most of their time at the rear of their pens. But when the back gates were finally removed, the wolves moved out. Before they did, each wolf was outfitted with a radio collar so that scientists could follow the animal's movements and study its behavior.

Yellowstone's new wolf population fared surprisingly well. The first 14 animals quickly bore two litters, totaling nine pups. By the spring of 1997, 13 litters totaling 64 pups had been born. In addition, 10 young orphaned wolves were released into the park in early 1997. Today, more than 700 wolves live in Yellowstone, and about 1,500 total live in Wyoming, Montana, and Idaho. All of those are descendants of the original Yellowstone wolves.

CRYING WOLF

Good news, right? Sort of. The resurgence of the wolf population in the western United States angered ranchers, who argued that the animals' growing numbers put their livestock at risk. In fact, over the last 35 years, ranchers have maintained that the wolf problem was getting out of hand and that government protection needed to be lifted.

In 2008, they found an ally in President George W. Bush, whose administration declared that the wolves no longer needed protection and removed them from the endangered species list. This left the job of protecting the wolves up to the individual states of Montana, Wyoming, and Idaho. The response of Idaho's governor, C. L. Otter, who "bid for that first ticket to shoot a wolf myself," wasn't reassuring to environmentalists. They argued that for the wolf populations to really rebound, between 2,000 and 5,000 animals should occupy the three states—not the 1,500 there now. Debate and legal wrangling continue as the wolves (and the folks who love them) await their fate.

*　　*　　*

WOLF BITES

- Alaska has America's largest gray wolf population, estimated at around 7,000 individuals. Canada has the largest population worldwide.

- Wolves usually chase their prey only 1,000 yards.

- In North America, there have been only three documented wolf attacks, none of which was fatal.

The first three digits of a 13-digit bar code indicate the country of origin.

THE FAMOUS FOR 3 WORDS AWARD

Clara Peller and Wendy's "Where's the Beef" Commercial

A feisty octogenarian put some sizzle into a simple ad line and made it into the history books.

CAUSING A COW-MOTION

Tuesday, January 10, 1984, was the first time Americans heard the phrase "Where's the beef?" It definitely wouldn't be the last. Almost instantly, the question asked by a 4'10", 83-year-old shrill-voiced actress named Clara Peller, in a commercial for fast-food giant Wendy's, became a popular catchphrase. And even though the commercial featured two other senior ladies trying to order a burger at a fast-food restaurant, Peller was the attention-getter.

A POWERFUL STATEMENT

The ad is deliciously simple compared to some of today's commercials. In it, three senior ladies, whose heads barely reach the counter of a restaurant that bills itself as the "Home of the Big Bun," are less than impressed by the hamburger they've ordered. Two of the women marvel at the size of the fluffy bun, but Peller asks three times, "Where's the beef?" (Peller's only other lines in the ad are "Hey" and "I don't think there's anybody back there.")

"Where's the beef?" became such a recognizable catchphrase that Peller recorded a single of the same name (with Nashville shock jock Coyote McCloud). More famously, the phrase took on new meaning in the 1984 Democratic presidential candidate debates, when Walter Mondale used it against Gary Hart. (A decision that bumped Mondale up in the polls, too). "Where's the

---

A gallon of water weighs 8.34 pounds.

beef?" was licensed in a major merchandising deal and emblazoned on T-shirts, underwear, coffee mugs, and towels.

Not bad for a commercial that almost didn't make it on the air. Just one week before it was scheduled to run, Wendy's got cold feet when test audiences reacted negatively to the ad. The ad copywriter had to talk the Wendy's team into sticking with his vision. And it paid off. Annual revenues for Wendy's jumped 31 percent after the spots began airing, and the fast-food chain moved from fifth to third place in the industry. In 1988, the ad spot was named a "Clio Classic" at the annual Clio Awards, the most prestigious prize given in the advertising industry.

THE TEAM BEHIND THE FLUFFY BUN

Wendy's had wanted to bump up its sales in the early 1980s, so the company turned to a 41-year-old copywriter named Clifford Freeman, employed by the Madison Avenue advertising agency of Dancer Fitzgerald Sample. Freeman had created several ads that used humor to make their point (like "Sometimes you feel like a nut; sometimes you don't" for Mounds and Almond Joy). Wendy's was betting that his approach could give them a bigger bite of the market.

What Freeman came up with was called "Fluffy Bun," even though the world would forever remember it as "Where's the beef?" Freeman wrote the simple line before he knew which actress would deliver it. He left the job of hiring to director Joe Sedelmaier.

Sedelmaier was famous in the ad business, too. He was the guy behind a 1980s Federal Express commercial featuring the fastest talker in the world, and he had a knack for picking out nonactors and "personalities" instead of professional actors for his spots. It was Sedelmaier who cast the little-known Peller based on her work in a previous commercial for a truck-rental company called Jartran. (In that commercial, Peller played a woman moving her belongings—which included a lot of pet rabbits—while her husband slept.)

A STAR IS BORN

Peller was a Russian native who'd come to the United States as a girl. She'd worked as a beautician and manicurist for 35 years and had only decided to give acting a try after she retired. She made her commercial debut for Jartran in 1983, but it was the Wendy's spot that made her a household name. Peller's lack of theatrical training shows in the spot; she looks a bit confused and out of sorts. But it didn't matter. Her presence and grouchy delivery of her short lines were comedic gold.

She made only the actor's union scale—$317.40 per day—for the first Wendy's commercial, but for her follow-up commercials for the chain—a total of 10 in all—she reportedly made $500,000. She was quoted later as saying, "I made some money, which is nice for an older person, but Wendy's made millions because of me."

When all was said and done, Peller was a celebrity, making appearances on *Saturday Night Live* and in the 1985 movie *Moving Violations*. She continued to get commercial work as well, but when she proclaimed, "I found it!" in a Prego spaghetti sauce commercial in 1985, Wendy's had a beef with her. She would no longer star in any more ads for the chain. William Welter, an EVP for Wendy's, told the *New York Times*, "Unfortunately, Clara's appearance in the [Prego] ads makes it extremely difficult for her to serve as a credible spokesperson for our products."

In 1987, exactly one week after her 85th birthday, Peller passed away. But her legacy lives on in American pop culture.

*　　　*　　　*

FACTS ABOUT WENDY'S FOUNDER DAVE THOMAS

- He got the idea for the distinctive Wendy's square hamburgers from Kewpee, a restaurant in Kalamazoo, Michigan.

- In the 1960s, he owned several Kentucky Fried Chicken locations in Columbus, Ohio, but sold them in 1969 to start his own hamburger chain. He said there weren't any good burger places in Columbus.

- His two-year-old daughter Melinda could only pronounce her first name as "Wenda." Thomas fashioned it into "Wendy" and named his burger restaurant that.

- Thomas dropped out of high school at age 15, but earned a GED at the age of 60.

- From 1989 to 2002, Thomas was Wendy's commercial pitchman, appearing in more than 800 commercials.

The 25 windows in the Statue of Liberty's crown represent the 25 gemstones known in 1886.

THE "VIDEO MADE THE RADIO STAR" AWARD

"Take on Me" by a-ha

The third time was the charm for this catchy hit—thanks to a groundbreaking video that rocked the music video world.

OFF THE HOOK

It took a while for the world to take to "Take on Me." Luckily, the Norwegian band a-ha had a record company that believed the group was destined for stardom thanks to the band members' matinee-idol good looks and the vocal range of lead singer Morten Harket. The trio (Harket, guitarist Paul Waaktaar Savoy, and keyboardist Magne Furuholmen) moved to London in the early 1980s to try to get a record deal and finally succeeded in late 1983 when Warner Bros.' U.K. division signed them. They released "Take on Me," a catchy pop song about the nervousness of falling in love, in the fall of 1984, but the song lacked a hook. Its midtempo beat was overpowered by synthesizer effects that distracted listeners from Harket's powerhouse voice. The familiar chorus of "Take on me/Take me on/I'll be gone/In a day or two" was there, of course, but the energy of the song was plodding.

Nevertheless, Warner Bros. still felt they had a potential hit band on their hands, and they wanted to recoup the initial investment they'd made in the group. They hired producer Alan Tarney, who'd had success working with such 1970s artists as Cliff Richard and Leo Sayer, to remix "Take on Me," along with some other songs on the album. Tarney's direction for the song worked. He rearranged the synthesizer line, bringing it to the forefront to create the hook that would make the song immediately recognizable.

The words loosen and unloosen mean the same thing; so do flammable and inflammable.

He also sped up the tempo, creating a tune that would have the potential to entice people onto the dance floor.

IF AT FIRST YOU DON'T SUCCEED . . .

Still, a second release of the single didn't change matters. Outside of Norway, sales of a-ha's album *Hunting High and Low* were tanking. This time around, though, the American section of Warner Bros. Records had an idea. When the band had visited their offices, all the women had gone crazy for the three band members, Harket in particular. Warner Bros. wasn't going to let that opportunity get away. They convinced their British counterparts that the song needed just one more thing—a good video.

In the spring of 1985, everyone would be humming along to Harket's almost glass-shattering chorus and reciting the song's simple lyrics ("Talking away/I don't know what I'm to say/I'll say it anyway"). But ultimately, it was the medium of television that would get the message of "Take on Me" across and help it achieve sales of nearly 10 million copies worldwide.

REANIMATING A HIT

A performance video for the original version of "Take on Me" had already been filmed, but Warner Bros. was looking for something new, different, and captivating. Director Steve Barron had worked on movie sets for years and had already made an impact in music videos with Michael Jackson's "Billie Jean," the Human League's "Don't You Want Me," Culture Club's "Do You Really Want to Hurt Me," and others. In 1985, he was ready to break out of the mold of traditional music videos (which usually had slim budgets that left little room for creativity). "Take on Me" was given £100,000—an enormous budget at the time, especially since the band was unknown and had a sketchy track record. But Warner Bros. believed the investment would pay off. Barron went to work creating a story that mixed live action and animation.

The video's story opens with comic-book art of a motorcycle race. A cartoon version of Harket fights off the attacks of his competitors to win the race fair and square. The scene then shifts to a woman in a café who's reading the comic while a waitress serves her coffee. Suddenly the woman notices movement on the page. An animated Harket winks at her, and then his hand pops through the table to invite her into his world. She follows, and their flirtation begins.

The couple's happiness is short-lived, however. The waitress believes the woman has left without paying her bill, and she crumples the comic and throws it in the garbage. Meanwhile, the thugs from the motorcycle race return with wrenches in hand to beat Harket. The couple runs away, and Harket pushes the woman back into the real world, where she emerges in the trash. She grabs the comic, runs from the restaurant, and hurries home to finish reading to find out the fate of her new love.

She reads on and feels helpless when she sees that Harket has been beaten savagely and may be dead. As her tears fall, she sees him awaken to struggle against the boundaries of the comic book, a scene that also plays out in the hallway of her apartment. As Harket crashes against the walls, his body transforms from animation to real over and over again. As the song ends, Harket emerges, sweaty but flesh and blood, and the two embrace.

LOVE BITES

The video was partially shot on a soundstage and at a real restaurant, Kim's Café, in the Wandsworth section of London. The woman in the video was played by Bunty Bailey, an actress, dancer, and model. Romance sparked for Bailey and Harket on the set, but it didn't last. After dating Harket, Bailey appeared as a backup singer in the video for Billy Idol's hit "To Be a Lover," which reached #6 on the Billboard charts in 1986.

Things didn't work out much better for the fictional lovers in "Take on Me," either. The video for the follow-up song, "The Sun Always Shines on TV," opened with the couple staring into each other's eyes when Harket begins to switch back to his comic-book form. He doubles over in pain while Bailey helplessly watches, and then he runs off. A strong burst of light follows, and "The End" pops up on the scene.

THE TAKE ON "TAKE ON ME"

For its animation, "Take on Me" relied entirely on rotoscoping, a process in which live-action film is projected onto a surface and traced by an animator. Barron asked the record company for three months to work on the video (most were produced in a couple of days), and he got it. Lead animator Michael Patterson and 13 other illustrators embarked on the painstaking process involving more than 2,000 drawn images for the video.

The video's tumultuous finale was an homage to the 1980 movie *Altered States*, which starred William Hurt as a man who evolves and devolves in an attempt to learn the meaning of life through sensory deprivation. The ending of the movie features Hurt violently switching between humanity and primordial sludge while his wife watches helplessly.

THE FINAL CHAPTER

Shortly after the release of the new video for "Take on Me," the song became a hit around the globe. It went to #1 in the United States and became the second best-selling single of 1985. ("We Are the World" took the top spot.) At the 1986 MTV Video Awards, a-ha won Best New Artist, and "Take on Me" won the following awards:

- Most Experimental Video
- Viewer's Choice, Best Special Effects
- Best Concept Video, Best Cinematography
- Best Direction
- Best Editing

Dire Straits' "Money for Nothing," which used state-of-the-art computer animation with some rotoscoping thrown in to tell the song's story, won Video of the Year. Barron couldn't have been too disappointed in that, though: he also directed the Dire Straits video.

*   *   *

ANOTHER GREAT MUSIC VIDEO

"Buddy Holly" by Weezer (1994)

The alternative rock band is seamlessly spliced into actual footage of *Happy Days*. In the clip, the band, dressed in 1950s sweaters and nerdy glasses, play at Arnold's Diner as Fonzie wins a dance contest.

THE TANGLED UP IN BLUE AWARD

Jeans We Can Live Without

From humble origins to haute couture, blue jeans have seen it all . . . and clothed nearly everyone—even Uncle John. But some of the newest blue jean trends are enough to make even a dedicated denim-wearer say "no thanks."

BLUE JEANS HISTORY—THE SHORT VERSION

The Dongarii Fort in India gave birth to dungarees; the Genoese fabric industry gave birth to blue de Gênes (one theory for the original "blue jeans"), and textile work in Nîmes, France, led to a material that became known as "de Nîmes," or denim. Then, in 1873, a tailor named Jacob Davis and a merchant named Levi Strauss teamed up and got a patent for their copper rivets sewed onto the stress points of denim dungarees. Popular blue jeans were born.

Once used exclusively by sailors, laborers, and cowboys, jeans have become universal outerwear. But lately, some new trends in denim have emerged that stink . . . and may even have some toxic side effects.

FOREVER IN BLUE JEANS

Jeans have been popular with everyone from California gold miners to today's CEOs. One reason is that they continue to look clean for a long time between washings and don't show dirt or stains as easily as other types of pants do. But one of the latest trends in blue jeans is "raw denim" jeans, which pushed the bounds of cleanliness. Raw denim is the fabric that comes right off the production line: it's unwashed, untreated, stiff, and dark blue. The benefit of raw denim is that, if someone wears it long enough, it should completely conform to his or her body, creating a nearly custom fit. Some raw jeans aficionados even put objects (wallets, pens, calculators) in their pockets so the outlines of the objects will remain visible in the denim as a style feature.

But even the most devoted dirty-denim fan might balk at the recommended care instructions on raw jeans: "Do not wash for six months." One company that makes the jeans, A.P.C., actually encourages no washing for a whole year. At the end of 12 months, A.P.C. designers recommend that you take your unwashed jeans to the ocean, give them a good dip and scrubbing with sand, and then rinse with fresh water and dry them in the sun. As for cleanliness and odor control, one fan sprinkles his jeans with baking soda and puts them in a plastic bag in the freezer—the cold kills bacteria and the soda absorbs odors.

DENIM COUTURE

In Japan, the latest trend is custom-made jeans. Yoropiko Denim, designed by Martin Ksohoh, features tailor-made, decorated denim, complete with jeweled buttons (sometimes made of rubies, emeralds, diamonds, and sapphires) and large pieces of embroidery fashioned from ultra-soft kimono thread.

Ksohoh's denim jeans and jackets have become favorites of hip-hop stars like S.A.S. (brothers Sean and Melvin Williams) and Dizzee Rascal. And each piece is a work of art that takes hours to create—and hours to earn. A pair of Yoropiko jeans costs anywhere from $475 (for plain denim with your choice of gems) to $995 (for embroidered denim) and up (for custom designs).

DISTRESSING THE ENVIRONMENT

Raw denim and custom-made jeans may be extravagant, but recently a popular form of treating denim has come under fire for being environmentally unfriendly. Stonewashed jeans were really popular in the 1980s and 1990s, and many people still like them because the jeans are soft from the first wearing, look good, and can be customized with all sorts of frayed threads, holes, slashes, and worn bits. But some of the processes that make denim more comfortable for wearers are polluting land and rivers in central Mexico—specifically the Tehuacán valley, where more than 700 clothing manufacturers process jeans to sell to U.S. companies.

Once called the "city of health," Tehuacán used to be best

known for mineral springs. Today, toxic runoff from the denim plants has poisoned the area. The water in Tehuacán's irrigation canals has turned blue and is so full of toxins that it burns seedlings and sterilizes farmland. And much of the dirt along the canal's banks is an ashy gray.

There are alternatives. Some smaller companies like Edun and Fair Indigo offer organic and fair-trade denim that's processed in environmentally friendly ways.

FAVORITE FABRIC

Today's denim often contains Lycra and other fibers, but it's typically an all-cotton fabric. The natural fiber and the strong weave make leftover denim useful for all sorts of things:

- Recycled denim can be made into pencils—sure, they're blue, but the lead is still charcoal gray.

- Recycled blue jeans, known as "Cotton Batt," have become a new eco-friendly choice for insulating homes. Cotton even has a better insulation value than fiberglass.

- Crane's, the famed stationery company, has been using denim scraps in its all-fabric paper for more than 200 years. It now even has a "Denim Blues" line.

*   *   *

FILLER

At the BRI, we call these little extra tidbits at the end of articles "filler." The Academy Awards has its own version: In the auditorium on Oscar night, the Academy enlists a few dozen "seat fillers"—volunteers whose job is to hang out in the wings during the four-hour ceremony, waiting for audience members to go the bathroom. Then the seat filler quietly runs in and occupies the vacant seat until its owner returns. The reason: Whenever the camera pans the audience, it must always appear to be a packed house. The seat fillers are under strict orders not to talk to or engage in any way with the movie stars they are sitting next to. (We now return you to your regularly scheduled Golden Plunger Awards.)

The first governor of the Bahamas, Woodes Rogers, was a former pirate.

THE STATE OF THE ART AWARD

Christo and Jeanne-Claude

If your average person decided to take thousands of yards of fabric and drape them over a well-known landmark, it might be seen as weird and intrusive. But contemporary artists Christo and Jeanne-Claude combine determination and lots of patience to make their visions work.

GOOD COP, BAD COP

Christo and Jeanne-Claude describe themselves as "environmental artists" because they take an environment and work with it to make art. Urban or rural, land- or water-based, Christo installations take every element of a place into account.

For years, the artworks were signed and marketed under the name "Christo," so people believed that he was the sole creator. Now, the pair refer to themselves as "the artists Christo and Jeanne-Claude." Christo Javacheff was born in Bulgaria on June 13, 1935—Jeanne-Claude was born on the same day in France. They met when Christo did a painting of Jeanne-Claude's mother in 1958. Jeanne-Claude describes their collaboration as a "good cop, bad cop" dynamic—he focuses on the vision; she focuses on business logistics.

Christo has vowed never to repeat himself. He won't wrap another bridge (as he did to Paris's Pont Neuf) or surround another set of islands (as in the Bay of Biscayne). Every project is unique.

A PROLIFIC PAIRING

Christo and Jeanne-Claude's six-decade career includes more than 18 completed installations. Here are some of their major works:

1. *Iron Curtain—Wall of Oil Barrels*: On June 27, 1962, in protest of the Berlin Wall, the artists closed the Rue Visconti, one of the narrowest streets in Paris, for eight hours by blocking it with 240 industrial oil barrels.

Until the 19th century, an "accident" referred to anything that happened, good or bad.

2. *Wrapped Fountain & Tower*: Completed in Spoleto, Italy, in 1968, this was Jeanne-Claude's first work without Christo, who was working on #3, the Wrapped Kunsthalle, in Switzerland. Jeanne-Claude wrapped a medieval tower and a Baroque fountain in white polyethylene; it remained on display for three weeks.

3. *Wrapped Kunsthalle*: Christo's first installation without Jeanne-Claude, this was the first fully wrapped building that the artists conceived. It was installed in Bern, Switzerland, for the 50th anniversary of the city's art museum.

4. *Museum of Contemporary Art Wrapped*: The Bern Kunsthalle was wrapped in translucent plastic, but Christo chose to wrap Chicago's boxy, anonymous Museum of Contemporary Art in greenish-brown tarpaulin to play up its industrial feel—and for a greater contrast with the January 1969 snow.

5. *Wrapped Coast*: Christo and Jeanne-Claude wrapped the rocky, cliff-lined shore of Little Bay in Sydney, Australia, in the fall of 1969. It required one million square feet of erosion-control fabric and 35 miles of polypropylene rope.

6. *Valley Curtain*: Plagued by problems, including protests from environmentalists and financial shortfalls, this bright-orange curtain at Rifle Gap, Colorado, which required 142,000 square feet of cloth and 200 tons of concrete, had to come down just 28 hours after it was finished . . . because gale-force winds shredded it.

7. *Wrapped Roman Wall*: In 1974, Christo and Jeanne-Claude wrapped a 2,000-year-old wall built by Emperor Marcus Aurelius to surround Rome. Set at the end of the crowded and cosmopolitan Via Veneto, this work highlighted the coexistence of ancient and modern worlds.

8. *Running Fence*: A dramatic, 24½-mile white fence running through California's Marin and Sonoma counties, this 1976 installation brought the artists to the forefront of the American art scene. Charles Schulz gave the authors a nod in a *Peanuts* cartoon strip with Snoopy coming home and finding that his doghouse had been "wrapped" à la Christo. Twenty-five years later, in 2003, Christo and Jeanne-Claude presented the Charles Schulz Museum with a life-size wrapped Snoopy doghouse that is now on permanent exhibit.

Archaeologists have found ancient "Beware of Dog" signs in Pompeii.

9. *Surrounded Islands*: Of course, an installation in Miami's Biscayne Bay would be done in flamingo pink. The 1980–83 work involved surrounding 11 islands with 6.5 million square feet of polypropylene fabric. It also highlighted an unintentional but significant aspect of the artists' work: cleaning up debris and leaving natural places the same or better than when they started. Forty tons of garbage were removed from the islands before the project began.

10. *Pont Neuf Wrapped*: It took years to get permission to wrap this historic bridge in Paris that connects the Île de la Cité with the Right and Left Banks. When it was complete, the installation highlighted the heart of Paris.

11. *The Umbrellas*: This was a joint project—3,100 fabric umbrellas were set up in Japan and California (blue for Japan, yellow for California) and unfurled in 1991. The Japanese umbrellas were positioned close together and the Californian umbrellas spread out in many directions.

12. *Wrapped Reichstag*: The Reichstag building, home of Germany's first parliament, has been a symbol of democracy in Berlin for more than 100 years. But it's also endured many decades of conflict. So perhaps it's fitting, then, that it took 24 years for Christo and Jeanne-Claude (with the help of 90 professional climbers) to wrap this building.

13. *The Gates*: The original design for New York's Central Park included a number of gates that were never installed. In 2005, Christo and Jeanne-Claude created their own version of the gates, a series of 7,500 gates made of billowing, saffron-colored fabric panels. It stood for two weeks, spread over 23 miles, and was the largest created artwork since the Great Sphinx of Egypt.

GATED COMMUNITY

The artists are as famous for their fortitude in fighting the approval process as they are for the scale and audacity of their breathtaking works. In February 2005, *The Gates* was unveiled in Central Park. The $20 million installation was conceived in 1992 and had been rejected by several mayoral administrations until Mayor Michael Bloomberg finally approved it. Bloomberg told the *New York Times*, "I can't promise . . . particularly since this is New

---

Lighthouse keepers were nicknamed "wickies" because they tended the lamp's wick.

York that every single person will love *The Gates*, but I guarantee that they will all talk about it."

In fact, many people had been talking about it for years. The work's official title was *The Gates: Central Park, New York, 1979–2005*. That 26-year span in the date is no typo. It represents the length of time it took the artists to persuade New York City officials to install this work. (That includes 41 formal presentations in 1980 alone.)

THAT'S A WRAP

Let's cover some fun facts about the creative couple:

- With the exception of 11 architecture students who refused payment for their work on Australia's *Wrapped Coast*, there are no volunteers who work on the installations; everyone is paid.

- According to the artists, there are three things Christo and Jeanne-Claude don't do together:

    1. Fly in the same aircraft.

    2. Jeanne-Claude doesn't make drawings. Christo commits all of their ideas to paper and has never had an assistant in his studio.

    3. Christo never talks to their tax accountant.

- The couple does not take vacations, and they work seven days a week; he works an average of 17 hours per day, and she works about 13 hours a day.

- They immigrated to the United States in 1964 and, for their first three years, were illegal aliens. They have lived at the same address in New York City since their arrival.

*   *   *

"I'd like to thank the rest of the cast. To give a really bad performance like mine, you need to have really bad actors."
> **—Halle Berry, Worst Actor Razzie for *Catwoman*,
> also starring Benjamin Bratt and Sharon Stone**

THE SNACK
ATTACK AWARD

Popcorn

*The American Cancer Society includes popcorn on its short list
of "11 Things That Don't Cause Cancer." Pair that with its
soul-satisfying tastiness and you have an award-winning snack.*

A PIECE OF POPCORN A DAY

A cup of air-popped corn has just 20 calories, and according to a 2004 survey by Jolly Time Popcorn, 86 percent of respondents considered popcorn to be a healthy snack—even though 58 percent also want an intense buttery taste.

Americans eat about one billion pounds (59 quarts per person) of popcorn every year. Sure, we also nosh on potato chips, pretzels, peanuts, crackers, and rice cakes, but popcorn is special. Crunchy and buttery, fluffy and salty, it's good hot or cold. (Some people even float it in soups as a garnish!) Popcorn, a starchy carbohydrate, is an indigenous all-American food product that is cheap, wholesome, and low-calorie (in its unadorned form). Did we mention versatile? Throw on some butter or cheese, some sugar or spice—popcorn tastes great any way you serve it.

YE OLDE CORN

Actually, the word "corn" doesn't refer to the green-sheathed cobs we're used to finding at roadside stands. "Corn" is an Old English word that means simply "local grain." The "corn" mentioned in the Bible probably meant barley. In England, it meant wheat, and in Scotland and Ireland, oats. So when European settlers came to the New World, they began calling the most common grain found here "corn," though its proper name is maize.

Maize has been growing for thousands of years in the Americas. Ranging from smaller than a penny to about 2 inches high, the oldest ears of popcorn were discovered in the Bat Cave of west central New Mexico in 1948 and again in 1950. Those Bat Cave ears may be nearly 2,500 years old. The Aztecs used popcorn in many ways, including as a decoration for statues of the god Tlaloc, who governed rain and fertility. In many countries, including the early U.S. colonies, popcorn was the original breakfast cereal, served variously with milk, cream, sugar, and fruit. And the Wampanoag tribe of Massachusetts, which introduced popcorn to the first Thanksgiving feast in Plymouth, even made popcorn beer.

The colonists were also the first to invent an alternate popcorn flavor: kettle corn. It's mentioned in the diaries of Pennsylvania Dutch settlers (whose ethnic origin is German), and its sweet-and-salty flavor comes from a combination of salt and sugar, honey, or molasses, though some people use two or more.

MOVIE BUTTER

It wasn't until the 1890s that popcorn became a popular snack food, but when it did enter the scene, one of its attractions was in the "pop." When heated, moisture inside the kernel turns to steam and the pressure of the steam causes the corn to pop. (The kernels left behind are called "old maids.")

A popped kernel of corn is called a "flake," and there are two main types of flakes: "mushroom" and "butterfly." The former have fewer "wings," and are sturdy enough to take heavy coatings (like caramel), while the latter have that typical "winged" shape and feel lighter. Most commercially produced popcorn is from white and yellow corn strains.

The more popular popcorn became, the more venues vendors found for its sale. When street vendors hawking the fluffy stuff started cutting into snack stand sales at movie theaters in the 1920s, the theater owners decided to bring the vendors inside. Thus, a classic pairing began, as moviegoers realized that popcorn was the perfect food to eat while their eyes were glued to the screen. Those savvy theater owners also realized that they could sell more popcorn if they offered butter to pour over the top. Soon a tub of popcorn and a stack of paper napkins were as essential for going to the movies as ticket stubs.

114 million carats of diamonds are produced every year.

SMART POP

Most popcorn is bought and consumed at home (70 percent, both unpopped and prepopped), and the main popcorn producers are Illinois, Indiana, Iowa, Kansas, Kentucky, Michigan, Missouri, Nebraska, and Ohio. People buy the most during the fall and winter, when they spend more time indoors. Perhaps one of the most nostalgic popcorn-making methods today is the 1960s–era Jiffy Pop, an aluminum pie pan with a foil top and a handle that the maker shook over an electric burner until the kernels burst and turned the top into an aluminum mushroom cloud.

The most popular flavors for popcorn include plain, butter, cheese, and caramel, but there are plenty of variations available, including a Halftime Chili and Sour Cream, green apple and blue raspberry, Irish Cream Coffee with white chocolate, loaded baked potato, and even root beer float.

NUKE IT!

A new trend in modern popcorn snacking came in the 1980s with the boom in home microwave ovens. Microwave popcorn accounted for $240 million in annual popcorn sales in the United States in the 1990s. Recently, however, microwave popcorn has come under fire as posing possible health hazards. In particular, people who work in the plants where the popcorn's butter flavoring is made have complained of lung problems (from breathing in the chemicals), though plenty of manufacturers claim there's no risk for consumers.

KERNELS OF FUN

- Old-fashioned method of making popcorn: Heat 2 tablespoons of oil in a pan, add ½ cup of kernels, cover, shake, and enjoy!

- October is National Popcorn Poppin' Month, as proclaimed in 1999 by then–Secretary of Agriculture Dan Glickman.

- *Guinness World Records* says that the "World's Largest Popcorn Ball" was created in October 2006 by a company called The Popcorn Factory. It weighed 3,423 pounds, measured 8 feet in diameter, and had a circumference of 24 feet, 6 inches.

- Popcorn is a whole grain and contains fiber. If you don't drown it in butter, it's a healthy low-calorie snack.

The music for California's state anthem was written by a man named Frankenstein.

THE COMING SOON AWARD

Best Movie Taglines

A picture is worth a thousand words—or at least five or six really good ones.

THAT PERFECT LINE

Movie posters excite movie buffs and collectors, who value the art as a snapshot in time of culture and society. In 2005, a collector bought an original movie poster for *Metropolis*, Fritz Lang's 1927 science fiction classic for $690,000—the highest price ever paid for a movie poster. But the words on the posters also help to excite interest in an upcoming movie. According to one film industry marketing executive, a good tagline reinforces a film's iconic image. The words suggest the experience that awaits the viewer, and are themselves an art worthy of recognition. In some cases, the tagline is more memorable than the poster it's printed on—and sometimes it's even better than the movie.

Los Angeles design firms employ copywriters to come up with the words to sum up a movie. They brainstorm the concepts and words months in advance of the poster's release. As the first step in the process, ad copy can cement the direction for a motion picture's multimillion-dollar-marketing campaign. The tagline's goal is always the same: entice, lure viewers in, and don't give away too much.

Since 1971, *Hollywood Reporter* has been honoring creative movie marketing at its annual Key Art Awards, but it was only in 2004 that a category was added for the best copy line. So far, the paper has honored the following:

- 2004: *The Incredibles* ("No gut, no glory").
- 2005: *Scary Movie 3* ("You'll die to see these rings").
- 2006: *The 40-Year-Old Virgin* ("The longer you wait, the harder it gets").

In a 1988 poll, Batman comic readers voted to have Robin killed by the Joker.

DON'T GO IN THE WATER!

Perhaps the best-known tagline, though, comes from a movie that was first a major best-selling book that scared people out of the ocean. In 1975, thousands of people heeded the warning of *Jaws*'s tagline: "Don't go in the water." Three years later, the poster for *Jaws 2*, released in 1978, used another effective tagline: "Just when you thought it was safe to go back in the water . . ."

Jaws 2's tagline stands out in movie history for many reasons:

- It became an international catchphrase—one that's still in use.

- It's better than the image on the poster. (Everyone remembers the first movie's shocking depiction of an easygoing swimmer unaware of a rapidly approaching shark. But few recall *Jaws 2*'s picture of a water skier being trailed by a giant great white.)

- *Jaws 2* is a terrible movie. Vincent Canby, writing in the *New York Times*, remarked that the movie "simply drones on and on and on" and the shark "looks like something one might ride at Disneyland." But the tagline built up enough excitement to make the film the highest-grossing sequel ever up until then.

PLAYING ON YOUR FEARS

Many movie taglines employ the fear factor. Our other favorite scary taglines:

- "Pray for Rosemary's Baby." *Rosemary's Baby* (1968)

- "There's only one thing wrong with the Davis' baby . . . it's Alive." *It's Alive* (1974)

- "In space, no one can hear you scream." *Alien* (1979)

- "They're heeere . . ." *Poltergeist* (1982)

- "Be afraid. Be very afraid." *The Fly* (1986)

- "After a decade of silence . . . the buzz is back!" *Texas Chainsaw Massacre 2* (1986)

- "To enter the mind of a killer, she must challenge the mind of a madman." *The Silence of the Lambs* (1991)

- "We dare you again." *Saw II* (2005)

George W. Bush is the only U.S. president to have fathered twins.

MEET SOMEONE ON THE EDGE

Movie taglines aren't always out to scare you, though. Some-times they want to say just enough to get audiences excited to learn more about the characters in the story. These are the best enticements to spend a little time with someone who's a little different.

- "I hate him! I love him! He's a scoundrel! He's a saint! He's crazy! He's a genius!" *Citizen Kane* (1941)

- "Jim Stark . . . a kid from a 'good' family—what makes him tick . . . like a bomb?" *Rebel Without a Cause* (1955)

- "This is Benjamin. He's a little worried about his future." *The Graduate* (1967)

- "Not since the dawn of time has America experienced a man like Howard Beale!" *Network* (1976)

- "Nobody knows Rupert Pupkin, but after 11:30 tonight no one will ever forget him." *The King of Comedy* (1983)

- "If adventure has a name, it must be Indiana Jones." *Indiana Jones and the Temple of Doom* (1984)

- "The story of a rebel and his bike." *Pee-Wee's Big Adventure* (1985)

- "His story will touch you, even though he can't." *Edward Scissorhands* (1990)

- "You'll laugh. You'll cry. You'll hurl!" *Wayne's World* (1992)

- "If you can't be famous . . . be infamous." *Chicago* (2004)

MASTERS OF HYPE

They may overstate their case, but there's no denying these taglines have a point.

- "The most awesome thriller of all time." *King Kong* (1933)

- "The more he yearns for a woman's arms . . . the fiercer he lusts for the treasure that cursed them all!" *The Treasure of the Sierra Madre* (1948)

- "They had a date with fate in Casablanca!" *Casablanca* (1942)

- "His whole life was a million-to-one shot." *Rocky* (1976)

- "They're young. They're in love . . . and they kill people."
  Bonnie and Clyde (1967)

- "It's time to kick some asteroid." *Armageddon* (1998)

- "On my command—unleash hell!" *Gladiator* (2000)

KEEP IT SIMPLE

Sometimes you need to get right to the point and sum up the entire movie in one short line. It may seem like the easiest way to go, but it's probably the most difficult to get right. Here are the ones that did it best:

- "Simple. Powerful. Unforgettable." *High Noon* (1952)

- "Love means never having to say you're sorry."
  Love Story (1970)

- "A long time ago in a galaxy far, far away . . ." *Star Wars* (1977)

- "He is afraid. He is alone. He is three million light years from home." *E.T.* (1982)

- "The first casualty of war is innocence." *Platoon* (1986)

- "Can two friends sleep together and still love each other in the morning?" *When Harry Met Sally* (1989)

- "The story of two people who got married, met, and then fell in love." *Green Card* (1990)

- "One ring to rule them all." *The Lord of the Rings: The Fellowship of the Ring* (2001)

- "Bigger, squarer, spongier!"
  The SpongeBob Square Pants Movie (2004)

- "Love is a force of nature." *Brokeback Mountain* (2005)

*   *   *

"What does the Academy Award mean?
I don't think it means much of anything."

—**Sally Field, after winning the Best Actress
Oscar for *Norma Rae* (1980)**

Right shoes wear out faster than left shoes.

THE PERSONAL ASSISTANT AWARD

Baboon Jack, the Signalman

*James Wide nearly lost his job twice, but a trusted
baboon named Jack saved him both times.*

OUCH!
Railway guard James Wide earned his nickname,
"Jumper," because he liked to jump from one railway car
to another—often while they were still moving. He worked in the
town of Uitenhage, South Africa, during the late 19th century,
and he did his job well, even if he had an unorthodox way of
doing it. But jumping from car to car was a dangerous game, and
one day he paid a terrible price for it.

Wide slipped during one of his jumps and got his legs caught
under the train. They were amputated below the knees. In most
cases, that would have been the end of his career as a guard.
Instead, he changed jobs, became a signalman (who used a series
of flags to signal to trains that the needed to stop or slow down),
and also found help so he could continue to do his job. Who was
Jumper's great assistant? A baboon named Jack.

JACK OF ALL TRADES
Wide constructed pegs to complete his legs and even built a small
trolley to make it easier to move around. But living and working
alone were tough with his disability, and he began to look for solutions. One afternoon in 1881, he found the perfect one.

There are a couple of theories as to how Wide found his
baboon friend: One says that he spotted the animal pulling an ox
wagon in the town center and pleaded with the animal's owner to
give him up. The reluctant owner was finally persuaded, but he
entrusted Wide with the baboon, named Jack, with one admoni-

tion: give Jack "a tot of good Cape brandy" every night, or don't expect him to do any work the next day. Wide agreed.

A second story says that Wide found Jack as a baby, in a cage at the local market. He bought the animal and brought him home.

Whichever is the real story, the first thing Wide trained Jack to do was push him the half-mile from his house to the train station in his trolley. Jack took to his new job very well.

JACK TO THE RESCUE

Wide's job as a signalman involved listening to the whistle blasts of the passing locomotives. The three tracks were assigned a number of whistle blasts: one blast for track one, two for track two, and three for track three. Four blasts meant the conductor of the train needed the keys for the coal sheds.

Wide didn't expect Jack to do this job for him, but it turned out that Jack was quite a listener. After only a few days, the baboon had figured out the codes and rushed to get the keys for a conductor who sounded his whistle four times. Wide was astounded but knew he—and Jack—were on to something.

Wide started training the baboon to make the appropriate track changes, too. Jack's performance was flawless, and Wide knew he had found an assistant who could take on the demands of the tough job.

TATTLETALE

Unfortunately, it wasn't long before Wide's unconventional assistant was noticed. A local woman saw the baboon working the railways and complained to the authorities. A team of inspectors visited the station to see what was going on, and when they learned the truth, they fired Wide on the spot.

But Wide was never one to give up . . . and certainly not when it came to the job he loved so much. He pleaded with the inspectors to put Jack to the test. When Jack performed the tasks perfectly, the amazed men gave in and admitted he was no ordinary baboon—this was Jack the Signalman. Wide and Jack were reinstated. Jack even received an official employment number from the local government, making him a full-time employee.

Gentoo penguins have pink poo.

KNOWING JACK

Jack was so good at his job that he even looked at the oncoming trains before changing the signals, a sign that he wasn't just going through the motions. He actually understood the importance of what he was doing. But more importantly, Jack and Wide developed a true friendship. Jack's loyalty helped him learn to do all kinds of jobs for Wide, including helping to clean the house where they lived in and acting as night watchman.

Jack died in 1890, but he still inspires people today. The Albany Museum in Grahamstown, South Africa, has an exhibit dedicated to him. And a photographic museum recently opened at the site of now-closed Uitenhage station, where locals still marvel at the story of Jack the Signalman.

*　　*　　*

MEMORABLE OSCAR ACCEPTANCE SPEECHES

"I'm speechless now. I, well, I, thank you life, thank you love, and it is true, there is some angels in this city."
> —Marion Cotillard (Best Actress for *La Vie En Rose*)

"Marlon Brando very regretfully cannot accept this very generous award. And the reason for this being is the treatment of American Indians today by the film industry."
> —Sacheen Littlefeather (refusing Brando's Best Actor award for *The Godfather*)

"This is one night I wish I smoked and drank."
> —Grace Kelly (Best Actress for *The Country Girl*)

"Thank you to Martin Scorsese. I hope my son will marry your daughter."
> —Cate Blanchett (Best Supporting Actress for *The Aviator*)

THE JULIA WILD CHILD AWARD

Insect Delicacies from Around the World

Tired of chicken cooked 100 ways? Or the tried-and-true, but boring, rotation of beef, poultry, seafood, and a vegetarian meal? We've got the perfect solution to make your meals take flight.

NOBODY EATS COCKROACHES
Gene Defoliart, professor of entomology at the University of Wisconsin at Madison, and publisher of The Food Insects Newsletter, told the *New York Times*, "Nobody eats cockroaches. They're unsanitary. Kind of disgusting, when you think about it." Well . . . yes. But fans of entomophagy (insect-eating) universally agree that people who don't eat insects are missing out on an abundant, low-calorie, easily sustained protein source that has been appreciated for thousands of years.

Ancient Greeks and Romans often ate insects—the latter particularly enjoyed beetle larvae. Today, biting into a fried cricket or spreading a spoonful of ant pâté on a cracker gives most Americans the willies, but people in other countries and cultures eat them all the time. An estimated 80 percent of the world's population are entomophages—people who consume insects as food. (Yes, on purpose!) Dragonflies, cicadas, crickets, grasshoppers, and giant water bugs are all on a menu somewhere at any given time.

Cultivating insects as a food source has many advantages:

- Insects create far more edible protein per pound than chicken or beef.

- According to *National Geographic*, insect farming is more efficient than cattle production: 100 pounds of feed produce 10 pounds of beef, but the same amount of feed yields 45 pounds of crickets.

There are two talking animals in the Bible: the serpent and Balaam's ass.

- Hamburger is roughly 18 percent protein and 18 percent fat, but cooked grasshopper contains up to 60 percent protein with just 6 percent fat. (Other insects like caterpillars, termites, and beetle grubs are high in fat, though like fish, insect fatty acids are unsaturated and healthier.)

- Insects are faster to raise than other meat.

- They're also easier to hunt. (One 19th-century observer of Paiute Indians watched tribe members dig trenches and drive crickets into them.)

BEYOND ANT FARMS

Nutritional aspects make bugs a smart crop, and new demand is making them a cash crop. The *Seattle Times* reported in 2005 that when farmers near Mexico City realized that they could get as much money for trapping and selling grasshoppers as they were spending on pesticides, they began deliberately planting crops as "traps" for the protein-rich insects.

HAVE ANOTHER APHID, MY DEAR

Types of insects that people around the world eat include ants, beetles, caterpillars, cockroaches, crickets, grasshoppers, earthworms, fly larvae, bees, mealworms, may flies, moths, rolli-pollies, silverfish, snails, slugs, termites, water bugs, and wasps. They all have distinctive flavors. Male giant water bugs have a minty taste; leaf-cutting ants have a walnut flavor; fire-ant pupae taste like watermelon; and many grubs taste sweet and creamy.

These varied flavors were highlighted in a menu from a New York Entomological Society "Bug Banquet" held at the Explorers Club:

Assorted Crudites with Peppery Delight Mealworm Dip
Wax Worm and Mealworm California Rolls W/ Tamari Dipping Sauce
Wild Mushrooms in Mealworm Flour Pastry
Cricket and Vegetable Tempura
Mealworm Balls in Tomato Sauce
Mini Fontina Bruschetta with Mealworm Gannouj
Wax Worm Fritters with Plum Sauce
Seasoned Cricket Breads and Butter
Assorted Insect Sugar Cookies.

Q: If you had $1 million in $100 bills, how much would it weigh? A: 20.41 pounds.

Most authorities (both entomologists and chefs) recommend that would-be entomophages stick to farmed insects. Not only are they disease-free—they're more likely to be toxin-free, too.

DOWN THE HATCH

You've been reading along, and you're probably still squirming. You'd never go near a fire-roasted tarantula, or coconut-milk-marinated grubs. On the other hand, maybe you would. Most people already eat shrimp and lobster, which are arthropods, just like insects. They stir honey, an insect-made sweetener, into their tea. And although only a few of us have eaten one, we've all heard of the agave worm at the bottom of a tequila bottle.

Still not convinced that "mixed-bug" products are for you? Well, like it or not, you've already been consuming them. The FDA doesn't ban insect parts in our food, because that would be—well—impossible. Insects are present in many different foodstuffs, especially grains. (Sacks of rice always include rice weevils.) One Ohio University resource on unintentional entomophagy estimates that people eat the equivalent of one to two pounds of insects a year. Regulatory agencies around the world do try to limit the acceptable quantities of insect parts in food. For example, 100 grams of chocolate can contain up to 60 insect fragments. We needn't go on. You're already an entomophage.

*   *   *

OTHER BUGGY FOOD ITEMS

- Shellac is a well-known wood finishing product. Applied to wood, it makes furniture shine. It's also used to make food shiny, most commonly jelly beans and apples. But exactly what is "shellac"? It's an excretion of the *Kerria lacca* beetle, found in Thailand. To stick to trees and leaves, the beetle excretes a sticky substance. Collectors scrape it right off of the trees.

- Food labels may list any of the following: crimson lake, cochineal, natural red 4, E120, or even natural color. These are all other names for carmine . . . which is just another name for finely ground red beetle abdomen.

According to his "official biography," Popeye is 34 years old, 5'6" tall, and weighs 154 lbs.

THE BURIED TREASURE AWARD

Geocaching

Under every leaf and rock, there might be a "cache."

T HE SEARCH IS ON!
Most of us can't dive for Spanish gold and sunken treasure on shipwrecks, but plenty of people comb beaches and fields with metal detectors, hoping to stumble on something valuable. But there's an opportunity to search for treasure that you may not have known about—geocaching. Geocaching is an activity that combines new technology—a Global Positioning System (GPS)—with old-fashioned fun, and a chance to find hidden caches of trinkets and other items.

SIGNED, SEALED, DELIVERED

Geocaching has an oddball predecessor: the "sport" of letterboxing, which has been around for more than a century and a half. Letterboxing began on England's lonely moors, specifically at Dartmoor's Cranmere Pool in 1854, when a Victorian tour guide named James Perrott left a bottle there to collect people's notes and letters.

It took a while for Perrott's idea to catch on—the next message didn't appear for 40 years, and the third for another 44! But once people did catch on, they started making the letters more and more elaborate, and then began hiding the letterboxes to make searching for the container part of the fun. By the 1970s, letterboxing had morphed into a combination of orienteering, puzzle, and craft, as serious hikers looked farther, wider, and harder for hidden boxes, and filled them with elaborately designed letters, poems, maps, and drawings. At this point, letterboxers decided that their sport needed a Code of Conduct so that the natural

---

King Arthur's Round Table had seating for 150.

landscape, historic sites, and landowners wouldn't be disturbed. The job fell to an Englishman named Godfrey "God" Swinscow, who drafted the following rules, which remain in place today:

- The letterboxes couldn't be attached to any walls, buildings, or other ruins.

- The boxes couldn't be hidden in hazardous locations or anywhere that someone could get injured retrieving them.

- The boxes couldn't be affixed to anything, and the people setting them up weren't allowed to use cement or other building materials to secure them.

NO STASH IN THE CACHE

After an article about letterboxing appeared in a 1998 issue of *Smithsonian* magazine, the activity gained popularity in the United States and adopted new technology and a new name: geocaching. On May 2, 2000, selective availability became "open" for all GPS units, meaning that anyone could precisely pinpoint a location. Tech enthusiasts wasted no time finding interesting ways to use this technology . . . and geocaching was one of them.

Originally called "GPS stash hunting" (the name change was suggested to avoid the negative drug-related connotation of "stash"), the game involves burying a geocache—a small (waterproof) container that holds a logbook and trinkets—for other people to find using their GPS.

A typical hunt works like this:

- Someone lists the location coordinates of a cache on a geocaching Web site.

- A participant chooses that site and enters the coordinates into a GPS.

- The participant travels to the location and starts looking. Geocaches can be underneath logs, hidden in a manmade structure, under water, or hidden by shrubs—the possibilities are endless.

- The geocache is usually a box that contains a log book, an information sheet, and some kind of "treasure." Treasures range from money, jewelry, tickets, maps, and antiques to CDs, pins,

---

It costs a zoo five times more to keep a panda than it does to keep an elephant.

buttons, books, maps, tools, or figurines. The only rule of the game is that the finder must sign the book, but most geocache enthusiasts also try to "up" the find by leaving something nicer than what was there.

- Common sense should prevail for deciding what treasures to leave, though. Don't leave food because animals may destroy the cache, and use common sense and don't leave explosives, alcohol, and weapons because geocaching is an all-ages sport.

- People usually write down who they are, what the weather was like when they found the cache, how easy or hard it was to find, and other pertinent details. Geocaching devotees also bring their own special signature stamps and leave that "mark" in the log book.

TRACKABLE TREASURES

Some types of geocaching treasures are themselves trackable. Travel Bugs and GeoCoins are among the most popular. Travel Bugs are tags (they look like dog tags) with an embedded electronic chip, and they're usually attached to a "treasure" (a plastic doll, for example).

GeoCoins are silver-dollar-sized disks with embedded chips that have become collector's items in their own right and often include some kind of logo or insignia.

Travel Bugs and GeoCoins aren't meant to be kept; they're meant to be found and moved to another cache. That way, geocache enthusiasts can track them online and see where the items have been, where they're heading, and sometimes even some information about the finders.

COLLABORATE AND NAVIGATE

Just as there are lots of different kinds of "treasure," there are lots of different hiding places for caches. Some are easy to track, others are more hidden. Some are even meant to be located at night, with the help of flashlights to find reflectors.

One "cool cache" identified by *Today's Cacher* magazine is North Carolina's "Tube Torcher." Hunters of this geocache are encouraged to bring "flashlights, climbing harness with carabiner and safety rope, gloves, and kneepads"—whew! This requires a lot more energy than combing a beach, but it's also a lot more fun.

There are different kinds of caches, too:

Traditional: There's always at least a container (usually waterproof) and a log book. Some "microcaches" are tiny plastic bags or tubes that have just a log sheet inside of them.

Multi-Cache (or Offset Cache): These can have two sites or more. The first cache contains clues to the one with the log book and treasure.

Mystery or Puzzle Cache: A mystery cache includes some clues that a participant must solve in order to find the cache's location.

Letterbox Hybrid: to find these, seekers use clues (like the old art of letterboxing) instead of GPS coordinates.

Event Cache: Local geocachers often get together to discuss the sport and go on group hunts.

Mega-Event Cache: An event cache with 500 or more people.

Cache In, Trash Out: A type of Event Cache that includes cleaning up trails and areas while caching.

EarthCache: Instead of finding treasure, cachers find information about geosciences, the earth, or the area where the cache is located.

GPS Adventures Maze Exhibit: A traveling exhibit that helps teach people about geocaching.

HIGH-TECH HUNTING

Geocaching hasn't even been around for a decade, but the technology that has made it possible has increased the community of geocaching fans. Because it would be easy for a cache to be stolen or vandalized, most geocachers abide by a code of ethics involving being safe, considerate, and honest. At sites like Geo-Caching.com, players can find cache lists, discuss the activity, and download coordinates so they can engage in completely paperless geocaching.

Ready, set . . . search!

THE NUTS TO YOU AWARD

Colorful Squirrel Towns

Black squirrels, white squirrels—who's got the right squirrels? Lots of people try to get rid of squirrels, but these five communities deserve kudos for putting out the welcome mat for the frolicsome rodents.

EVERY SQUIRREL FOR HIMSELF

Most unusual subject of regional competition in the United States? Squirrels . . . Yes, squirrels. The bushy-tailed rodents have inspired fierce competition in quite a few towns, based not on usefulness (most people regard them as vermin) or rarity (every suburban yard has a few), but on color. Brown and grey squirrels need not apply.

WHITEST WHITES

Squirrels adapted to their habitats by turning brown and grey to camouflage themselves from predators or their prey (squirrels are omnivores). But in several towns around the country, white squirrels flourish. The Albino Squirrel Preservation Society (ASPS) has nine campus chapters, including its founding group at the University of Texas at Austin. And although the ASPS chapters vary in their amount and constancy of activity, their mission—to help save and foster albino squirrel populations—is shared by the towns that proudly claim white squirrels as their mascots, too.

Five towns use white squirrels as their calling card, but only two—Olney, Illinois, and Kenton, Tennessee—claim to have populations of true albino squirrels—meaning the animals have little or no melanin pigment in their hair and eyes.

1. In Olney, there are two opposing theories about how the little white ones came to town, though both arrived around the turn of the 20th century:

During an average Easter season, Americans buy 600 million marshmallow Peeps.

- The George W. Ridgely Hypothesis involves Ridgely and a neighbor capturing two squirrels (one cream and one white), breeding them, and bringing them to Olney.
- The William Yates Stroup Hypothesis involves a resident named Stroup finding two baby white squirrels and raising them.

Either way, Olney is proud of its usual wildlife. The town bills itself as "Home of the White Squirrel," and local police wear a shoulder patch with a white squirrel logo.

2. Olney claims its white squirrels are the only true albinos, but Kenton, Tennessee, residents disagree and claim their squirrels are the true albinos. Kentonians also say that their white squirrels are the oldest U.S. population, having escaped from a gypsy caravan around 1869. When asked where the other town's white squirrel populations came from, Kentonians imply theirs was the source.

3. Marionville, Missouri, also uses the slogan "Home of the White Squirrel." People there acknowledge that the town's white squirrels are not albinos, but residents suggest that Olney's squirrels are descendants of white squirrels stolen from Marionville.

4. Brevard, North Carolina, is yet another "Home of the White Squirrel." This town boasts a White Squirrel Research Institute, an annual White Squirrel Festival (complete with a Squirrel Box go-cart race), and the White Squirrel Shoppe in the Blue Ridge Mountains, which sells white squirrel earring, spinners, Christmas cards, ornaments, and videos.

5. Exeter, Ontario, Canada, has the white squirrel population that is farthest north. To honor their squirrely population, Exeter residents created a mascot named White Wonder, and they celebrate the annual White Squirrel Festival, which they promote through a song and music video. (We urge you to look these up on YouTube.)

SQUIRRELFESTS
Billboards, municipal logos, festivals, and all kinds of knick-knacks help white-squirrel towns fight their good fights on behalf of their pale-furred creatures. Residents also go out into the field to keep an eye on the populations themselves. Olney, which once had 800 white squirrels, conducts an annual squirrel

Studies show that having guilty feelings may damage your immune system.

count. If the number drops below 100, the town takes preventive measures, which include careful monitoring of the most dreaded squirrel foes—domestic cats. (During the 2002 counting, which was also part of the town's 100-Year White Squirrel Celebration, visitors were invited to participate in the count, the dedication of a white squirrel monument, and a blessing of the squirrels ceremony.)

Marionville also conducts an annual count, although many residents believe that the official counts—from 100 to 120 in most years—are usually low because some locals, like Bob Smart, nurture small populations on their own property. Smart, who estimates that he has from 50 to 75 squirrels and buys "about a ton" of feed for them each year, brings mature squirrels to town when he gets too many, since they are protected there.

The oddest tribute to white squirrels has to be Sam Sanfillipo's dead white squirrel dioramas in Madison, Wisconsin. Sanfillipo (a retired mortician) has friends in Marionville who, on discovering his hobby of making taxidermy dioramas, sent him some dead white squirrels: "the ones that had been hit by cars or died of heart attacks or whatever." Some of Sam's handiwork includes six white squirrels riding motorcycles, six white squirrels on racehorses, and even a few playing basketball. (At least the beloved white squirrels aren't in the Topless Girlie Show—yet. That diorama uses common brown squirrels wearing little grass skirts.)

BACK IN BLACK

There aren't any white squirrels in Council Bluffs, Iowa; Marysville, Kansas; Kent, Ohio; and London, Ontario, Canada, but that doesn't bother these towns one bit because they are proud boasters of black squirrels. Black squirrels are mutations of gray squirrels, and some people think that global warming is responsible for the change in pigmentation.

Council Bluffs has had black squirrels since the 1840s, but Marysville has an official town "Black Squirrel Song." And it was the Marysville squirrels that "seeded" a population in Hobbs, New Mexico. (Unfortunately, the red fox squirrels there—imported from Sadler, Texas—killed the newcomers.)

Black squirrels at Kent State University in Ohio have inspired the annual Black Squirrel Festival and the campus's Black Squirrel run, but alas . . . the rodents aren't natives. The Kent State black squirrels were imported from London, Ontario, in the 1960s. Black and white squirrels represent only a small percentage of the world's 300-plus squirrel species, but they certainly have left their paw prints on these North American towns.

*　　*　　*

NOBEL PRIZE TRIVIA

- The awards were founded by scientist Alfred Nobel, who invented dynamite in 1866. After his death in 1896, 94 percent of his fortune—31 million Swedish *kronor*—was set aside for the Nobel Prize.

- The Nobel Prize is awarded annually for "outstanding contributions" in five categories: physics, literature, chemistry, medicine, and peace. It's presented by the Royal Swedish Academy of Sciences.

- Four people have won the Nobel Prize more than once. Linus Pauling won for chemistry in 1954 (for hybridized orbital theory) and in 1962 for peace (for his work in trying to ban nuclear testing). Marie Curie won for physics in 1903 (for discovering radioactivity) and for chemistry in 1911 (for isolating pure radium). For inventing the transistor, John Bardeen won for physics in 1956 and in 1971 in physics for the theory of superconductivity. And Frederick Sanger won for chemistry in 1958 for discovering the structure of the insulin molecule and in chemistry again in 1980 for virus nucleotide sequencing.

- One group won the Nobel Peace Prize three times. The International Committee of the Red Cross was honored in 1917 and 1944 for humanitarian work during the two world wars and in 1963 to commemorate its centennial.

- Curiously absent from the Nobel Prize is an award for mathematics. It's unclear why Nobel didn't account for it, although an urban legend says his wife cheated on him with a mathematician.

- To receive the Nobel Prize, you have to be alive (although you are still qualified if you die during the annual nomination process).

The "Mexican Hat Dance" is the official dance of Mexico.

THE JOLLY GREEN GIANT AWARD

Organic Funerals

Going green means going all the way . . . even to the grave.

COLD, WASTEFUL DEATH
In *The American Way of Death*, a 1963 exposé of the funeral industry, Jessica Mitford argued that too many of our funeral processes and rituals are artificial, cold, and wasteful. Mitford would likely approve of a recent trend in the United States—the "green burial." First it was recycling glass bottles and aluminum cans; now it's recycling Grandma Beatrice and Aunt Cora. Natural funerals (green burials and clean cremations) involve thinking carefully and conscientiously about what we take from—and put back into—the earth.

For centuries, the only burial possible was a natural one. When people died, they might be burned, buried in a simple shroud, or laid to rest in a plain wooden box. Many cultures attempted to preserve bodies in accordance with spiritual beliefs. Chinese royal tombs were filled with life-sized clay models of loyal retainers and soldiers. The Egyptians embalmed their dead because of their belief that a body needed to arrive intact in the underworld. While their methods were effective (we've got the mummies to prove it), they weren't particularly harmful to the Earth, just space consuming. Modern Western funeral preparations, on the other hand, involve lots of different artificial and toxic substances, from formaldehyde embalming fluid to lead-lined caskets.

THE GREENEST GOODBYE
In most states, embalming is optional. Without synthetic liquids

in it, the human body decomposes more quickly and cleanly. But an organic funeral does not necessarily mean you simply dig a pit and dump a body in. Many beautiful natural coffins and containers are available, from plain formaldehyde-free wooden jointed caskets to "ecopods" made of hardened recycled paper to woven reed baskets. Pressed fiber, paper, and recovered hardwood cremation urns are also available.

Green funeral advocates recommend burial over cremation; ashes are alkaline and can't be as easily decomposed as a body. But there is a "green" way to perform cremation. Having it completed "cleanly" means that a cremation machine reclaims energy and recycles it, filters mercury, cleans bodies completely first (no synthetic materials are burned), and has less-frequent startups so that it uses less energy.

LAWN CARE

However, all these natural preparations would be spoiled if the containers went into highly processed, artificially fertilized ground, the kind that most American cemeteries currently use. Organic burial is best done in woodland burial grounds (there are many like these in Europe) that reclaim soil, build habitat, provide oxygen, sequester carbon, store water, and create urban green space.

The simplest option of all is being tried in Scandinavia: flash-freezing of a body in liquid nitrogen, then breaking it down into a fine powder that can be spread directly on the earth as compost. That's "dust to dust" for you.

WITH YOU FOREVER

If organic burial or cremation still leaves you feeling lonely, consider a new, unique, and permanent option: have your loved one's carbon processed into a LifeGem diamond. Created by a "special process," these gems are supposedly identical to diamonds in every respect, and can be shaped, colored, and set to personal tastes.

But don't be put off by the LifeGem. It's not made from leftover ashes, but rather from the carbon in your loved one's locks of hair.

In Japan, when a man reaches 60, he is considered free of the responsibilities of being an adult.

THE WORMIEST TOWN AWARD

Wiscasset, Maine

Does any town really want to be famous for worms?
Wiscasset does, but it's got a fight on its hands.

PRETTIEST AND WORMIEST

Located on Maine's southern coast between Penobscot Bay and Portland, Wiscasset's motto is "Maine's Prettiest Village." If you head into town on a sunny morning, you'll agree: its early prosperity left a heritage of fine Federal architecture and well-planned streets.

So how did Wiscasset add "wormiest town" to its reputation? By Yankee ingenuity, of course. In the 1920s and '30s, the town's shipbuilding industry had fallen off, and most of Wiscasset's narrow-gauge railway tracks and cars were converted to scrap metal. What remained had been there for centuries: coastal flats bursting with sandworms and bloodworms. In the early 20th century, they numbered in the billions, and as *Time* magazine noted, most Maine fisherfolk considered them a "damnuisance," because bloodworms sting and sandworms pinch—quite painfully.

THAR'S GOLD IN THEM THAR WORMS

But the "damnuisance" started to look mighty fine when someone realized that worms, properly packed and shipped (100 worms per bag, plus "five for breakage," packed between layers of seaweed), could be marketed to sport fishermen. True, worms aren't as glamorous as lobsters or blueberries, but in 2003, baitworms accounted for $7.9 million worth of Maine's marine harvest, making them its fourth most-valuable fishery crop—ahead of cod, crab, scallops, and sea urchins.

Once upon a time, Wiscasset shipped 2.5 million saltwater

The majority of home burglaries occur during the daytime.

worms per month to fishermen far and wide. Citizens of this southern Maine coastal town could lay claim to living in "The Worm Capital of the World," and did so proudly.

THE WORMS CRAWL IN, THE WORMS CRAWL OUT

Diggers, who pay $43 for an annual license, are independent contractors who buy their own equipment, including specially made hip waders with tight ankles that can't be pulled off in sucking mudflats. Worm digging is backbreaking work, with 1,000 state-licensed diggers spending up to six hours at a time at low tide in knee-high mud scratching through the mud with wooden-handled, nine-inch-tinned hoes to find the worms. State regulations restrict the tools used for the harvest to "devices or instruments operated solely by hand power" in order to protect the worm flats. When the temperatures are high, the worms make things tougher by burrowing deeper to stay cool.

It's a short season, peaking in July and August, so many pick blueberries, make Christmas wreaths, split wood, or process lobster in other seasons. Some families have been working in the bait-worm business for over 50 years, but are concerned about the future. Other communities up the coast have gained on Wiscasset's worm output, but the potential loss of their livelihood altogether is more worrisome to Wiscassians than who's number one.

GLOBAL WORMING

Worm populations have been steadily and rapidly declining. A 1991 biologist's review of the baitworm fishery found that bloodworm landings—the amount of worms harvested in a particular area—were at a maximum between 1960 and 1976, ranging between 140,000 and 215,000 pounds annually. A sharp decline began in the late 1970s with landings ranging between 102,000 pounds in 1988 and 168,000 pounds in 1982.

One scientist said that in eastern Maine, things are even worse: about 20 years ago, you could harvest 2,000 worms per tide, which have dwindled to between 250 and 500 per tide. Explanations for the decline range from the natural cycles of tidal ecology, to overharvesting, to poor fishing practices like mussel dragging, in which heavy iron baskets are pulled across mudflats to harvest mussels, damaging worm habitats in the process.

Statistically, scuba diving is safer than table tennis.

Another problem facing Wiscasset and surrounding worm towns is that most state research funding goes into better-known and more lucrative species like lobster and cod, while ignoring the worms, as well as the socioeconomic impacts of their scarcity.

THE FARMER TAKES A WORM

One solution being tried is a worm farm, the effort of a British entrepreneur named Peter Cowin who got the idea while working on his doctorate in worm biology. Cowin's company, Seabait, is fully operational in the United Kingdom, and with a loan from the State of Maine, he's launched a facility there.

But while the state sees aquaculture as an industry of the future that could enhance its economy and create jobs, many of the worm diggers of coastal Maine believe it is a threat to their livelihood and way of life. Of course, without worms, there won't be any way of life to protect, so many Mainers believe Seabait technology should be used to re-seed wild worm beds.

*   *   *

THE WORST GUEST AWARD

If there's one worm you don't want around, it's a tapeworm. Tapeworms have afflicted human beings for 10,000 years. They attach to the human host's intestinal wall through hooks on their heads. Although tapeworms start out tiny, they grow . . . sometimes several feet long (an adult human has about 25 feet or more of intestine for the worms to make themselves at home in). They also cast off portions of their bodies in human waste. Those worms then go in search of their own hosts.

Traditional effects of having a tapeworm include constipation, diarrhea, malnourishment, and weight loss, but the parasites can do far more damage. A pork tapeworm can cause lesions and cysts and, at its worst, damage the brain and central nervous system. The kind of tapeworm that lives in dogs or sheep (though this one is pretty hard to catch) can affect the liver and other organs. So rumors may persist that tapeworms once made good diet aids (*read about that on page 4*), but really, they're a wiggly hassle.

(*read about that on page 4*)

Pine cones are female.

THE MIRACLE CURE AWARDS

Standing Up, Laughing, and Getting a Pet

Some unexpected ways to get healthy are easy and even fun. That's a health plan everyone—including Uncle John—can get behind.

NOT-SO-SECRET MEDICINE

The best medicine isn't always a pill or a treatment. And if there were an alternative to surgery, most people would take it. It turns out there are three methods that are easy to implement and inexpensive. And even though they've been around for ... well ... ever, science is just starting to understand how they help people stay fit and healthy.

GET UP! STAND UP!

Common sense says that if you lie around too much, you'll put on weight. And even though a lack of exercise is one of the main reasons people pack on pounds, it's not the only one. These days, people spend lots of time sitting at desks and in front of their computers and TVs. In April 2008, Marc Hamilton (a professor of biomedical sciences at the University of Missouri-Columbia) presented a new study that said sitting down dramatically decreases the body's ability to dispose of fat.

Hamilton found that fat tends to collect in tissue when people are sitting down. Also, while we're sitting, our bodies produce only about 10 percent of the lipase, a natural enzyme that breaks down fat, than it does normally. HDLs, the "good" cholesterol, also went down while people were sitting.

Hamilton's suggestion: stand up and walk around a little bit. Standing up while watching TV would be one start. Stand up while on the telephone at home. Apparently anything that decreases the amount of time spent sitting will do a body good.

In the Middle Ages, people added carrot juice to butter to make the color more appetizing.

WHAT ARE YOU LAUGHING AT?

The average four-year-old will laugh more in an hour than the typical adult. And toddlers usually laugh once every four minutes, while adults get in just 10 to 15 laughs a day. Does that matter? It seems to. The healing power of laughter is finally getting its due.

In 2005, the University of Maryland School of Medicine released the results of a study showing that laughter could help prevent a heart attack. The study worked like this: A group of people was shown a funny movie. As they watched and laughed, they were monitored. The result: Laughter caused their endothelium linings—the inner part of blood vessels—to expand, which increased blood flow, necessary for a healthy heart. Sad or stressful movies, in contrast, made the endothelium linings contract. The research bore out what science had long thought—stress harms cardiovascular health, while laughter helps it.

One of the pioneers of laughter research was Stanford Professor William Fry, who documented the intense benefits of laughter back in 1971. He found that laughter, like exercise, increases the heart rate. In fact, all the effects of hearty laughter mirror what the body goes through during a workout—in particular, an increase in blood pressure and oxygen consumption. The effects drop back to normal levels after it's done, just as with exercise.

Other studies have shown that laughter also helps with respiration, diabetes (laughter lowers blood sugar levels), stress levels, pain management, and even productivity at work (happy workers get more done). So even though some scientists (probably the grumpy ones) say that the studies are inconclusive and don't prove that laughter is a form of medicine, everyone agrees that laughter doesn't hurt and that if there's a chance it can help, it's worth trying.

WOOF! PURR . . .

At the 2008 International Stroke Conference in New Orleans, Dr. Adnan Qureshi of the University of Minnesota delivered some surprising news: According to a study of 4,435 people, cat owners were less likely to die of cardiovascular disease. On the other hand, people who didn't own cats were 30 to 40 percent more likely to die from it.

That was good news for the more than one-third of U.S. households that own a cat. Dog owners were not so elated—their pets didn't decrease their chances of having a heart attack at all. But dog owners can still take solace in the fact that a 1995 American Journal of Cardiology study found that all pet owners are more likely to survive a heart attack than those who don't have one. The National Institutes of Health seems to agree, saying that all pet owners have lower blood pressure, triglyceride, and cholesterol levels and feel less lonely than the pet-less. Also pet owners make fewer visits to the doctor.

Some dogs also seem to be able to warn of oncoming seizures. "Seizure-alert" dogs can be trained to predict a seizure up to 15 minutes before it comes on, giving their owners ample time to take safety precautions. People with Parkinson's Disease who suffer from a condition called "freezing"—wherein their feet freeze up while their bodies are in motion—can be helped by dogs too. When a dog touches their feet while the situation is occurring, they become unfrozen.

Pets' abilities to detect problems like cancer cells are being studied as well. Someday, scientists may figure out how to get Fido to sniff out cancers in the body before they become untreatable. In the meantime, pet owners can relax in the knowledge that their best friends provide many long-term health benefits.

*   *   *

MATCH THE SPORTS TROPHY TO THE SPORT

1. Larry O'Brien Trophy	**a)** Canadian Football League
2. Commissioner's Trophy	**b)** PGA Championship
3. Grey Cup	**c)** National Basketball Association
4. Vince Lombardi Trophy	**d)** NFL
5. Sprint Cup	**e)** NASCAR
6. Wanamaker Trophy	**f)** Major League Baseball

1. c, 2. f, 3. a, 4. d, 5. e, 6. b

The average American spends 500 percent more time sitting in a car than on vacation.

THE SULTRY VOICE AWARD

Lauren Bacall

A great speaking voice is paramount if you want to become a Hollywood legend. All of the greats have their own unique vocal qualities: John Wayne's monotone drawl or Marilyn Monroe's breathy whisper. But when it comes to the ultimate sultry, sexy voice, we think of Lauren Bacall. Here's how she found that voice . . . and then broke free of it.

VOCAL TRAINING

The pretty teenager who would one day become one of Hollywood's most glamorous movie stars had one big problem: her high, nasally voice. That was the only thing keeping director Howard Hawks from hiring 19-year-old Betty Bacall for his 1944 film adaptation of Ernest Hemingway's *To Have and Have Not*. Hawks's wife, Slim, had seen a picture of Bacall on the cover of *Harper's Bazaar* and convinced Howard to fly the young model and aspiring stage actress from New York City to California for a screen test. Bacall (born Betty Joan Perske in 1924) had the acting ability and the look that Hawks was looking for—plus she seemed wise beyond her years—but what to do about that voice?

Hawks worked with Bacall for two weeks, modeling her speaking on the low timbre of his wife Slim's. Still not quite there, Bacall went home to New York and practiced for two more weeks. Then she traveled back to Los Angeles and wowed Hawks with her new husky, sultry voice . . . and got the part. At the insistence of Hawks, she changed her first name to the more alluring Lauren (though she still goes by Betty to her friends and family). "He wanted to mold me. He wanted to control me," Bacall said of Hawks. "And he did . . . until Mr. Bogart got involved."

TO HAVE AND HAVE MORE

He was 44; she was 19, but the chemistry was there from the

Humphrey Bogart was buried with a gold whistle.

beginning. On the set of *To Have and Have Not*, Humphrey Bogart and the newly christened Lauren Bacall sparked a romance, and their attraction translated to the screen. In the film's most famous scene, Bacall, as Marie "Slim" Browning, says to Bogie in her new sultry voice:

> You know you don't have to act with me, Steve. You don't have to say anything, and you don't have to do anything. Not a thing. Oh, maybe just whistle. You know how to whistle, don't you, Steve? You just put your lips together and blow.

Both the line and the movie became instant sensations, propelling young Bacall to stardom.

Yet, as Hawks pointed out (and rumor had it that he was quite jealous of Bacall's affections for Bogart), it was the character she was playing that Bogart had fallen in love with, "so she had to keep playing it the rest of her life." Good thing that the role of a confident woman was easy for her to live up to, both on and off the screen . . . although that voice would one day catch up with her.

BACALL OF THE WILD

The public was enamored with Hollywood's most glamorous couple, eagerly awaiting each new film noir picture they costarred in, most notably *The Big Sleep* (1946), *Dark Passage* (1947), and *Key Largo* (1948).

Off the screen, Bacall was making waves for, very simply, living life on her own terms. Even though she was happily married to Bogart, she went against the grain of the 1950s woman—she was outspoken, refused to take roles simply for a paycheck, and even protested against McCarthyism while campaigning for democratic presidential candidate Adlai Stevenson in 1952.

Showing off her comedic talents in 1953's smash hit *How to Marry a Millionaire* (also starring Betty Grable and Marilyn Monroe), Bacall used her sultry voice to poke fun at her screen persona. "I've always liked older men—look at that old fellow what's-his-name in *The African Queen*. Absolutely crazy about him." The movie-going public loved the reference. And although Bacall was enjoying the life of a celebrity, all she cared about was the acting part of it—that and being a good citizen, wife, and

---

First city in modern history to reach 1 million people: London (1811).

mother. In the spotlight, people were always telling her what to do, and she hated that. "Let people push you around, and you deserve whatever bad things happen after that."

Statements like that, plus Bacall's insistence on only taking on scripts she approved of, gave her the reputation of being "difficult." But she felt—after being immediately accepted by the public—that she didn't have to prove anything to anyone . . . except herself. That became a lot harder after Bogart died from throat cancer in 1957. (At the funeral, Bacall placed a whistle in Bogie's coffin.) Devastated by the loss of her husband, Bacall, now a 33-year-old single mother with two children, took on fewer film roles, not finding them as much fun as before. A brief romance with Frank Sinatra didn't work out, and Bacall was tired of being a "movie star."

THE PLAY'S THE THING

It always came back to acting, the only constant in her professional life. But Bacall wanted more out of it than she was getting. "I never even thought I'd be in movies," she recently admitted. "I only wanted to be on stage. I wanted to see my name in lights. I wanted to take that curtain call."

So Bacall moved back to New York and focused her talents on Broadway, where she became one of the theater world's biggest attractions. She fell in love with actor Jason Robards and married him in 1960, only to file for divorce in 1969 due to his excessive drinking. Bacall has remained happily unmarried ever since. "If you want a good marriage, you must pay attention to that. If you want to be independent, go ahead. You can't have it all."

Again, she focused on acting, earning Tony Awards for the musical *Applause* in 1970 (based on the 1950 film *All About Eve*, which starred Bette Davis), and for *Woman of the Year* in 1981. In that time, Bacall still acted in the occasional movie, including John Wayne's last film, *The Shootist*, in 1976. Even though the two were political opposites, they became close friends.

SMALL TALK

Her days as a sex symbol long behind her, Bacall was able to rest her sultry speaking voice. Had she kept at it, she could have caused

According to the experts, the smaller the bubbles, the better the champagne.

severe damage. The medical field even named a vocal "misuse" disorder after the affliction called "Bogart-Bacall syndrome" (BBS). Technically, it's a form of muscle tension dysphonia. Actors as well as singers can suffer from BBS after years of speaking or singing in a lower register than their natural voice. Thankfully, Bacall caught it in time, never suffering the full effect of the disorder named for her. Now, she only turns on the huskiness if the role requires it.

THESE KIDS TODAY

Over the last 25 years, Bacall has taken on mostly smaller, arty roles. And even now, her voice is still one of her greatest attributes: Bacall's done voice-over work for animated films such as *Howl's Moving Castle* (2004), where she played an evil witch, and *Firedog* (2005), where she played a cat. On the small screen, she has appeared on *Chicago Hope* and *The Sopranos*. Her recent big-screen credits include *Dogville* (2003) and *Birth* (2004), two independent films she starred in with Nicole Kidman.

So what does the outspoken movie star from Hollywood's Golden Age have to say about outspoken movie stars of today? "We live in an age of mediocrity," she says. "Stars today are not the same stature as Bogie, James Cagney, Spencer Tracy, Henry Fonda, and Jimmy Stewart." She calls most of today's major films "artless" and takes exception with overrated movie stars, especially Kidman's ex-husband. "When you talk about a great actor, you're not talking about Tom Cruise. His whole behavior is so shocking. It's inappropriate and vulgar and absolutely unacceptable to use your private life to sell anything commercially."

LIVING LEGEND

But when Bacall looks back at her own life, she realizes she has little to complain about. "Although I beef about a lot of things, I think I've been extremely lucky." And though she's never won an Oscar, Bacall did win a Golden Globe Award for her role in 1996's *The Mirror Has Two Faces*. She also received the Kennedy Center Honors in 1997, and two years later was named one of the "25 Most Significant Female Movie Stars in History" by the American Film Institute. But at 83 years old, and with nearly 40 films to her credit, Bacall just wants to keep on acting. "I am still working, I've never stopped and, while my health holds out, I won't stop."

People who eat beans regularly tend to have smaller waist sizes.

THE WAY WE WERE AWARD

A Host of Wonderful, Missing Things

Remember making crystal radios when you were a kid?
We do, too. And gosh darn it—we miss it.

AULD LANG SYNE

Times keep changing, and simple little things we take for granted go the way of the Studebaker and bell bottoms—but that doesn't mean we have to forget them. Here's Uncle John's salute to a few of our favorite (nearly) forgotten things:

Crystal radios: When Uncle John was a kid, every mechanically inclined child, and many who were not, got a crystal radio kit. It was a very simple radio that you had to assemble yourself. And through the seeming magic of a tiny quartz crystal—it didn't plug in and had no batteries—it received radio signals that you could listen to through earphones. He still doesn't know how they worked . . . maybe they *were* magic.

Network sign-offs: In a slower and saner world, there were no all-night TV stations, so networks would go off the air around midnight with their own unique "sign-off": often just a quick "thank you" message from the staff along with a playing of the "Star Spangled Banner," but sometimes they aired a several-minutes-long, specially made, "arty" public service announcement with a witty and informative message. They're almost completely nonexistent today, and have been since cable TV took off in the 1980s.

Blank checks: Tell the kids about this one and they won't believe you: In the old days stores had "counter checks" from the local bank at their checkout counters. They were blank checks that had the bank's name and address printed on them, along with a place for a date, the payee, dollar amount, and your signature. If you had an account at that bank, you could use them to pay for your items.

First comic strip artist to win the Pulitzer Prize: Garry Trudeau, for *Doonesbury* (1975).

Not surprisingly, less-than-honest people—who didn't have accounts—figured out that they could fill in any name they wanted and get free stuff. Counter checks were history by the 1970s. (We're surprised they lasted that long.)

Wild Kingdom with Marlin Perkins: Every Sunday, we'd gather round the TV and watch Marlin—and his buddy Jim—whiz across a marsh on their fan-driven boat, and we'd learn about exotic animals like lions, tigers, and elephants. Who knew those animals lived in marshes? (Maybe we just remember it wrong.)

Watches that tick: Uncle John can't remember the last time he saw someone wearing a watch with mechanical parts that you could hold up to your ear to listen to that tiny, magical "tick tick tick . . . " It brings back memories of grandma and grandpa just thinking about it.

House calls: Someone in your family is sick. You're worried but an emergency room visit would be overreacting and too expensive, so you make a call and a doctor comes to your house. This was common until the late 1960s, when insurance companies stopped making it financially viable for physicians. The practice has been making a small comeback recently, due to a change in Medicare law—but not enough for us!

Hand-written letters: The ease and speed of e-mail is truly a wonder, and we're glad we have it. But the fact that it has nearly killed the ancient art of writing, by hand, a lengthy letter to a friend or family member—well, it's just a shame.

Rolling down the window by hand: Looking back, you have to wonder what genius automotive designer thought, "You know what we oughta do? We oughta make electronic controls for rolling windows up and down . . . because doing it by hand is just so gosh-darned hard!" Thanks to that person you have a much better chance of not being able to roll the windows up or down *at all*—because the car's electronics have gone haywire.

"Choking" the engine: In the old days, driving a car was an interactive experience. In addition to rolling down the windows by hand, you had to pull out a knob on the dashboard before you could start the engine. This controlled a flap that limited the amount of air entering the carburetor ("choking" it), making for a

---

Some people are able to hear AM radio through their dental fillings.

"richer," more fuel-laden, combustible mix—which cold engines need. As the car warmed up you pushed the knob in until it was fully open again. Chokes have been automatic on virtually all engines with carburetors since the 1970s, and today's more common fuel-injected models have automatic equivalents.

Daisy BB guns: Uncle John remembers getting his first "official Red Ryder carbine action two-hundred shot range model air rifle with a compass in the stock and this thing which tells time"—just like Ralphie in *A Christmas Story*. Ah, but those were more innocent times, and though Daisy Outdoor Products still exists and you can still get a BB gun today—they're not nearly as popular as they used to be. (Because, of course, those things could put somebody's eye out, for goodness' sake!)

Hank Aaron as Home Run King: Henry Aaron was a 6-foot tall, 180-pound baseball player—for just about his entire 22-year career. Barry Bonds was a 6-foot tall, 185-pound player . . . when he entered the league in 1986, and for about 10 more years. But between 1996 and 2001, the year he set the record for most HRs in a season with 73, he ballooned from 190 up to 228 (listed) pounds. (And that was just his head!) He only broke Aaron's career record of 755 in 2007, we know, but we miss the simple and untarnished legacy of Hammerin' Hank already.

Straight razors: We really don't know why we miss them—but we do. They're just cool.

The Concorde SST: Like you, we had dreams of someday becoming insanely wealthy and renting a Concorde supersonic transport jet for a wild party with a few hundred of our best friends, during which we would fly back and forth from Paris to Las Vegas six times in one day for no good reason whatsoever. Alas, supersonic transport isn't economically viable, and the last Concorde flight landed in 2003. One more dream down the toilet.

Drive-in theaters: Huge movie screens . . . outside . . . with parking lots in front of them . . . that you drove your car into . . . and made out with your sweetie while Elvis and Annette Funicello did the twist. Does life get any better than that? You can still find a few of these across the United States, but most of them are just nostalgia . . . along with Annette and the twist.

There are almost 800 different brands of bottled water available for sale in the U.S.

THE CLOCK IS CUCKOO AWARD

Daylight Saving Time

Love it when you gain an hour but hate it when you lose one? Daylight Saving Time causes a lot of confusion. Is it really worth all the trouble?

SPRING FORWARD, FALL BACK

Daylight Saving Time (note: it's "Saving," not "Savings") has been with America in one form or another for roughly a century. It was first used in 1918 and 1919, during World War I, to help conserve energy for the war effort (and it ended six months after the war, because it was so unpopular). The government rolled it out again during World War II, but that time around, time never fell back—the country stayed an hour ahead until the war ended.

After 1945, Daylight Saving Time became a free-for-all. Some states observed it, some didn't. It was confusing all around, until Congress decided to make things official with the Uniform Time Act of 1966, which decreed that from the first Sunday in April until the last Sunday in October the clocks would move forward one hour—unless a state didn't want to participate, which was fine. Parts of Indiana, and Arizona, and Hawaii decided not to change their clocks, but the rest of the country adopted the rule.

Americans aren't alone in recognizing Daylight Saving Time. From Canada to the European Union to Central America to Africa to the Middle East, countries and entire regions all over the world put their citizens through it. Even scientific stations in Antarctica get in on the Daylight Saving Time action. (There are too many participating countries to list here, but if you're interested, check them all out at worldtimezone.com/daylight.htm.)

Kite flying is a professional sport in Thailand.

BLAME BEN

Most people think that Daylight Saving Time began to help farmers. Not true. In fact, after World War I, farmers were the biggest opponents of Daylight Saving Time. (They called for the country to return to "God's time.") People have been complaining about it ever since, and in 2005, Congress responded, revising the bill so that Daylight Saving Time would be extended to begin in mid-March and end in mid-November, giving everyone just a little more light before and after the long winter.

Those who truly hate Daylight Saving Time continue to place blame. So if you really want to take out your frustration on someone, blame Benjamin Franklin.

A MODEST PROPOSAL

Franklin was living in Paris as an ambassador in 1784 when he pitched a time-saving idea in a letter he wrote to a friend, who was the editor of *Journal de Paris*. In the letter, Franklin explained how much less oil would be needed to fuel lamps if the time were changed so people actually awoke with the sun. (Franklin was kidding. He had no intention of living that way himself. He liked to play chess well into the night and sleep until noon.) Even though his letter was written in jest, Franklin's friend published it under the title "An Economical Project."

Frugal people were intrigued by the suggestion for saving candles, and the idea remained part of governmental discussions for more than 100 years. Then in 1905, British builder William Willett put forth a similar idea—he thought that people were wasting their time sleeping away the early morning hours of summer when they could be out enjoying themselves. Willett tried to get a clock-changing idea recognized by the British parliament, but it wasn't popular. When changing the time showed promise as a way to help economies during the expensive time of World War I, however, countries around the world got on board—first the Germans, then the British, and then the Americans.

ENERGY SAVING TIME?

Economics was also the reason the U.S. Congress expanded Daylight Saving Time in 2005; the representatives wanted to save

The first typewriters typed only in capital letters. (The SHIFT key wasn't invented until 1878.)

money—some $180 million on energy. That number came from Michigan Congressman Fred Upton, who cosponsored the bill and estimated that the country would use 100,000 fewer barrels of oil per day (at $60 per barrel at the time) if Daylight Saving Time were lengthened.

PROS AND CONS

How true that assessment is, though, is another story. In decades past, Daylight Saving Time worked on the principle that people used less electricity because they needed fewer lights when the sun was out and that they enjoyed more outdoor activities when during daylight. But today, most households have a computer or a TV, and one is likely to be on any time someone is awake, meaning that electricity savings may be minimal. A study by the University of California–Santa Barbara, released in 2008, seems to support this. The study determined that Daylight Saving Time actually costs households more money—$3.19 more a year in electricity. (However, the study focused entirely on Indiana, where part of the state observes Daylight Saving Time and part doesn't; it's not clear if the added expense would be equivalent across the entire country).

Good news does come in the form of fewer car accidents, though. A 1995 study by the Insurance Institute for Highway Safety found that motor vehicle crashes decreased when Daylight Saving Time was in effect, particularly fatal accidents involving pedestrians. This group even called for year-round Daylight Saving Time, saying that "the predicted net benefit for retaining daylight saving time was a reduction of 727 fatal pedestrian crashes and 174 crashes fatal to vehicle occupants." So, as annoying as the idea of changing all the clocks can be, the tradeoff of an hour of sleep once a year isn't so bad when you consider that it's a good way to save some lives.

*　　　*　　　*

"I want to thank my father, the man who, when I said I wanted to be an actor, he said, 'Wonderful. Just have a back-up profession, like welding.'"

—Robin Williams, after winning the Best Supporting
Actor Oscar for *Good Will Hunting*

The average wedding has four bridesmaids.

THE VIDEO GAME "GATEWAY DRUG" AWARD

Donkey Kong

It introduced mainstream kids to the interactive on-screen world, spawned an incredibly successful sequel, and launched the "career" of one of the industry's most famous characters . . . oh, and it was fun too.

BROTHER, CAN YOU SPARE A QUARTER?
Before Donkey Kong, video games were a mild addiction at best. Sure, you had your Pong enthusiasts, Space Invaders had quite a few fans, and Pac-Man enticed a lot of the world's youth to turn over their hard-earned quarters. But Donkey Kong showed us how simple and compelling a console could be. The intervention should have occurred then—before Wii, Nintendo DS, Game Boy, and all the rest were injected into our lives.

When Donkey Kong was released, America was in a video game frenzy. About 10,000 arcades had sprung up across the nation, and video game consoles could be found in bars, movie theaters, bowling alleys, laundromats, and grocery stores—anywhere people could be tempted to spend a few minutes and a few quarters.

This is when the video game pastime became a full-fledged addiction. The giant machines gobbled up 20 billion quarters in 1981 alone. And the success of the arcade and video game industry was due in large part to a game called Donkey Kong.

HELP!

Let's start at the beginning. The year was 1981, and Nintendo introduced Donkey Kong. What's in a name? The Japanese video game company needed a good one to identify its new product: the game's developer Shigeru Miyamoto thought the word "donkey" meant "stupid" in English, so he chose it to modify "Kong," a word associated with apes. It was a good way to sum up the game's giant ape villain. Although most players didn't care about the story behind the game, there was one: The ape escaped from the zoo after being mistreated by his trainer, Jumpman (later called Mario). Kong kidnaps Mario's girlfriend, Pauline, for revenge and takes her to a construction site, which he partially demolishes by jumping up and down. Mario, of course, comes to the rescue. While the ape throws barrels and other objects at Mario in an effort to kill him, the player (as Mario) continues trying to rescue the girl. As he gets closer, the ape climbs up another level, and there are more ladders to climb and barrels for Mario to jump over.

The game sounds deceptively easy, but it takes a certain skill to jump over the barrels—the player has to time pressing the jump button just right. And sometimes the barrels double up, meaning the player's finger dexterity is about to get tested. (Most likely, a generation's worth of Nintendonitis can be traced back to here.)

THE NEXT GENERATION

No video game is an island. During the 1980s, the industry's hey-day, gamers' attention was easily diverted to newer, bigger, and shinier things. Video game developers had to keep coming up with new projects to lure players in, and sequels to popular video games were one way to do it.

This is where Donkey Kong really shines. Some people argue that Pac-Man and its successor, Ms. Pac-Man, deserve the kudos for getting us all seriously addicted to video games. They did their part, to be sure, but Pac-Man is monotonous—its maze never changes, so you're stuck playing the same board again and again. Ms. Pac-Man is a contender, with its six mazes, constantly chang-ing colors, and several different unpredictable ghost enemies.

But Ms. Pac-Man is a hack. It was an unauthorized sequel orig-inally produced by a couple of small-time computer programmers as a Pac-Man knockoff. In quality, though, it far surpasses the orig-inal, so much so that Namco (the Japanese company that pro-duced Pac-Man) and Midway (the American licenser of Pac-Man) eventually brought it into the family. Still, it loses points for not being original.

Kevlar is five times as strong as steel.

What about other sequels, like Baby Pac-Man and Professor Pac-Man? They were lemons. Baby Pac-Man tried to combine pinball action with the Pac-Man grid (it didn't work), and Professor Pac-Man had trivia questions built in. Not really what the Pac-Man enthusiasts were after.

Donkey Kong, on the other hand, managed to produce a sequel—Donkey Kong Jr.—that was every bit as fun as the original. In that one, Donkey Kong's son tried to rescue the captured ape from the evil Mario. The first screen started with a tropical theme, and successive screens got progressively more challenging. The game was still based on moving up levels, but the scenery changed. And in a twist on the original, the industrial barrels and ladders were replaced with vines to swing on and falling fruit to dodge.

OUR HERO

Beyond delivering a great sequel, Donkey Kong created an industry in Mario, who (along with his brother Luigi) would return to star in more than 200 games. Mario also became one of the most (some people say *the* most) recognizable characters. Just as you can't keep a good ape down, you certainly can't keep the Mario brothers down, either.

*   *   *

MEET MARIO

- Mario didn't officially become "Mario" until the release of the game Mario Bros., which also introduced his brother, Luigi.

- Mario is the older brother.

- In the early 1980s, Nintendo executives were thinking of giving the Jumpman character a name and expanding him to other games. One day, their landlord, Mario Segali, interrupted and demanded a late rent payment. Like Jumpman, Segali wore a red cap and had a mustache. Jumpman became Mario (and Italian).

- Mario wears a cap (with an "M" on it) because the character's designer, Shigero Miyamoto, has a hard time drawing hair.

THE LOST IN SPACE AWARD

Interstellar Messaging

As radio and TV waves travel through space, they may be our first contact with life outside of Earth. And if something's out there, we want it to know that we come in peace.

EARTH TO ETs . . . COME IN
In 1936, the world sent its first intergalactic greeting card. That year's Olympic games, hosted by Germany and officially opened by Adolf Hitler, became the first broadcast powerful enough to travel into space. Even the weakest radio waves can escape the Earth's surface. The distance a signal can travel is really only limited by the amount of background noise and the quality of the receiver. A stronger signal will go farther because it is easier to pick out from the background noise. Before 1936, transmissions weren't strong enough to leave Earth's atmosphere. The broadcast of the Olympics happened to be the first transmission that was powerful enough to go out into space. And in the 70-plus years since then, hundreds of thousands of hours of television and radio have streamed their way out beyond the Earth's atmosphere.

Whether it's possible for intelligent life out there to detect and decode these waves is a question that scientists continue to ponder. Radio waves are wide—sometimes up to a mile wide—and cannot be "read" completely by just one radio telescope . . . unless it's as wide as the signal itself. So scientists have had to create several large radio telescopes—like the aptly named "Very Large Array" in New Mexico, which has 27 telescopes lined up to form the equivalent of one 22-mile-wide telescope. (The installation provides the resolution a much larger, single antenna but at a fraction of the cost.)

The U.S. Army includes Tabasco sauce in every ration kit.

REACHING A TARGET AUDIENCE

The farther radio wave signals travel, the more they widen and weaken. They also can be disrupted or broken up by planets, comets, stars, and other objects. Still, scientists believe that the signals could continue to travel, even in a weakened state, for several hundred light years. And even if they were indecipherable, they might still be recognizable as the product of intelligent life. Some programs are even sent out especially for audiences far, far away.

- In 1974, Carl Sagan and astronomer Frank Drake sent out a message directed toward the M13 star cluster—25,000 light years away. Encoded in the signal was a message set in binary code and depicting numbers, DNA, and Earth, among other things. Fears that the message would be compromised by its long journey through space, spurred scientists to resend the message in 2001—just in case.

- In 2006, a French space agency beamed a television program to a point 45 light years away. The scientists had done research that showed the area could conceivably host life (although there's no evidence it does at this point). The program was hosted by a nude man and woman (to give potential alien viewers the opportunity to see what human bodies look like) and featured conversations about sociology and science.

- On February 4, 2008, NASA sent a Beatles song, "Across the Universe," toward the North Star—431 light years away. The date commemorated the 50th anniversary of NASA and the 40th anniversary of the song.

- In June 2008, scientists in Norway planned to broadcast a 30-second "commercial" (promoting Earth and its inhabitants) to a solar system in the Great Bear constellation—42 light years away. (The first commercial sent into space was a collection of thousands of Craigslist ads in March 2005.)

Other people are getting in on the act, too. At least one Web site on the Internet sells a "service" that allows anyone to send a text or phone message into space. (Uncle John's message: "Go with the Flow.")

The space between your eyebrows is called the *glabella*.

IS ANYBODY OUT THERE?

SETI (Search for Extra Terrestrial Intelligence), a research institute in Mountain View, California, says its mission is "to know our beginnings and our place among the stars." To that end, it transmits radio messages with the hope that a living being outside of our solar system will receive it.

Some people, though, think that talking to the heavens is a potentially dangerous activity. In 2006, an editorial in *Nature* challenged scientists (and amateurs) who send out these radio transmissions to stop because the practice is irresponsible. People could be establishing contact with . . . well, anything. Their other issue was with anyone setting themselves up as a self-appointed spokesperson for the planet. Many scientists also feel that the search for life in the universe is a waste of time. Even if there were extraterrestrials out there and radio waves reached them, it would take the same amount of time for them to send a message back. Hundreds or even thousands of years could go by, and that's a really long time to wait for a return call.

*   *   *

TAKE THIS JOB AWARD: 11 UNUSUAL (BUT REAL) OCCUPATIONS

1. Porta-potty scrubber
2. Earthworm farmer
3. Roller coaster inspector
4. Wine cave digger
5. Alligator egg collector
6. Dysentery stool sample analyzer
7. Armpit sniffer (for deodorant companies)
8. Jaw massage therapist
9. Ice cream taster
10. Orangutan pee collector
11. Easter Bunny

Every day, the sun's heat evaporates about a trillion tons of water.

THE LOST TREASURE AWARD

Russia's Amber Room

Grab a shovel and put on your thinking cap, because it's time to go hunting . . . for treasure. The location of Russia's Amber Room, which vanished during the chaos of World War II, remains one of the Western World's greatest mysteries. But a crafty bunch of art hunters may have finally tracked it down. (For more Lost Treasures, turn to page 169.)

THAT'S QUITE A GIFT

It's been called the "most valuable missing artwork in the world" and the "Eighth Wonder of the World," and it's worth more than $250 million. But after World War II, Russia's Amber Room—a room decorated entirely with amber that dated back to the days of Peter the Great—vanished, and people around the world have been looking for it ever since.

In 1701, the first king of Prussia, Friedrich I, hired craftsmen to panel his study in amber, the fossilized resin of ancient trees. It was completed in 1713, the same year the king died. Three years later, Friedrich Wilhem I dismantled his father's showpiece room and gave it to Czar Peter the Great to cement a new alliance. The room traveled to St. Petersburg in 18 large boxes and was initially displayed as part of an art collection . . . until 1755 when Peter's daughter, Czarina Elisabeth, decided to have the room installed in St. Catharine's Palace in Pushkin (the Russian royals' summer home).

BIGGER THAN A BREADBOX

The part of the palace where Elisabeth wanted to set up the Amber Room, though, was larger than Friedrich's original study. So Russian artisans added additional jewel-encrusted panels. These included four Florentine mosaics fashioned from gems like jasper, marble, jade, onyx, and quartz. Also among the furnishings were display cases containing precious amber objects like chess sets, candlesticks, and jewel boxes.

When Catherine the Great came to power in 1762, she ordered even more improvements and had the room moved a second time to her new summer home outside St. Petersburg. The job was finally complete in 1770, and the Amber Room was a marvel. It included more than 100,000 pieces of carved amber paneling that covered about 592 square feet. Catherine showed the room off by installing 565 candles to illuminate its six tons of amber, semi-precious stones, gold leaf, and silver.

(NOT) PRESERVED IN AMBER

The room stayed at Catherine's palace until 1941, when the Nazis invaded the Soviet Union and the Amber Room went missing. How does an entire room simply vanish?

As the Nazis advanced, the Soviets tried to hide the amber panels by wallpapering over them. (First, they tried to disassemble the room but couldn't figure out how to take it apart without the amber crumbling.) The Nazis easily uncovered the ruse, tore down the room (they didn't care so much about the crumbling stones), and shipped it to Germany. Then they set it up at their own museum in Königsberg, where it was on display for two years.

In 1943, the Americans bombed the town of Königsberg, and no one is sure if the Germans got the room hidden away before the bombs razed the museum or not. Supposedly, the museum's director had been warned of the raid and was told to save the amber, but there's no evidence that he actually did. And since then, the Amber Room has been missing.

ROOM ON THE RUN

The missing room, though, and all of the gems, jewels, and other treasures that went along with it have inspired many theories as to its fate:

1. The amber was loaded onto a ship that sank in the Baltic Sea.

2. The Soviet Army destroyed the room themselves before the Americans bombed the museum in an effort to keep the world's attention on Western atrocities as one way of justifying the Cold War.

Fossilized termite farts have been found preserved in amber.

3. Then there's the Amber Room Curse—the idea that the room doesn't want to be found. Lots of people associated with the missing room have died. The museum director in Königsberg (and his wife) died of typhus during the KGB's investigation of the missing room. A Russian intelligence officer was killed in a car crash after he talked to a reporter about the room. And in 1987, an Amber Room hunter was murdered in Bavaria.

FOUND ART?

In February 2008, however, treasure hunters started digging up an abandoned mine in the German town of Deutschneudorf. They looked there on a tip from the son of a former German pilot who said that the Nazis had stashed art, gold, and silver there when they realized they were going to lose the war.

Further investigation led authorities to believe that the underground location might contain parts of the famous Amber Room, but because of possible booby traps and adjoining mines, they haven't yet been able to enter the site to find out what's in it. If the material below ground does turn out to be surviving relics of the Amber Room, Deutschneudorf's mayor Hans-Peter Ulstein says they'll be returned to Russia.

AMBER ROOM REDUX

Whether or not those finds prove to be the original Amber Room, the Russians unveiled a reconstructed Amber Room in 2003. They government had been working on the new room since 1979, and it was finally dedicated to mark the 300-year anniversary of the original room. It took six tons of Baltic amber and $11 million to re-create the Amber Room, and it's on display in the town of Pushkin outside of St. Petersburg.

*　　　*　　　*

"Looking out on these tuxedos tonight, it's like seeing the movie again. Thank you for this homage."
　　　　　　　**—Yves Darondeau, when his *March of the Penguins*
　　　　　　　won the Academy Award for Best Documentary**

THE JOLLY GREEN GIANT AWARD

Envirolet Composting Toilets

They were all a flush when they heard they'd won.

A **BIG GREEN FLUSHING MACHINE**
They say if you build a better mousetrap, the world will beat a path to your door. Here at the BRI, we feel obligated to beat a path to the door of someone who builds a better toilet. It takes a special kind of talent to improve on something so popular and widely used. When we noticed someone had made an improvement in composting toilets, we knew we had to give him a thumbs-up for doing the green thing.

YOU ARE WHAT YOU POST
Composting takes organic waste (manure, plant trimmings, leftover food, things like that) and lets it break down over time. When added to soil, it can add nutrients back into the environment and work as a sustainable fertilizer for new plant growth and vegetation. Composting saves a lot of material from going to landfills, too. It's a win-win all around for the environment.

It's easy enough, and human beings have been doing it for thousands of years. But when it comes to adding human waste to the compost pile, most people turn up their noses. Not so with Envirolet Composting Toilets. It's sometimes easier to use a composting system in a cabin or a remote place that doesn't have access to plumbing, which these toilets work well for, but Envirolet has broken into the home bathroom market. In a good home system, a holding tank for the waste is kept somewhere remote from the toilet itself. And in that special holding tank, the composting magic begins.

From field to fork, the average American dinner travels 1,500 miles.

WATER, WATER NOWHERE

Most of the waste people generate is water—up to 90 percent, in fact. Composting toilets let that water evaporate back into the air as the . . . ahem . . . deposits that people make in the toilet are collected in a special aeration basket. The obvious concern here is smell—and in this case, fans, microbes, and a little bit of peat moss do the dirty work of eliminating odor.

For home use, the baskets need to be placed in a waste treatment container, and most people don't want that in the bathroom. Outside or in the basement is better (the principle is the same as home plumbing; it's just that the journey is shorter—instead of going to the main collection spot, the waste goes into the holding tank). The system takes care of the rest of the compost creation process. You only have to empty it out once a year too.

The Envirolet toilet systems are designed to use either no water or very little of it, depending on the model. A typical regular toilet uses about three gallons of water every time it's flushed; low-flow toilets use about half that. That's a lot of water being wasted on waste. Composting is a huge benefit to the environment, too, especially when yard waste and disposed food products are added in. The Environmental Protection Agency praises composting for helping regenerate soil, suppressing plant diseases, helping create larger crop yields, and reducing the need for water, fertilizers, and pesticides. Waste not, want not, we say.

*   *   *

COMEBACK KID?

Pia Zadora was a child actress, appearing in 1964's *Santa Claus Conquers the Martians* . . . but then nothing. She didn't get another role until 1982, when she starred in *Butterfly*, a drama in which Zadora's character has a romantic relationship with her father. The movie was financed by Zadora's husband, Israeli businessman Meshulam Riklis, and was a critical and commercial flop. Zadora especially earned poor reviews. Nevertheless, she won a Golden Globe Award for Best New Star of the Year. But that might have had something to do with the lavish trips Riklis gave members of the Hollywood Foreign Press Association, the Golden Globes' voting body.

THE FASHION ON A ROLL AWARD

Toilet Paper Wedding Gowns and Duct Tape Prom Dresses

These creations are the very definition of "throwaway chic."

A SILK PURSE OUT OF A SOW'S EAR

The idea of making something from nothing springs from that all-American pioneer spirit: if you can make a doll from a corncob or build a house out of sod and a few boards, you can do anything! So instead of purchasing expensive off-the-rack garments, these people are using their ingenuity and skills to create elaborate and intricate garments out of the most mundane and humble materials.

THE BRIDE WORE TWO-PLY

The women behind the Web site Cheap Chic Weddings wanted to help budget-conscious brides (and publicize their site). So in 2005, they launched the first "Toilet Paper Wedding Gown Competition."

Rules: the gowns must be complete, wearable, and made of nothing except TP, tape, and glue—no buttons, snaps, hooks and eyes, or zippers!

Prize: $500 (squeeze the most out of every penny, ladies!) The real prize, though, is that the contest's sponsor foots the bill to turn the winning design into a fully finished fabric gown.

TYING THE KNOT

From day one, Cheap Chic contestants took the contest seriously. Bustles were incorporated into long, full-skirted designs; bustiers accented the bosom. But some of the most creative work involved the toilet paper appliqués and delicate toilet paper "lace." One

---

Americans recycle enough paper every day to fill a 15-mile-long train of boxcars.

woman managed to construct a floor-length lace veil. Another gown's floor-length veil had delicate scalloped edging. And working buttons were one of the more challenging elements of 2007 first runner-up Katrina Chalifoux's strapless two-piece design.

Hanah Kim, the 2007 winner and 2006 first runner-up, makes miracles with toilet paper. Her 2007 gown featured looped fringe trim and pieced cap sleeves, while her strapless 2006 entry consisted of angled accordion pleats. (Kim and her 2007 creation even made it on *The Martha Stewart Show*.) Kim isn't a serial bride, though; she's an aspiring designer. After her second entry won the top prize, she was invited to design a toilet paper dress for a real wedding that took place in the temporary "Charmin Restrooms" erected in New York's Times Square. The winners of the all-expenses-paid wedding contest (Jennifer Cannon and Doy Nichols of Lexington, Kentucky) tied the knot after Kim tied the bow on the back of Cannon's custom creation. "You may kiss the bride," said the Reverend Debra who performed the ceremony, "but please don't squeeze the Charmin dress."

STUCK ON YOU

Going to a prom usually requires a lot of money and advance planning, but you know it's true love when your date agrees to wear or even help to design clothes fashioned from duct tape. That's right: duct tape, the one item that can solve nearly any household emergency. No material of any other kind can be used, but since the company that sponsors one duct-tape prom contest makes the sticky stuff in nine different colors, at least there is a choice of palette. (College scholarships are the prizes.)

Efforts range from the supremely simple (a short, strapless, A-line dress in a single color) to the sublimely complex (a floor-length gown with a train of realistically fringed peacock feathers). Some couples match precisely; others sport completely different outfits but follow a theme like the pair who constructed medieval Japanese jousting costumes. The attention to detail is amazing, too; some pieces are completely woven out of duct tape, some have strands of "pearls" fashioned from duct tape, and one gown even featured embroidered flowers made of duct tape.

Accessories are one of the wackiest aspects of the prom contest: handbags, cummerbunds, ties, hats, bouquets, capes, tiaras, and shoes carefully crafted out of duct tape to match the suits and dresses. Anyone who bemoans the state of today's youth should admire the stick-to-it-ness of these crafty teens.

BAG LADIES

If you're not prepping for a wedding or a prom, you still can participate in the do-it-yourself couture trend. A recent fad in charity events is the Trashy Ladies Ball. Rather than drop thousands on the latest Valentino, attendees garb themselves in garbage-bag creations and donate the money they would otherwise spend on couture dresses to worthy causes. The Pittsburgh, Pennsylvania, "Garbage Bag Gala" is now entering its seventh year. Creations range from cocktail dresses to ball gowns, and the "fabric's" provenance doesn't matter, as long as it's a plastic trash bag! (Some additional trashy material is allowed, such as newspapers and aluminum can tabs.) Many women fashion their frocks from classic black, but others whip up frothy fake marabou from white, blue, and pink bags. Ruffles and boas are common, but even an "I-couldn't-be-bothered plastic toga" will do. It's all throwaway chic.

BRIDEZILLA BONANZA

They come bearing signs that read "Simple A-line Size 10-16," sporting neon headbands and deelybobbers, and wearing T-shirts with slogans like "Team Alison June 28th." Who are they? They're brides-to-be (some aren't even engaged yet), accompanied by their moms, sisters, best friends, and the occasional fiancé, and their object is Filene's "Running of the Brides." This twice-a-year sale offers designer wedding gowns originally priced from $900 to $9,000, now marked down to just three prices: $249, $499, and $699.

Filene's began the sale in 1947 at its downtown Boston store and now has "Running" events at a handful of others around the country. It's not an event for the faint of heart; within about 60 seconds of the store's opening, all 2,500 gowns will be stripped from the metal racks and guarded by a designated "dress-watcher." Women huddle in groups while the bride, stripped down to her undies, tries on as many dresses as possible until she finds "the one." No returns are allowed, so the gown has to be just right!

. . . a rubber duckie that wears an inflatable crown.

THE THINK OUTSIDE THE BOTTLE AWARD

Champagne in a Can

*What do Sofia Coppola and Paris Hilton have
in common? Hint: it comes with a pull-tab.*

CHAMPAGNE BY ANY OTHER NAME

Champagne is a popular drink for celebrations, and since not all celebrations involve several people, wine producers started packaging champagnes and other sparkling wines in small bottles known as "splits."

Splits of wine (remember, the name "champagne" applies only to sparkling wines produced in that region of France by the time-honored "méthode champenoise") hold about 12 ounces, or two glasses. However, splits have their disadvantages: They're heavy for their size, since the same thickness of glass is used even though the bottles are smaller. It takes a minute or two (and some practice) to unwrap and unwire the cork before removing it without spraying champagne all over the place. And there are places where you might like to enjoy a bit of bubbly, but glass is prohibited (boats, pools, beaches, and so on). What's a bubbly lover to do?

PRETTY IN PINK

Turn to Hollywood, of course. A few years ago, director and wine-maker Francis Ford Coppola wanted a different way to package his Niebaum-Coppola Winery's "Sofia Blanc de Blancs," a sparkling wine named for and created in honor of his daughter, herself a noted film director.

"Sofia" is a combination of pinot blanc and sauvignon blanc grapes—a bit drier than most French sparkling wines. It's blended with 8 percent Muscat grapes to make it sweeter, too. Coppola and his team wanted to put the wine into splits, but couldn't find a small enough cork of sufficiently high quality. Then they thought . . . why not cans? Wine in a can is more portable, chills more quickly, and has a hipper feel than screw-top bottles.

Today, Niebaum-Coppola packages single-servings of Sofia Blanc de Blancs in cool pink cans adorned with posh-looking type and an extendable pink straw. The four-pack—in its metallic pink octagonal box—looks like a classy hostess gift.

THEY'LL ALWAYS HAVE PARIS
Niebaum-Coppola has banked the success of its canned bubbly on a younger crowd, more *Sex and the City* than *The Sopranos*. After all, many twenty-somethings don't have the cash to shell out for a full-sized bottle, but don't mind ponying up $4.99 for a can. Of course, if they did the math, they'd realize that at $20 for a four-pack, Sofia Blanc de Blancs is priced in the same league as some really excellent full-sized bottles of sparkling wine. But no matter. The younger generation loves it.

To keep that younger crowd happy, other wine-makers started putting their sparkling wines in cans too and hiring hip people to hawk it. In 2007, wine-maker Rich Prosecco signed Paris Hilton as its spokesperson.

Hilton, a hotel heiress who is famous for . . . well, being famous . . . has done a number of scantily clad ads for this particular canned treat, made with one of Italy's better-known sparkling wines. (The Rich Prosecco cans come in original, passion fruit, and strawberry flavors.) Hilton's latest photo shoot features her in a desert, covered with nothing but gold body paint.

NOT-SO-SNOOTY "FLOOT"
With Sofia Blanc de Blancs packaged in pink and Rich Prosecco available in fruity flavors, one of the best attributes of canned bubbly might be overlooked: the trend takes a drink that for decades was the province of the monied classes and makes it fun and accessible to all.

Another brand, Floot, makes that point. Its name is a playful spelling of the kind of glass often used for champagne, and its yellow-and-orange cans have a more unisex appeal—its semi-dry,

---

You can use pine cones to forecast the weather: When rain is on the way, the scales close.

unfruity taste has a more unisex appeal, too. And Floot can be ordered by the case, making its per-serving cost a little more wallet-friendly than the other two brands.

TINY BUBBLES, TINY RATINGS

But wait! These mini-cans of sparkling wine are cute, chic, fun, and easy. Does their taste live up to its packaging? (Niebaum-Coppola and others line the cans with plastic so that the wine won't pick up an unpleasant metallic tang.) *Consumer Reports* brought in wine consultants who sampled Sofia Mini in blind taste tests and noted that it is a "simple, light-bodied" wine that rates "good" overall, though it tastes better consumed from a glass than the can.

We couldn't find a review of Rich Prosecco, but last year, it sold 10 million cans worldwide, so somebody must like it. One group that doesn't, though, is the wine growers association of Treviso, the Italian region where "prosecco" (a specific type of wine) is made. The association wants stricter standards for what can be labeled prosecco, much like the rules that govern what can be called champagne. Since its fruit flavors are lower in alcohol than its "original," Rich does not label those as prosecco.

The jury is still out on Floot, too, but according to the press on its Web site, it's being seen at lots of places and parties. So maybe we'll get to try it soon.

*　　　*　　　*

WEIRD JAPANESE DRINKS

- **Kidsbeer.** It looks like beer, it comes in six-packs of tallboys, but it just tastes like an extra frothy regular soda.

- **Canned Coffee.** Sold primarily out of vending machines, coffee in eight ounce cans are extremely popular in Japan. Some brands include BM Coffee, Deepresso, and God Coffee.

- **Pepsi Ice Cucumber.** Cucumbers are cool and refreshing, sure, evidently even more so if you add their flavor to fizzy water. It's one of Pepsi's bestselling products in Asia.

- **Mother's Milk.** Exactly how it sounds. It's a carton of actual human breast milk.

Popular drink in Greece: White wine mixed with Coca-Cola.

THE BELLS AND WHISTLES AWARD

Cupholders

*Whether you've got a hot cup of coffee or a cold soda,
cupholders make it easy to drive without spilling.
How did we ever manage without them?*

THE POWER OF THE CUPHOLDER

A survey posted on carsmart.com revealed that more than 70 percent of drivers use their cupholders every day or at least two to four times a week. Nearly 25 percent of responders wanted bigger holders to accommodate our nation's growing use of giant bladder-bursting beverages. Forty percent were more creative—they wanted cupholders that would expand and contract to hold large and small beverages equally well. The most surprising finding, though, was that more than a quarter of those surveyed said they'd base their decision to buy a car on whether or not it offered the perfect cupholder. So much for horsepower or a GPS.

SERVINGS PER CUP

G. Clotaire Rapaille is a French cultural anthropologist who has a second career as a consultant for American automobile manufacturers. His research into the car-buying habits of the general public has led to some interesting revelations. First, he found that there was a correlation between the presence of cupholders and feelings of safety in many consumers. In 2004, he told the *New Yorker,*

> [W]hat was the key element of safety when you were a child? It was that your mother fed you, and there was warm liquid. That's why cupholders are absolutely crucial for safety. If there is a car that has no cupholder, it is not safe [in the car buyer's perception]. . . . It's amazing that intelligent, educated women will look at a car and the first thing they will look at is how many cupholders it has.

Star Wars **creators modeled Yoda's face on Albert Einstein's.**

It's not just women, though. Overall, consumers are attracted to cupholders. A 2008 study conducted by CNW Marketing Research found that cupholders and heated seats were more important to consumers than gas mileage—73 percent ranked the first two amenities as important, compared to 67 percent for gas mileage. Also, a research paper commissioned by BMW in 2007 called "The Secret Life of Cars and What They Reveal About Us" contained this rather telling notion about cupholders:

> For all the sophisticated electronics now at their disposal, for all the issues affecting drivers in contemporary society, few things prompt more eager debate than the humble cupholder . . . One could even talk of the 'cupholder principle' in connection with small, emotional experiences that prompt disproportionately warm, positive feelings in the user.

HAVE A SIP

Early automobiles offered much too bumpy rides for anyone to even consider taking a drink of something while the car was moving. But by the early 1960s, car suspensions improved, and some manufacturers—thinking that people needed a place to put a beverage while at a drive-in movie—put small indentations on the inside of the glove compartment door. These first cup holders worked well enough when the car was parked, but they didn't hold the drink in place when the car was in motion.

Over the following years, cupholders took on different forms—even standalone devices that clipped onto the window. Those weren't terribly popular with consumers, though, because they left the drink to be jiggled when the door was opened. During the Space Race of the 1960s, some cupholders even came in the shape of *Mercury* capsules, although those didn't keep the drinks particularly steady either.

By the 1980s, cupholders were standard inside nearly all American cars—sometimes as a pop-out plastic contraption in the console near the radio and sometimes in the doors. European and Asian car manufacturers didn't catch on until the 1990s. Today, many carmakers don't just offer a couple of cupholders in each car—multiple cupholders have become a great selling feature, and in a large SUV, you might find more than a dozen.

CUPS THAT DON'T RUNNETH OVER

For the carmakers, keeping up with lifestyle changes can be tricky. Here are some of the things, they have to consider:

- Cupholders have had to adapt as average American beverage sizes have gotten larger. Now, they have to fit 12-, 32-, and 64-ounce drinks—and even larger. It's much harder than it seems, because larger drinks have a different center of gravity than smaller ones. So one drink might be fine while turning a corner, but a larger one in the same cupholder might spill.

- Different sizes have to be comfortably accommodated in convenient places, too. If a cupholder doesn't hold its drink securely, it can rattle while the car is moving, and prospective buyers don't like that at all. (Carmakers know that little things like this turn consumers off and make them less likely to buy the same model in the future.) It gets even worse if a retracting cupholder breaks inside its compartment and causes a constant rattle. Cupholders have to be sturdy and withstand years of wear and tear.

- People don't just drink soda and coffee in their cars, so the cupholders have to be able to accommodate an aluminum can, a coffee cup, a plastic cup, a juice box, a water bottle, and more.

*   *   *

CUPHOLDER TRIVIA

- In 1998, 7-11 redesigned the Big Gulp cup so that it would fit in standard cupholders.

- Cars in the United States (even foreign makes designed to be sold in the United States rather than overseas) have larger cupholders than in the rest of the world.

- Companies have started to design consumable products other than drinks to fit into car cupholders—like fruit cups, salads, and soup.

Every year, one ton of concrete is poured for every person on Earth.

THE "NICE TEAMWORK, GUYS" AWARD

The International Space Station

The International Space Station symbolizes a lot more than the end of the Cold War. It stands out as an international effort to propel humanity into the 21st century.

A ND . . . THEY'RE OFF!
In 1961, President John F. Kennedy announced that the United States would put a man on the moon by the end of the decade. Amid a staggering arms race between the U.S. and the U.S.S.R., as well as threats of aggression and war, the space race became the symbol of economic and scientific superiority. The race to the moon was as much about bragging rights for who got there first as it was about scientific discovery.

Perhaps nothing symbolizes the end of the Cold War as much as the construction of the International Space Station (ISS). It wasn't that long ago when several of the countries involved wanted to destroy, or at least outdo, each other. Instead, now they're working together to build a home in the vast ether surrounding the globe.

It all began when America's team lost funding for its own space station and had to turn to a former enemy for help.

LIFTOFF

While America began its race to the moon with the *Gemini* and *Apollo* programs, the Soviets turned their attention toward building a satellite, one that could sustain a crew for an extended period of time. They built the first space station, the *Salyut*

Sixty-five percent of Elvis impersonators are of Asian descent.

1, in 1971—two years after American Neil Armstrong walked on the moon.

America followed suit in 1973 with *Skylab*. Not to be outdone, the Soviet Union continued to launch space stations, including a military space station, throughout the 1970s. Space stations didn't have a very long life span, and technical problems plagued the entire program. But the Soviet's persistence paid off in 1986, when they launched the first piece of the space station *Mir*.

Mir was operable as a space station immediately, but it wasn't officially completed until 1997, when it reached its full weight of 137 tons. For 10 years, from 1989 until 1999, *Mir* was occupied by humans—and in a precursor to the peaceful cooperation of the International Space Station, *Mir* entertained both Soviet and American guests, as well as astronauts from 10 other countries. All told, 23,000 experiments were performed there in the name of science.

WHAT IT TOOK

Mir laid the foundation, but the origin of the International Space Station begins in 1984, when President Ronald Reagan announced plans for the American space station *Freedom*. But building *Freedom* would be costly, and by 1993, the project was stalling amid lack of funding and support.

Under President Bill Clinton, the plan for *Freedom* changed, and the former Soviet Union (now Russia) came in as a partner—along with Japan, Canada, and several European countries (under the European Space Agency). The project got a new name: the International Space Station. Russia had been planning its own new space station (*Mir-2*) and folded plans for that into the international effort. The space station would have to be built in sections, because it was so big, and the Russians launched the first component into orbit in 1998.

Today, 17 countries are part of the effort to build the ISS. When it's finished (NASA hopes for 2010), the space station will be 356 feet long and 100 feet high, and will weigh more than 900,000 pounds—or at least it would weigh that much on Earth. And when it's completed, the space station will have the largest laboratory ever built in space, with six separate and fully functional research stations.

If all the ice in Antarctica melted, sea levels would rise by about 200 feet.

CALL THE LANDLORD FOR REPAIRS

Who owns the space station, however, is a bit tricky. Complex agreements have been drawn up between all the participating countries that include basic laws and codes of conduct for astronauts onboard, as well as strict guidelines for who can use which lab and when. Teamwork only goes so far, and all the participants want to protect their own little piece of the investment.

NASA's estimated costs alone are in the neighborhood of $30 billion for the entire project (from 1994 to completion). Although the space station is the most expensive thing ever built, its success will be short-lived; it will shine in the sky only from 2010 to 2016 because space stations (like all satellites) still degrade over time and aren't known for their longevity.

* * *

WEIRD GRAMMY MOMENTS

- At the 1998 awards, Bob Dylan performed his song "Love Sick" while surrounded by young fans in a mock coffeehouse setting. Somehow, a performance artist named Michael Portnoy leapt onto the stage and danced wildly with the words "Soy Bomb" written on his bare chest. Security removed him, and Dylan didn't miss a note. (We still don't know what "Soy Bomb" means.)

- Also in 1998, at the end of the show, as Shawn Colvin took the stage to accept the award for Record of the Year for "Sunny Came Home," Wu-Tang Clan rapper Ol' Dirty Bastard got to the microphone first and went on a strange rant about how it was disgraceful that the Wu-Tang Clan lost the Best Rap Album grammy to Puff Daddy because "Wu-Tang is for the children!"

- In 1988, Metallica performed the hit song "One" and waited in the wings of the stage. The next award to be presented was the Best Hard Rock/Heavy Metal Grammy, for which they were considered a lock. The winner was announced and it was . . . 1970s progressive rock band Jethro Tull, who was so far removed from heavy metal that its lead singer played a flute.

- In 2001, country rock singer Shelby Lynne won the award for Best New Artist. It was a strange honor for Lynne. She'd recorded her first album in 1988 and had released six albums since.

Only countries whose names start with "A" but don't end with "A": Afghanistan and Azerbaijan

THE SCI-FI IN 2-D AWARD

Michael Whelan

By definition, every painter is a visionary—but only a select few can envision worlds that have never been seen by human eyes. Here's the best in the business.

THE GO-TO GUY

Even if you're not into fantasy or science fiction, chances are you've seen at least a few of this heavily influential artist's images—especially if you browse bookstores. Over the last 30 years, Michael Whelan's art has graced the covers of more than 350 books and dozens of album covers, including Meat Loaf's *Bat Out Of Hell II* and Michael Jackson's *Victory*. But it is in the world of fantasy and science fiction novels that Whelan has made his biggest impact, illustrating covers that boast the names of such prominent genre writers as Isaac Asimov, Arthur C. Clarke, Robert A. Heinlein, Ray Bradbury, H. P. Lovecraft, Anne McCaffrey, and Stephen King—who said on more than one occasion that Whelan illustrates the horror author's characters "exactly as I had imagined them."

And writers aren't the only ones who have recognized Whelan's abilities—he's picked up 16 Hugo Awards, which celebrate sci-fi and fantasy works, as well as a slew of other awards and honors. He's also done commissioned work for the Franklin Mint and the National Geographic Society.

AN ENGROSSING EDUCATION

When looking back at Whelan's formative years, it's not surprising that he ended up painting strange creatures in alien landscapes for a living. Born in Culver City, California, in 1950, Whelan spent his childhood moving to a different town nearly every year (his father worked in the aerospace industry). The one constant was art. He's always had a natural ability to draw and as a kid he loved the work of popular artists like Norman Rockwell and Maxfield Parrish. Combine Rockwell's expressive people with Parrish's imaginary worlds, and you get an idea of Whelan's work.

Perhaps an even bigger inspiration, though, came from the year Whelan spent living near a missile testing site in White Sands, New Mexico. The teenager was awe-struck by the rockets as they emerged from the desert landscape and trailed off into the haze. "It was always thrilling to watch them go up," he recalled, "and sometimes blow up!" The missile tests helped to plant the seed for the strange new worlds he'd eventually create. But what about the creatures that live in those worlds?

Whelan began to perfect those when he studied art at San Jose State University in the early 1970s. In addition to taking the traditional art classes, he spent a lot of time learning anatomy in the physiology department. Among his duties: building skeletons out of piles of bones and preparing cadavers for medical tests. He gained extensive knowledge of the human body . . . in all its gory detail. "You have to learn to draw the real before you can turn it into fantasy," Whelan advises.

MORE THAN JUST A PRETTY (STRANGE) PICTURE

It didn't take long for Whelan to get noticed—he illustrated his first book cover in 1975 and by '80 was among the most renowned genre artists in the world. So what exactly is it that makes Whelan's work stand out? Lots of conceptual artists have created some bizarre worlds, but Whelan tries to take it a step further. Whether he's drawing humans or aliens, he goes for what he calls "imaginative realism." In an otherwise otherworldly picture, the viewer must be able to identify with something, be it the sadness of the heroine or the courage of a winged beast flying into a fiery horizon. The "realism" aspect comes into play in his landscapes as well: Whelan must first learn everything about the universe where his image will take place before he can fill in the tiny part he has to paint. And although these universes may be pure fantasy, each one must adhere to its own specific set of rules.

It's that combination of intricate detail and recognizable emotion that has touched so many people, much in the same way the grit and dirt on the space ships in the original *Star Wars* film helped the audience believe those really *were* ships in space. That same quality holds true for Whelan's art: Look at one of his images and you can almost imagine him standing on a cliff in the foreground furiously painting the action before it flies away—or the soft, ethereal light before it vanishes.

THE ARTIST'S WAY
Whelan will be the first to say that these creations do not come easily: When commissioned to illustrate a book cover, he goes through a lengthy process. First, he'll read the entire book "two or three times" before creating sample drawings that he sends off to the author. It's always a collaborative effort, but much of what he paints "must come straight from my own mind."

And like it is with most painters, these elaborate images aren't completely created from nothing. Over the years, Whelan's traveled extensively and has taken thousands of photographs of landscapes, castles, and sunsets that he uses for reference. He's also collected thousands more images that chronicle everything from armor to animals to airplanes. For the humans who inhabit his worlds, Whelan uses models—either himself (via a self-portrait photo in the desired pose), or more often, friends or even fashion models who don elaborate costumes and pose for him. Then, using mostly oil paints and some acrylics (and these days, computers), Whelan hunkers down in his studio in Danbury, Connecticut, and gets to work on his next masterpiece.

R-E-S-P-E-C-T
Yet no matter how hard Whelan works or how many accolades and awards he receives, one thing has eluded him for a long time: respect as a true "artiste." Technically speaking, Whelan has spent the bulk of his career working as an *illustrator* for hire, an artist who is commissioned to create visual representations of other people's ideas. But over the last decade or so, Whelan has been trying to broaden his horizons. "There has been a deep-seated bias against illustration in the fine art world for a long time, but there are signs that it is easing somewhat," he said in 2007. "It probably had more to do with the fact that most illustrators worked realistically than for any other reason. Now that Realism seems to be on

the rebound, the barriers against illustrators seem to be lifting a little. Just think of all the famous American artists who began as illustrators: Winslow Homer, Edward Hopper, Remington, Parrish, Andy Warhol, to name a few." Will Michael Whelan's name be added to that list of famous artists some day? Only time will tell, but he'll definitely always be known as the most successful illustrator of fantasy and science fiction at the turn of the 21st century. For now, though, all he really wants to do is keep on painting.

DOING IT HIS WAY

Now in his late 50s, Whelan has stopped taking on commissioned works altogether, preferring to create worlds from the depths of his own mind. Although he says he "couldn't care less if they are 'accepted' or not," the bulk of these new pieces have been. "I'm in the happy but awkward position of selling most of my personal work," he admits. Still, Whelan realizes that he is in the minority of sci fi and fantasy illustrators trying to break into fine art galleries. Perhaps his success, along with the ever-changing tastes in popular art, will inspire the younger generation of fantasy painters to start branching out as well. Could an "Imaginative Realism" artistic movement be just around the corner?

Whelan doesn't know. His only worry, at this point in his life, is having enough time to paint all of the worlds he has imagined. "Much has been written by artists on the 'fear of the blank canvas,' but I have the opposite problem—I have too *many* ideas."

So one more won't hurt, will it? How about a surreal alien landscape, its flowing valleys dotted all the way to the horizon with porcelain monoliths . . . and floating high above it all in the azure sky—a shiny, golden plunger. (Mr. Whelan, if you happen to be reading this: hint, hint.)

* * *

"Fantasy, abandoned by reason, produces impossible monsters; united with it, she is the mother of the arts and the origin of marvels."

—**Francisco Goya, Spanish painter (1746–1828)**

In competition, the average dart hits the board at 40 miles per hour.

THE MAKING FACES AWARD

Forensic Artists

Re-creating a human face from minimal remains may seem impossible, but to forensic artists, it is an art and a science . . . and their livelihood. The results of the painstaking process—putting together clues to reconstruct a face—are astounding.

A NEW KIND OF ARTIST

In matters of history or crime, forensic artists are helping us see the unknown. Typically, they're brought in as a last resort, when clues to a crime have dried up and the victim is unknown.

Their work is also helpful in happier situations. The physical appearance of a historical figure who never had a portrait painted or photograph taken is a mystery to us. But now forensic artists can help fill in the blanks.

IDENTITY THEFT

Police know they can't expect exact replicas of a deceased person's face without any other evidence—that can be virtually impossible. But they hope the artist can reconstruct enough visual details so that someone who knew the victim will be able to identify him or her. In the United States alone, there are an estimated 40,000 unidentified human remains.

In the event of a major explosion, fire, or other catastrophic event, faces may be blown off. All that's left to analyze are bones or other body fragments. Forensic artists fill in the details.

Forensic artists are also the ones police call on to age existing photographs to determine what a person might look like years from now. This technique is often used for children who have been missing for years.

Antarctica has one active volcano, Mount Erebus, and one river, the Onyx.

PUTTING IT TOGETHER

Without a skull, forensic artists can't do much to re-create a face. But even an incomplete or badly damaged skull is a start. First, the forensic artist must rebuild the skull using modeling wax. A 1996 study at the University of Manchester determined that skulls can be re-created even if significant parts, such as the occipital bone, are missing. No one's skull is exactly symmetrical, but most are close enough. So mirror imaging (mirroring one side of the face after the other side) can be used to fill in blanks. (The mandible is the only bone whose absence can cause significant discrepancies in a re-created skull.) The success of the study led forensic artists to call the entire process the Manchester Method of Facial Reconstruction.

A complex look at the angle and shape of each part of the skull helps the artist determine the shape of the face, pointing to whether the deceased had a round, oval, or square face. Microscopic examination of the pieces of the skull can show scientists where the hairline was (hair follicles cause roughness on the bone), and even forehead creases can be seen based on muscular attachments in the area.

MATH MAKES THE DIFFERENCE

Mathematical equations are used to ascertain the shape of the nose. Caroline Wilkinson, in her 2004 book *Forensic Facial Reconstruction*, notes, "The width of the nasal aperture, at its widest point, is three-fifths of the overall width of the nose (at its widest point)." She further explains how to figure out the overall shape and size of the nose based on evidence found in the skull tissue. "A straight, thin nose usually has a weak glabella [the smooth space between the eyebrows]," she notes. A broad nose will show through "broad rounded nasal bones with simple contours and a bell shape." The nasal aperture will even show how far apart the nostrils were.

Dental analysis of the skull shows the thickness of the lips and the width of the mouth. The biggest missing details of the face are hair and eye color. Without any DNA evidence, they are difficult to determine.

Forensic artists earn up to $2,000 per skull they re-create. It takes about two weeks for them to do their job.

Grizzly bears eat moths—as many as 40,000 in a day.

PUTTING A HUMAN FACE ON THE PAST

Similar research has led to the re-creation of famous historical figures' faces. In 2005, French scientists were able to develop a bust of King Tut's head by analyzing 3-D CT scans of the boy king's skull. (*For more about Tut, turn to page 164.*) In September of that same year, forensics experts also began making models of George Washington's face at three different ages—19, 45, and 57, three pivotal moments of his life (when he became a major in the Virginia militia; when he fought at Valley Forge; and when he became the first president of the United States, respectively). Washington was 67 when he died, so the team reversed the aging technology to depict his image throughout these important years of his life.

Ongoing efforts to improve facial forensics may mean the world will deal with fewer cold cases, fewer mysteries will be left unsolved, and fewer of the missing or deceased will remain unknown. Forensic artists will continue to put a human face on the past.

*   *   *

NO THANKS

- In 1964, Jean-Paul Sartre (*Nausea, No Exit*) won the Nobel Prize for Literature. He turned it down, stating, "A writer must refuse to allow himself to be transformed into an institution, even if it takes place in the most honorable form."

- Russian novelist Boris Pasternak (*Doctor Zhivago*) was awarded the Nobel Prize for Literature in 1958, but had to turn it down because he feared that if he went to Stockholm, Sweden, to receive the prize, the Soviet Union would strip him of his citizenship.

- Sinclair Lewis, one of the most popular novelists in the United States in the early 20th century (*Elmer Gantry, Main Street*), was awarded the Pulitzer Prize in 1926 for *Arrowsmith*. He turned it down, saying, "The seekers for prizes tend to labor not for inherent excellence but for alien rewards; they tend to write this, or timorously to avoid writing that, in order to tickle the prejudices of a haphazard committee."

Do you read too much? If so, you are a bibliobibuli.

THE TRADING FACES AWARD

Extreme Plastic Surgery

Have you ever seen a movie star that you longer recognize? It turns out that plastic surgery can be addictive . . . with some interesting results.

PLASTIC FANTASTIC

Facelifts, breast augmentations, liposuction, and rhinoplasty have become commonplace as people try to stave off the appearance of old age. Plastic surgery is now de rigueur not only in Beverly Hills and Manhattan, but also in middle America. According to the American Society for Aesthetic Plastic Surgery, 11.5 million cosmetic surgical and nonsurgical procedures were performed in 2006. That's a lot of nipping and tucking.

But now that a great number of cosmetic surgical procedures have become prevalent, there's a whole subset of plastic surgery patients who are looking to take the scalpel to a whole new level—an extreme level.

Animal worship dates back to ancient times. Now, with the advent of modern medical science, humans can worship animals by altering themselves to physically resemble one.

For example, Austin, Texas-based artist/entertainer Eric Sprague reportedly spent $250,000 on surgery and other body modifications to transform himself into "Lizardman." To give himself a reptilian appearance, Sprague underwent an estimated 650–700 hours of tattooing, as well as having five Teflon horns implanted above each of his eyes to form horned ridges. Then he had four of his teeth filed into sharp fangs and his tongue bifurcated.

CAT WOMAN

Probably the most famous case of animal-inspired extreme plastic surgery, though, is Jocelyn Wildenstein, widely known as "The Cat

---

Enough Coca-Cola is consumed every year worldwide to fill 3.5 million bathtubs.

Lady" or "The Bride of Wildenstein." Jocelyn Wildenstein is the ex-wife of deceased millionaire art dealer Alec Wildenstein. In 1977, their first date, prophetically enough, took place over a dawn lion hunt in Kenya. Within a year, they were married.

At some point, perhaps fearing the loss of her husband's interest, she began a frenzied cycle of cosmetic procedures—collagen injections to her lips, cheeks and chin, along with at least seven facelifts and drastic eye reconstruction surgery. She did it all to appear more feline.

Needless to say, both her husband and society at large found her new look cat-astrophic. Scandal ensued—involving Mr. Wildenstein and an affair with a Russian fashion model, gunplay, and acrimonious divorce proceedings. Not exactly a purr-fect ending.

AMERICAN IDOLS

Plenty of cosmetic surgery candidates enter their doctor's office asking to have Angelina Jolie's lips or George Clooney's chin, but some patients take it too extremes. In 2004, MTV showcased a series entitled *I Want a Famous Face*, in which everyday people underwent major plastic surgeries in order to resemble celebrities, everyone from Brad Pitt to Carmen Electra. (On the side of sanity, when actress Drew Barrymore learned that a 23-year-old girl was scheduled to appear on the show to undergo procedures to look like her, she contacted the girl directly and convinced her not to go through with the surgeries.)

Other notable cases of idol insanity include Cindy Jackson, whose childhood fixation on her Barbie doll inspired her to undergo a total of 30 procedures to look like a real-life Barbie. Motivated by Jackson's transformation, Tim Whitfield-Lynn went through multiple surgeries in order to resemble Barbie's boyfriend Ken.

The reigning celebrity queen of extreme cosmetic surgery is most certainly the comedienne Joan Rivers, who has been candid about her many procedures. With her humor (if not her facial muscles) fully intact, Rivers even played up her self-described plastic surgery addiction in a 2008 Geico television commercial in which she delivered the lines, "Am I smiling? I can't tell! I can't feel my face!"

THE "NOW THAT'S UGLY" AWARD

Ugliest Dog Contest

With faces only their human mothers could love, these
pups take the prize for the cutest ugly dogs around.

TOP OF THE HEAP

Westminster it's not, but World's Ugliest Dog contest in Petaluma, California, has been entertaining dog lovers every June for 20 years. It started as a local summer attraction in 1988 but got so much media attention that now news cameras outnumber entrants, Internet voting climbs to the tens of thousands, and ugly aspirants travel from as far away as Florida to compete. (Winners get trophies, prize money, and the title, of course.) Back in 2006, suspense was especially high because Sam, the champion for three years running, had died at the age of 14, and the field was wide open for the 18 (really bad-looking) contenders. Here's a look at some of the ugliest winners ever to grace a dog show stage.

SAM
Awards: World's Ugliest Dog (2003, 2004, 2005)

Probably the most famous ugly dog, Sam was a 13-pound Chinese crested who was so ugly that his owner, Susie Lockheed, was scared of him when she first brought him home. (He was also so ugly that Japanese TV reporters compared him to Godzilla.) Sam was acne-riddled, blind, warty, and hairless (unless you count the straggly wisps sticking out of his head). He had crooked teeth, a fatty tumor on his chest, and a line of moles down his nose. But Lockheed loved him. Sam came to her as a rescue dog; his original owner lost her pet-friendly apartment and could no longer keep him. Early in their relationship, Lockheed was diagnosed with cancer. Sam slept with her, comforted her, and saw her through chemotherapy, proving that judging an old dog on bad looks is never fair.

Cuddly side aside, Sam was plenty cranky, and had a fascination with his back leg. To Lockheed, it seemed that he believed there was an imaginary foe attached to his back leg. He'd snarl at it and bite, and whenever she gave him a treat, Sam would keep a close eye on that back leg to make sure it didn't steal the snack away.

TATORTOT
Award: Ugliest Mutt (2005)

Sam may have gained worldwide fame for his hideousness, but his girlfriend—who is part Chihuahua, part Chinese crested—is pretty ill-favored, too. TatorTot, another dog belonging to Susie Lockheed, never did win the World's Ugliest title, but she did take Ugliest Mutt honors in 2005. TatorTot has her looks and personality working against her, it seems. She's only mostly hairless, not nearly as snarly as Sam, and has a tuft of white hair atop her head. Apparently, says Lockheed, TatorTot is just too cute to take home the top prize.

ARCHIE
Award: World's Ugliest Dog (2006)

In 2006, Archie (yet another Chinese crested) earned the title of World's Ugliest Dog. His owner, Heather Peoples, traveled all the way from Arizona to show off Archie's attributes at the contest. Unlike Sam, Archie does have hair—it sticks up erratically all over his head. His tongue hangs out of one side of his mouth because he has no teeth to hold it in place. His naked, liver-colored belly resembles a sausage. And he's so ugly that the animal shelter where he was living (and where Peoples worked) gave Peoples $10 to take him away. It was supposed to be just a temporary thing, but Peoples says her husband fell in love with the beauty-impaired beast: "Now when we go out, my husband carries Archie in his arms like a baby."

Archie was the winner in a year fraught with scandal. The ugliest dog is crowned after an Internet voting campaign that lasts several weeks, but during the 2006 process, computer hackers infiltrated the contest's Web site and erased votes from some of the top dogs. Fortunately, contest organizers discovered the crime

---

Steepest street in the world: Baldwin Street in Dunedin, New Zealand. Its incline is 38%.

and remedied the situation: they started the voting over from scratch. In the end, Archie pulled past favorites Munchkin, Rascal, and Pee Wee Martini to take the crown.

ELWOOD
Award: World's Ugliest Dog (2007)
This Chihuahua and Chinese crested mix took the top title after coming in second in 2006. He traveled all the way to California from New Jersey with his owner, Karen Quigley, who—despite the dog's new title—thinks Elwood is "the cutest thing that ever lived." Elwood's Internet voters, obviously, disagreed. With his dark, almost hairless body (Elwood does have a tuft of white fur atop his misshapen head) and a tongue that always droops from his mouth, Elwood is sometimes called "Yoda" or "ET"—affectionate nicknames, for sure. Besides winning the title and taking home $1,000, Elwood is somewhat of a local celebrity back in New Jersey, where he's a Good Will Ambassador for the SPCA. He and Quigley try to educate people about special-needs pets (from sick animals to ugly ones) and encourage residents to adopt homeless dogs and cats.

*   *   *

AWARDS GLUT
Do you like watching awards shows on TV? Then you have a lot more to choose from than just the Oscars and Grammys. There's the Critics' Choice Awards, the Screen Actors Guild Awards, the GLAAD Media Awards, the Golden Globe Awards, the MTV Movie Awards, the Independent Spirit Awards, the Billboard Music Awards, the Tony Awards, the American Music Awards, the World Music Awards, the NAACP Image Awards, the Primetime Emmy Awards, the Daytime Emmy Awards, the MTV Video Music Awards, the Nickelodeon Kids' Choice Awards, the Teen Choice Awards, the People's Choice Awards, the TV Land Awards, the Food Network Awards, VH1's Hip-Hop Honors, the VH1/Vogue Fashion Awards, the Clio Awards, the BET Awards, the Radio Music Awards, the ESPY Awards, Soap Opera Digest Awards, the Family Television Awards, the Spike TV Scream Awards, the Reality Awards, and the CMT Flameworthy Video Awards.

THE STINKY CHEESE AWARD

Vieux Boulogne

Some like it hot, some like it cold, some like it really smelly. Uncle John agrees with the experts—this cheese really stinks!

WHO CUT THE CHEESE?
When most people think of a smelly cheese, Limburger is what comes to mind. Comedians joke about its noxious stench, and even though Mighty Mouse had a weakness for it, the stuff's indescribable scent repels most people. Researchers at the Netherlands' Wageningen Agricultural University found that the mosquito species *Anopheles gambiae* "loves both stinky feet and Limburger cheese." Limburger's uniquely smelly properties come from *B. linens*—the same bacteria that attract malaria-carrying mosquitoes to stinking feet. But despite that fact, Limburger is *not* the world's stinkiest cheese.

The *B. linens* bacterial strain is shared by many other washed-rind cheeses, including Muenster, époisses, Taleggio, Pont l'Evêque Reblochon, and Port-Salut. During the ripening process for washed-rind cheeses, cheesemakers rinse the cheeses with a liquid (usually wine or beer), which encourages bacteria to grow and gives the cheeses a reddish-brown rind. Many people associate smelly with moldy, and moldy with old. But washed-rind cheeses are young cheeses, and the washing process is what brings this type of cheese to maturity. They're most common in mainland Europe, but are also made in England, like the pungent perry-washed Stinking Bishop. (Perry is hard pear cider common in Wales and Britain's West Country.)

NOTES OF GARLIC AND UNWASHED FEET
But even Stinking Bishop doesn't qualify as the world's stinkiest

---

The Arabic word for coffee means "excitement."

cheese. In 2004, scientists at Cranfield University in Bedfordshire, England, conducted a study to determine the most fetid fromage out of 15 contestants. The panel of pungency used 19 human testers backed up by an electronic "nose" to make its determinations. The electronic nose was made up of an array of sensors, each of which responded to the presence of chemicals in a slightly different way. The sensors were linked to a computer that interpreted their responses and rated them.

The winner was Vieux Boulogne ("Old" or "Aged Boulogne"), a washed-rind cheese from France that testers likened to a combination of garlic, unwashed feet, and unwashed cat. But like Limburger, the actual taste of Vieux Boulogne (also known as Sable du Boulonnais) isn't as disgusting as its description. It's tangier and alcoholic because of the bière blonde (pale ale) used to wash its square rind. In fact, the owner of Le Fromagerie, the only store in London that stocks Vieux Boulogne, describes it as "a young, modern cheese with a surprisingly mellow and gentle taste that's perfect served with some crusty bread and a beer. It's a great cheese to try, as it doesn't have the earthy, farmyardy flavours that some people find overpowering."

RUNNY AND ROYAL

Vieux Boulogne is made in the northernmost reaches of Normandy, a region of France renowned for its dairy products. The rich, flavorful milk from the cows near the city of Boulogne-sur-Mer contributes to its "mellow and gentle taste." But don't expect to sample it at your neighborhood grocery store. Vieux Boulogne is an unpasteurized milk cheese, so it's not legal in the United States. To savor its authentic runny, stinky (and yummy, to some) taste, you'll need to cross the Atlantic.

ANOTHER OLFACTORY ASSAULT

Although it ranked tenth in the Cranfield study, Époisses de Bourgogne is often considered the stinkiest cheese around, simply because it's more widely available in France and Europe. (A pasteurized version can be found in the United States, too.) French epicure Jean-Anthelme Brillat-Savarin called this washed-rind cheese from the Burgundy wine region "the king of all cheeses," and it was a favorite of Napoleon. Époisses needs to ripen at room temperature for several days before being served—you'll know it's at just the right runniness if you stick a spoon in it and it drips and swirls from the tip like thick caramel sauce.

GREEN BAY STATE'S STINKY SANDWICH

There is one really stinky cheese that's made in the United States: We're back to Limburger, which came to the New World with German and Belgian immigrants. For years, Limburger was a staple of Wisconsin's Teutonic-descended cheeseheads, whose legacy lives on in a Green Bay State tavern staple: limburger on pumpernickel bread with sliced red onion and hot mustard. However, there's only one place that still produces stateside Limburger: the master cheesemakers of Chalet Cheese Cooperative in Monroe, Wisconsin.

*　　　*　　　*

LIKE AN (UN)BROKEN RECORD

Ashrita Furman is the world-record world-record holder. He's set more than 189 official records over the past three decades—80 still stand. Here are some of his accomplishments:

- Longest distance traveled on a pogo stick (23.11 miles)
- Longest distance somersaulted (12 miles, 390 yards)
- Underwater jump roping (900 jumps in one hour)
- Longest distance carrying a brick with one hand (85.05 miles)
- Longest time juggling underwater (48 minutes)
- Most hopscotch games played in an hour (28)
- Most grapes caught in his mouth in a minute (77)
- Longest distance jumped on a pogo stick underwater (1,680 ft.)
- Most 20-ounce glasses balanced on his chin (81)
- Eating the most Jell-O with chopsticks in a minute (16.04 oz.)
- Fastest duct taping a person to a wall (2 minutes, 38 seconds)
- Fastest duct taping himself to a wall (8 minutes, 7 seconds)

THE DARK AND STORMY NIGHT AWARD

Ultra-Short Stories

Life is short, and sometimes, so is art. When it comes to fiction, less really can be more.

PAPA'S POINTED PROSE

Ernest Hemingway is famous for his economy with the written word. In novels like *The Old Man and the Sea* and *For Whom the Bell Tolls*, his sentences are spare and his adjectives sparer. But his sparest work? Just six words: "For Sale: Baby shoes, never worn."

Legend says that "Papa" Hemingway wrote this poignant line after being bet $10 that he couldn't write a story of six words or less. Even if it doesn't seem to meet the criteria of a real short story, there are two things to keep in mind: one, that the bet was all about writing a story of six words or less. Two, over the years numerous literary experts have included this "story" in their accounts of micro-fiction.

The "story" doesn't have a plot, resolution, or a back story of its own, but it does show how effectively a few words can deliver emotional impact—and make you want to know the rest of the story.

WHO WRITES SHORT SHORTS?

Hemingway wasn't the first to find extremely short-form fiction pleasing. From *Aesop's Fables* to Chekhov to O. Henry and beyond, writers have long packed punches in what is referred to variously as flash, micro, sudden, postcard, short-short, quick, minutes, furious, and skinny fiction.

Even if Hemingway didn't consider the "baby shoes" story his masterpiece, it's pretty close to genius for economy of scale. While writing less rather than more might sound like working less rather than more, nothing could be further from the truth. Flash fiction is rarely, if ever, composed in a flash of inspiration.

SHORTEST, SHORTER, SHORT

In the past several decades, the shortest fiction has enjoyed a renaissance among serious literary writers, but its most ardent practitioners are usually fantasy and science-fiction writers, which is where the term "nanofiction" probably gained popularity. Nanofiction, or "55 Fiction," is strictly limited to 55 words.

55 Fiction developed from a writing contest run by *New Times* magazine in 1987 and must contain at least one character, a setting, and a plot that includes conflict and resolution. Drama, suspense, and shock are important elements, too. Many devotees of "55 Fiction" try to include a "last sentence shock."

Next in line of increasingly longer short fiction is "The 69er," consisting of—you guessed it—69 words. However, its slightly longer (100-word) counterpart, "The Drabble," has a more interesting back story.

The Drabble has the distinction of being the only literary genre to grow out of a *Monty Python's Flying Circus* publication. In the British comedy troupe's 1971 *Big Red Book*, Drabble was a word game where the first person to write a novel wins. While this was of course a tongue-in-cheek jab at the popular board game Scrabble, where players compete to build words for points, Drabble captured the imagination of British science-fiction circles, and during the 1980s at Birmingham University, the first 100-word Drabbles were born.

SCREEN GEMS

Very short stories aren't written just in English. In France, they're known as *nouvelles*, and in China, there are lots of names for them: "little short story," "pocket-size story," "minute-long story," "palm-sized story," and the "smoke-long story" (one cigarette's worth of reading). But the latest innovation in short fiction comes from Japan: cell-phone novels. These backlit books aren't just read on tiny screens; they're composed on them, too. A new generation of cell-phone novelists has sprung up, and now that group is doing what all aspiring novelists do: trying to get their work published in print editions.

FLASH FORWARD

Most "flash fiction" is a bit longer, from 300 to 1,000 words. Its proponents think that anything over 1,000 words is a short story (or at least a "short short"). If this sounds a bit picky, remember—these are people ready to pick a story down to its bones.

Like a good poem, a good flashfic story can have a "lightbulb" quality, illuminating an image, an emotion, or an experience so that its intensity stays with the reader. But a good flashfic story isn't necessarily a poem. A poem doesn't have to have a beginning, a middle, and end—flash fiction does.

Although some types of very short fiction originated in the genre communities (science fiction, suspense, and so on), today these shortest of shorts aren't given short shrift by the best writers. Venerable authors like John Updike, Francine Prose, Amy Hempel, Joyce Carol Oates, and Raymond Carver tried their hands at flash fiction, proving that Hemingway's idea was no flash in the pan.

*   *   *

AWARD ORIGIN:
THE IRVING G. THALBERG MEMORIAL AWARD

Thalberg was president of MGM Studios in the 1920s and '30s. He sought to make films more respectable, and not just profitable. After he died of pneumonia in 1936 at age 37, the Academy of Motion Picture Arts and Sciences began presenting the Irving G. Thalberg Memorial Award. It's a lifetime achievement award presented at the Oscars to a well-established director or producer. Past winners include Alfred Hitchcock, Steven Spielberg, and Billy Wilder.

THE "SECOND BANANA" AWARD

Emma Peel

For an outstanding and unforgettable performance as sidekick.

THE INTRODUCTION

Choosing one Golden Plunger-worthy sidekick was tough—there have been so many great ones through the ages: Don Quixote's Sancho Panza, Sherlock Holmes's Dr. Watson, Ralph Cramden's Ed Norton, Frodo's Samwise, Lucy's Ethel, Andy Taylor's Barney Fife, Mary's Rhoda, Batman's Robin, Seinfeld's Costanza . . . the list is so long! In their own unique ways they all did what every great sidekick must do: made their star brighter without making their own *too* bright. Some simply provide comic relief; some give an otherwise aloof star opportunities to show emotion; some provide sexual tension; some even help highlight a star's negative aspects, thereby making the character more human. (Think of Dr. Watson and Holmes's cocaine habit.) It's a difficult job—but there have been many masters. But we chose one of the most unique sidekicks in history.

DUELING DUET

On October 2, 1965, British TV viewers sat down in front of their sets and watched the following scene unfold: An impeccably dressed, 40-ish British gentleman in a black bowler hat and carrying an umbrella/walking stick arrives at the apartment of an attractive, dark-haired woman in her late 20s. She is dressed in a tight, black leather body suit and is holding a fencing epee. He pours tea. She makes him duel her for cream for the tea, and during the sometimes seemingly real battle the two engage in witty verbal repartee rife with sexual tension. She is clearly the better fencer, but he is more devious—and he wins when he tricks her and "ties her up" in a curtain . . . and then smacks her on the bottom with his epee. "That was very, very dirty," she says . . . and so began the partnership of star secret agent John Steed and sidekick Emma Peel in the off-kilter, darkly humorous, surreal British spy series, *The Avengers*.

TOWERING VIOLET

Diana Rigg's Emma Peel gets our award for not only being a great sidekick, but doing it in a way that reached beyond the television screen. Emma Peel was a breakthrough character for women in television. Before "women's liberation" was a household phrase, she was a hero to young female viewers around the world. Before then, playing a female sidekick to a secret agent would have meant being easily frightened and prone to fainting, and being saved from bad guys by the star every week. And while sex appeal was certainly a part of her character, Peel was no fainter: during the three years she was on the show, she saved Steed as often as he saved her.

In that same episode, titled "The Town of No Return," Mrs. Peel (she's a widow) mentions that she has just finished writing an article for a respected science journal, disposes of two dangerous criminals with martial arts moves, knocks back a few brandies, and finishes the show driving off on a moped . . . with Steed sitting side-saddle behind her. Steed was the star of the show, so he of course performed a bit more of the bad-guy-beating, but Peel was clearly his match in many ways, and he obviously liked and respected her—and it made Steel (played by Patrick Macnee) seem more human and likeable.

BEHIND THE SCENES

Rigg wasn't the first sidekick to John Steed: *The Avengers* debuted in 1961 with a male partner for the spy. In 1962 Honor Blackman, best known as the Bond girl "Pussy Galore" in 1964's *Goldfinger*, became Steed's first female sidekick as Dr. (of anthropology) Catherine Gale. Like Peel, she was attractive, independently wealthy, intelligent, and knowledgeable in martial arts and weaponry—but, while the show was very popular, it hadn't matured yet. Steed was portrayed as a trench coat-wearing macho man during this period, and the humor had not yet developed the level of sophistication it later would. In any case, in 1964 Blackman quit the show when she was offered the role in the Bond film.

National pride? Only 19 percent of the Welsh population speaks Welsh.

That year more than 60 actresses showed up at Associated British Corporation studios in London to audition for the part. Among them was a 26-year-old actress from London's Royal Shakespeare Company, Diana Rigg. She had never seen the show before. But did she get the part? Not at first. Another actress, Elizabeth Shepherd (she has played small parts in numerous films, including 1978's *Damien: Omen II*) got it, but one-and-a-half episodes into taping for the 1965 season the producers decided she wasn't right for the part—and Rigg got the job.

EXTRAS

- The official bio of Emma Peel, as extracted from the show: She was born Emma Knight in the late 1930s, daughter of industrialist Sir John Knight. She was just 21 when he died and she took over Knight Industries, where she established a reputation for being hard-headed and ambitious—and became very rich. She married test pilot Peter Peel—but he died in a mysterious crash in the Amazon. Her need for danger and excitement led to employment at an unnamed British intelligence agency, where she was partnered with John Steed. IQ: 152. Martial arts: kung fu and tai-chi (among others). Height: 5' 8½". Weight: 130 pounds.

- Rigg studied judo for the role. She did most of her own fight scenes; Macnee did not.

- In one of the highest rated *Avenger* episodes ever, "A Touch of Brimstone," Peel infiltrates the murderous "Hellfire Club" disguised as "The Queen of Sin": she wears an extra-tight, extra-small corset, black bikini bottoms, knee-high high-heeled leather boots—and a collar with three-inch spikes on it. Rigg designed the outfit herself. (The episode was banned in the U.S.)

- During the Emma Peel era *The Avengers* was wildly popular, with an audience of 30 million viewers in 70 countries worldwide.

- Rigg left the show in 1968—and became a Bond girl herself in *On Her Majesty's Secret Service*. (She played the only wife of 007, Mrs. Tracy Bond.)

- How did they come up with the name "Emma Peel"? Before the role was cast, producers said they wanted somebody with "man appeal." That was shortened to "M. Appeal."

The shortest word ending in "ology" (meaning "the study of") is *oology*—the study of eggs.

THE CLASS IN A GLASS AWARD

The Martini

Given the number of drinks with the suffix "tini" in their names, you're forgiven for believing that anything in a conical stemmed glass qualifies as a martini. The real martini has a history, a recipe, and its own lore—and with good reason: it's elegantly simple, it packs a punch, and it's delicious.

THE MARTINEZ?

The martini has many creation myths, but most historians of potent potables agree that its precursor, "the Martinez," was first mixed up somewhere in California in the mid-19th century. Whether it was in San Francisco for an old miner en route to the town of Martinez, or in the town itself, the story always includes a miner placing a gold nugget on the bar and asking for "something special."

The San Francisco variation involves the bartender at the city's Occidental Hotel in the 1850s or '60s. He published his recipe in his 1887 *Jerry Thomas' Bar-tender's Guide*, and it included a maraschino cherry, a small wineglass of sweet (red) vermouth, Old Tom's Gin (sweetened), and "gum syrup" if the guest "prefers it very sweet."

That teeth-aching recipe eventually evolved into a much more bracing cocktail. By about 1910, the gin-based martini had made its mark. Today, a strictly classic martini consists of unequal portions of gin and dry vermouth (in a ratio of somewhere between 2:1 and 15:1) served chilled, in a conical stemmed glass, garnished with either a green olive or a lemon twist. The only deviation allowed is less vermouth . . . more on that in a moment.

The average speaker sprays 2.5 microscopic droplets of saliva for every word spoken.

A DRINK WITH SOMETHING IN IT

A martini is a "short drink," meaning that it consists primarily of alcohol, and that's what gives it its tingle. (A "long drink" involves alcohol with some type of nonalcoholic mixer like soda or juice.) When you order a classic martini from a bartender, you'll get a cold glass of the hard stuff, making it hard to believe that any work got done when the three-martini lunch was a staple of the businessman's day.

Dedicated martini drinkers have their own variations:

- Shaken or stirred?
- One olive or two?
- Plain olives or stuffed (with almonds, garlic, pimiento, blue cheese)?
- An olive or a lemon zest?
- Conical glass or six-ounce tumbler?
- Rocks or straight up?

Should the vermouth be stirred in with the gin or dripped on top—or maybe just even wiped in the shaker? In extreme cases, like Winston Churchill's, the recommendation is that a martini should consist of a cold glass of gin and a glance at a bottle of vermouth.

ABOUT THAT VERMOUTH

Churchill might disdain it (Hawkeye Pierce of TV's M*A*S*H went even further, saying that his perfect martini consisted of six jiggers of gin and a salute to "the photo of the inventor of vermouth"). But joking aside, without vermouth, there's no martini —just a tumbler of gin. (Straight gin was known in 19th-century England as "mother's ruin.")

Vermouth is a kind of fortified wine, and in its dry or unsweetened form is bitter, although not unpleasantly so. The Italian inventor of the liquor, Antonio Benedetto Carpano of Turin, named his concoction "vermouth" from the German *Wermut*, or "wormwood." Some martini aficionados like to lightly coat ice cubes with vermouth, and then use them in a cocktail shaker with gin; still others have special misting canisters to allow a light, oily coating to sit on top of the gin's surface.

How about you? 31 percent of American employees skip lunch every day.

IT'S A GIN THING

The Churchillian extreme, along with Ogden Nash's ode—"There is something about a Martini / I think that perhaps it's the gin"— conveys the importance of this liquor in the creation of a martini. Gin is a neutral white spirit, usually made from wheat or rye, flavored with various "botanicals" (herbs and spices). Most gins contain several botanicals, but the most important is the berry that gives the spirit its name: juniper, or *genever* in Dutch. Juniper's resin taste gives gin its distinctive kick.

Gin distillers use different methods to flavor their potions, from simple mixing to steeping to redistillation. For most of the 20th century, "London Dry" gin (made anywhere in the world) was most popular. But in recent decades, spicier or more floral blends—like Tanqueray Rangpur (limes, bay leaf, and ginger) and Hendricks (flavored with cucumber and rosewater)—have gained fans.

But regardless of where its ingredients are made, the martini is an American drink and an American symbol. Twentieth-century literary critic Bernard DeVoto said, "The martini is the supreme American gift to world culture." Although martinis are most popular in the United States and the United Kingdom, they are now enjoyed worldwide. A humorous British book published in 2003 by Gustav Temple and Vic Darkwood was titled *Around the World in 80 Martinis* because, during the authors' quick-and-dirty circumference of the globe, the martini was the only beverage they felt could always be relied on as safe and drinkable.

THE SILVER BULLET

Almost everything about a good martini requires cold: cold gin, cold vermouth, cold glass, and an even colder shaker. Keep everything you can in the freezer. A warm martini has never been in vogue.

The essential chill is what led connoisseurs to call the classic martini "the silver bullet." The fussiness around its preparation is in directly inverse proportion, of course, to the ingredients discussed above. It's one icon that isn't enshrined under glass—you can vary steps, ingredients, and methods to your liking.

There was a post office on the Russian space station *Mir*.

IN A PICKLE

The easiest and most common variation on the classic martini is known as the Gibson, and its recipe is exactly the same as its forebear's, with one change—instead of an olive, a Gibson is garnished with a cocktail (or pearl) onion. There are several theories of how the Gibson got its garnish:

- Artist Charles Dana Gibson (creator of the "Gibson girl") challenged Players Club bartender Charlie Connolly to improve on a martini.

- Gibson was a teetotaler who garnished his cocktail glass of water with an onion to distinguish it from martinis.

- A completely different Gibson, Walter K. Gibson, invented the drink at San Francisco's Bohemian Club.

As is so often the case with classic food and drink recipes, no one knows which tale is true. But we do know that you can't make a Gibson with a slice of Vidalia—you have to have good quality pickled cocktail onions to put in your drink. You never know when you might wind up savoring that garnish. After all, who could forget Bette Davis in *All About Eve*, pickled on Gibsons, chomping down on her onion before uttering the line, "Fasten your seatbelts, it's going to be a bumpy night!"

*　　*　　*

QUOTINIS

"I never go jogging. It makes me spill my martini."

—George Burns

"Martinis should always be stirred, not shaken, so that the molecules lie sensuously one on top of the other."

—W. Somerset Maugham

"Shaken, not stirred."　　　　　　　　　**—James Bond**

"I must get out of these wet clothes and into a dry martini."

—Robert Benchley

"The only American invention as perfect as a sonnet."

—H. L. Mencken

Most used metal in the world: iron. Second place: aluminum. Third place: copper.

THE TIMELESS FASHION AWARD

The Little Black Dress

You can always change accessories, but you can't improve on this fashion icon.

ALL YOU NEED IS LBD

Jane Austen wrote, "A woman can never be too fine when she is all in white." That was then—this is now. These days, black is always in fashion, but the best black to have is the LBD, or the "little black dress." Fashionistas have long repeated the mantra that with one LBD in your closet, you can conquer any sartorial situation, from boardroom to ballroom. OK . . . you might need two—one short, one long. But you get the picture.

MOURNING WEAR

Once upon a time, black was the color of mourning and considered far too drab for fashionable ladies. Black was historically (and superstitiously) used to make its wearers inconspicuous so that death would not claim them, too.

Tradition dictated that the length of mourning depended on the person's relationship to the deceased: a woman mourning her husband was required to grieve for at least a year. There were also strict rules about proper mourning attire, codified into three stages:

Stage 1: Dull black clothing, no accessories; women of good standing also typically wore a veil. (Lower-class women usually couldn't afford a veil.)

Stage 2: Still plain black clothing, but women could add some ornamentation—modest jewelry or black trim on their clothes.

Stage 3: Gradually, women could introduce accessories and clothing of other colors until they came out of mourning completely.

Because mourning clothes were needed quickly, they were among the first off-the-rack clothing offered by merchants. The poor made their own by dying regular clothes black.

COCO CHANEL'S REVOLUTION

It took a Frenchwoman to awaken the fashion world from its dreary slumber. Gabrielle "Coco" Chanel was born in 1883 to a poor family in Saumur, France, but over the years, she learned millinery and tailoring—and a bit about life. Thanks to a lot of hard work (and affairs with a couple of rich playboys), Chanel was able to open "Chanel Modes," her first dress shop, in the northwestern French town of Deauville in 1909.

Chanel's philosophy was "simplicity is elegance." Her most celebrated signature piece was the Chanel suit, introduced in 1923 and consisting of a knee-length skirt and a chic boxy jacket with gold buttons. The suits are still in style today.

But although the suit made Chanel's name famous, the Little Black Dress ensured her legacy. Chanel's devotion to keeping things simple extended to color. Why shouldn't practical black, which is versatile and doesn't show dirt, become a fashion ideal? Her first LBD, introduced in 1926, was a long-sleeved sheath with a slash neck and a hem cut just above the knee.

A SHOCKING SHIFT

Chanel wanted a dress that could act as a sort of canvas or backdrop for a woman's personal style. Depending on what a woman wore with it, the LBD could work for day (boucle jacket, pearl earrings) or evening (diamond necklace, silk shawl).

Chanel was responsible for two other important ideas that revolutionized fashion and the LBD:

- Dresses could be short, loose, and shiftlike, which set the tone for the next decade's flapper style.

- Dresses could be made from forgiving fabrics like jersey. Before Chanel, knitted material was mainly used only for things like men's underwear.

The brilliant part? It worked—and beautifully. Soon, women were mad for the LBD, and even Chanel's greatest rival, Elsa Schiaparelli, created a beautiful LBD. This was shocking, since that designer's signature color was the equally shocking "Schia-parelli Pink."

THROUGH THE DECADES

During the Depression and World War II, the LBD continued to gain fans, especially since its shorter style meant less fabric and its many uses meant women needed fewer frocks. The booming 1950s economy meant full skirts and fabulous trims made their way into fashion, but the LBD still reigned supreme as the dress that could take women from lunch through cocktails and on to dinner.

The most iconic LBD appeared at the end of this era, when Audrey Hepburn's character in *Breakfast at Tiffany's*, Holly Golightly, wore a sleeveless LBD with gigantic pearls and enormous sunglasses. Even during the late 1960s and early 1970s when the LBD declined somewhat in popularity due to the rise of Pucci and hemlines, the image of Golightly with her updo and white paper bag wearing that LBD remained a fashion icon.

The LBD's fortunes rose again in the 1980s as women entered the workforce in unprecedented numbers. Designers like Diane von Furstenberg, Norma Kamali, and Donna Karan realized that simple black dresses were ideal office attire.

STRIKE A POSE

The 1990s ushered in the golden age of the LBD, which can now, according to *Vogue*, fit into the following categories: day dress, date dress, dance dress, mourning dress, gothic dress, portrait dress, showstopper dress, and red carpet dress. And part of the fashion's renewed success is due to the groundbreaking TV series *Sex and the City*. The lives, fates, and fashions of four Manhattan female singletons revolved around pink drinks and LBDs. If women can wear the LBD to an art gallery, to brunch, to babysit, and to go grocery shopping—like the characters on *Sex and the City* did—well, that's what fashionistas call a "wardrobe builder."

One of the most fascinating things about looking at galleries and collections of LBDs is that it can be nearly impossible to tell which ones are from today and which ones are from 1920. It seems Chanel was exactly right when she deemed that simplicity was elegant.

THE BE HAIR NOW AWARD

Dreadlocks

Whether they're called dreads, dreadies, or "locks," this style is all about letting hair go its own way . . . so you can go yours.

ANYONE CAN WEAR THEM
Sometimes they're short, sometimes they're long; sometimes they're made from curly hair, sometimes from straight. No matter what they look like, though, hair in what's come to be called "dreadlocks" is formed by encouraging sections of hair to "lock up" against themselves. The result is a distinct, natural-looking style made up of separated pieces that don't need to be combed, untangled, braided, or elaborately styled.

LOCK LIKE AN EGYPTIAN
There is no definitive origin for the term "dreadlocks." One theory is that it comes from ancient religions that thought it was unholy to cut the hair and adherents lived in "dread" of the Lord. The term could also have derived from the idea that the wearer was either to be feared or that he looked dreadful. Regardless, the wearing of dreadlocks can be traced back much further than the Rastafarians of Jamaica—one of the best-known adopters of the hairdo.

Cultures have worn locked hair for centuries. Even Tutankhamen, the Boy King of Egypt, had images on the walls of his tomb of himself, his mother, and his wife wearing wigs styled like dreadlocks. The ancient Celts also wore dreadlocks (invading tribes described them as having "hair like snakes"), and the Bible describes Samson as having "seven locks on his head." Hindus, Pacific Islanders, Islamic Dervishes, and Coptic Christian monks have all sported dreadlocks at one time or another.

World's shortest street: Ebenezer Place in Wick, Scotland. (It's only 81 inches long.)

By far, though, the greatest ambassador for "dreadies" was Rasta-farian reggae master Bob Marley, famous for songs like "I Shot the Sheriff," "One Love," and "Jamming." Marley's long dreads usually hung free while he played concerts, and his soulful style appealed to many different people in the United States who wanted to emulate Marley's look.

MYTH-CONCEPTIONS

When it comes to dreads and their upkeep, myths abound. One of the most common is that dreadlocks are all unkempt and dirty. In reality, most dreadheads are meticulous about hair care and wash their locks three to four times a week. It's important to find sham-poos that don't leave residues behind, though, because those residues (whether fragrance or moisture) can trap grease and dirt in the dreads.

Another myth is that dreads can be formed simply by allowing hair to "go natural." Not so—if you do that, you'll just get big, flat, knotted mats. The one thing every lock-wearer needs is some dread wax (usually beeswax), because it helps keep dreads looking neat and not knotty.

Once you're done with your dreads, you needn't shave your head. Most people just let them grow for a couple of months and then cut them off, leaving a few inches of hair. But people who don't want to sacrifice any of their hair's length can spend a few hours soaking their hair in oil and working out the locks.

There's no Guinness world record for the longest dreads, but Ian Barron of Scotland grew his dreadlocks from age 15 to age 32 and then had them cut off when they reached 3½ feet long—and he raised 1,000£ for charity in the process.

KNOT A PROBLEM

To get real dreadlocks requires time and thought. As many peo-ple who love locks say, "It's not a hairstyle, it's a lifestyle." Get-ting hair to lock on to itself so that it forms even, attractive coils takes effort.

To get locked, you should definitely have a comb and some wax handy, and there are so many different ways of getting hair into locks—everything from back combing to perming to twisting—that you can probably find one to suit you. There's even one way of creating dreadlocks that involves rubbing hair repeatedly in a circular motion with a wool sweater, though experts warn that this method won't create the nicest-looking locks. Most sites and salons that specialize in dreadlocks can suggest reliable methods.

Once your hair has been sectioned and knotted to a greater or lesser extent (depending on the hair's length and texture), you need to take care of your "baby dreads" . . . waxing, twisting, and encouraging them along. The process can take weeks, months, or even more than a year. So it's definitely not a style for the fad-oriented. (Those people are disparagingly referred to as "rentadreads.") But once you've got the dreads, you'll be in good company, sporting a hairstyle that's adorned kings, queens, warriors, musicians, and even those counterculture kids up the street.

*   *   *

MORE HIGH-MAINTENANCE HAIRSTYLES

The Pompadour: Its name might be genteelly French—the high-tressed Madame de Pompadour was Louis XVI's favorite mistress. But this hairstyle's roots are in rockabilly. In the 1950s, edgy musicians started using hair cream to sculpt a 'do with slicked-back sides and a curled-over top; the more comb tracks, the better. It may not have made Elvis a King, but it definitely was his crowning touch.

The Beehive: Sculpted to resemble the nosecone of a B-52 Stratofortress bomber plane (hence its nickname "B-52," and the hairstyles of the 1980s band with that name), the beehive was born in the late '50s and had its heyday the following decade, but "big hair" has survived in the South, along with big cans of hairspray. Margaret Vinci Heldt, an Elmhurst, Illinois, native and the creator of the beehive, once told CNN that she hoped the most famous contemporary beehive queen, Marge Simpson, had been named after her. (She wasn't.)

The outdoor clothing fabric Gore-Tex is made from stretched Teflon.

THE TEENAGER OF THE YEAR AWARD

King Tut

At the age of nine, he was a pharaoh. By 18 he was dead.
Then he was forgotten for more than 30 centuries.

THE BOY KING

Tutankhaten was born in about 1341 B.C. His parents were Akhenaten (the pharaoh of Egypt) and Kiya, one of his wives. When Akhenaten died in 1332 B.C., Tutankhaten—at nine years old—became the king of Egypt. On being crowned, Tutankhaten married Ankhesenamun—his half-sister and the daughter of Akhenaten and his main wife, Nefertiti.

King Tut didn't make many (if any) important decisions, but his reign is notable for a measure enacted by his advisors. Official state business was conducted by Horemheb, the commander of the Egyptian military, and by Ay, his top advisor (who was also Ankhesenamun's grandfather).

Tut's father, Akhenaten, had tried to replace the ancient Egyptian religious system of gods (including Ra, the sun god) with a single, previously minor god (Aten, a light-giving force that was an aspect of Ra). In fact, Akhenaten named his son Tutankhaten because it meant "the living image of Aten." Two years into Tut's reign, Horemheb and Ay restored the traditional religion, built new temples to worship Ra, and changed the young pharaoh's name from Tutankhaten to the more widely known Tutankhamen, which means "living image of Amun." (Amun was the god of air.)

A CONDO MADE OF STONE

In 1323 B.C., when he was just 18 years old, King Tutankhamen died. He left no heirs, so Ay, his top advisor and de facto ruler of

Egypt, became the official ruler of Egypt . . . after he married Tut's wife and his own granddaughter, Ankhesenamun.

Because his reign was short and uneventful, Tut's mummified body (inside an ornate sarcophagus) was relegated to a small, out-of-the-way tomb in the Valley of the Kings, home to all the pharaohs' tombs. Over the years, stone chips that had crumbled off other tombs buried Tut's. When the tombs in the Valley of the Kings were looted during the 11th century B.C., Tut's was spared because nobody knew it was there.

UNEARTHED

So how did Tut become the most famous ancient Egyptian in the western world? The 1922 discovery of his nearly entirely intact tomb by British researcher Howard Carter was a major world event. Carter and his team took home lots of treasures for the British Museum, including Tut's sarcophagus, a silver trumpet, lots of jewelry, three golden coffins, and a throne. Carter removed Tut's burial mask—still *the* iconic image of the pharaoh and ancient Egypt as a whole—by peeling it off with scalding hot knives.

The team also unwrapped the mummified corpse to remove the jewelry from his body. Tut had a large indentation in his head, apparently the result of a head trauma, which fueled speculation that he'd been murdered, most likely by the power-hungry Ay.

REVELATION

Some key details about Tut's life and death came to light in 2005. A team of Egyptian scientists led by Dr. Zahi Hawass and radiologist Ashraf Selim performed a series of CT scans on King Tut's mummified corpse. They were able to decipher what the boy king looked like: he was 5'11", had an overbite, an elongated skull, and a slightly cleft palate. The team also discovered that the head trauma wasn't caused by an injury—it was the result of a hole being drilled into his skull after death, likely by an embalmer who'd removed Tut's brain.

Selim and Hawass also pieced together how King Tut died. The scan revealed a series of fractures to his left thigh bone, likely caused during a fall, probably from a horse. Tut got an infection from the open wound and died of blood poisoning. Gangrene killed the pharaoh in just a few days. There was no evidence of foul play.

Today's King Tut's body rests in its tomb in a museum in the Valley of the Kings. The corpse is unwrapped and sits in a climate-controlled glass case. Also on display: a computerized re-creation of what Tut's face actually looked like, based on the 2005 CT scans.

*   *   *

WHEN THEY WERE KIDS

Tutankhamen was pharaoh of Egypt from the ages of 9 to 18. But he was just *born* into it. Here are some other young people who also did some remarkable things between those ages.

9: Shirley Temple was already a millionaire.

9: Future Admiral David Farragut (who coined the phrase "damn the torpedoes, full speed ahead") joined the U.S. Navy as a midshipman.

10: Stevie Wonder signed with Motown Records.

11: Keyboardist Herbie Hancock performed with the Chicago Symphony Orchestra.

13: Mario Andretti started racing cars.

14: Nadia Comaneci achieved a perfect 10 in gymnastics at the 1976 Summer Olympics.

15: Isacc Asimov entered Columbia University.

16: Albert Einstein began researching what became the theory of relativity.

17: Pele scored the game-winning goal for Brazil in the World Cup title match.

18: Samantha Larson completed her quest to climb the tallest mountains on all seven continents.

THE TROJAN HORSE AWARD

Häagen-Dazs

*Rich, creamy, and Scandinavian . . . right? Not! We're
giving this ice cream manufacturer a Trojan Horse
Award for sneaky advertising.*

A BRONX CHEER FOR ICE CREAM

The Bronx is home to Yankee Stadium and a world-famous zoo, but it's not legendary for being the birthplace of a popular ice cream. It should be. Reuben Mattus, a Polish immigrant peddled his family's homemade ice cream to Bronx restaurants and stores for more than 30 years before he came up with his fortune-making idea for the super-premium ice cream he christened with a nonsensical name.

He introduced Häagen-Dazs in 1961, and at first, it came in only three flavors: vanilla, chocolate, and coffee. His ice cream was made with real (versus artificial) flavors and premium ingredients like real cream and expensive Belgian chocolate. He also added more butterfat and incorporated less air to create a richer, denser ice cream. Reuben and his wife, Rose, invented the name while sitting on their couch at home; they thought a foreign named would give the ice cream an air of sophistication and elegance.

Although it sounds spurious, Rose Mattus noted that the Danish-sounding name "Häagen-Dazs" was inspired by Duncan Hines—if you switch the "D" and the "H," you come close to the ice cream's name. In her 2004 memoir, *The Emperor of Ice Cream*, Rose also revealed that she and her husband chose Denmark for their ice cream's "home country" because they respected how well the Danes had treated Jews during World War II.

GIVE ME A SCOOP OF UMLAUT

Convinced they had a winner, Reuben and Rose packaged their ice cream in cartons and marketed it around New York City. They even added a map of Denmark on the cartons to give the brand more foreign cachet. But anyone who speaks a Scandinavian language knows that Häagen-Dazs isn't native to that geographic region. The words aren't native to any region, really. They're a dubious trick used to sell the ice cream. Only the savvy (or those who spoke Danish) noticed the deceit right away—the Danish language doesn't use umlauts, those two dots above the letter "a."

From its small origins, the ice cream grew into a phenomenon. With no money for advertising, Rose personally visited bodegas and delis around New York to get owners to carry it. It took a few years, but Häagen-Dazs became a hit, first in New York City, and then beyond. By the early 1970s, people all over America were enjoying it, and rumors about the ice cream's origin had already developed: some people believed that Frank Sinatra had discovered the ice cream overseas and introduced it to the United States. Häagen-Dazs was sold to Pillsbury in 1983 for $70 million; that company in turn sold it to General Mills.

KEEPING COUNT

All three original Häagen-Dazs flavors have the same calorie count: 270 calories per half cup. Decadent flavors like Chocolate Chip Cookie Dough, Sticky Toffee Pudding, and Triple Chocolate up the ante calorie-wise, but not as much as Chocolate Peanut Butter—that's the highest, with 360 calories in each half cup.

After selling the company, Reuben and Rose Mattus stayed on as consultants to Pillsbury. Häagen-Dazs was the first to market premium ice cream bars in 1986. And Reuben and Rose continued to be pacesetters in the industry. In 1992, they introduced a low-fat brand that contains only 3 percent fat. (Häagen-Dazs has about six times more than that.) They named their new venture the Mattus Ice Cream Company.

Reuben died shortly after that, at the age of 81 in 1994. Rose lived to 90 and passed away in late 2006. Their legacy lives on in a technology center they funded in Herzliya, Israel, just north of Tel Aviv. The Mattuses may have invented a fake Danish brand, but they definitely found their true flavor in the lives they lived.

THE LOST TREASURE AWARD

Murals by Hans Holbein and Diego Rivera

We introduced you to the first lost treasure on page 116. Here are two more masterpieces that met their demise due to human involvement.

LONDON'S BURNING

Back in the mid-16th century, England's Henry VIII—infamous for his wives, for his break with the Roman Catholic Church, and for establishing himself as the head of the new Church of England—desperately needed what a modern PR guy would call "rebranding." He needed a new (and better) image to maintain his supremacy over England. His brandmaster? The great Flemish painter Hans Holbein the Younger.

Holbein created "The Whitehall Mural"—a painting of Henry, his wife Jane Seymour, and his parents King Henry VII and Queen Elizabeth of York. In the mural, Henry stood in the foreground, dwarfing his father and looking directly at the viewer. Karel van Mander, writing in the early 17th century, described the painting: "[Henry] stood there, majestic in his splendour, [he] was so lifelike that the spectator felt abashed, annihilated in his presence."

The center panel of the mural contained a Latin verse that debated whether Henry was greater than his father and includes the following lines:

> But the son, born to greater things, drove out of his councils
> His worthless ministers and ever supported the just.
> And in truth, the overweening power of the Pope bowed to
> his resolve . . .

The painting hung in England's Whitehall Palace until 1698, when a maid left some laundry drying in front of a fire and the clothes ignited. The resulting blaze destroyed the palace—and the

---

Alpaca wool comes in 22 natural colors—the most color variety of any wool-bearing animal.

mural. However, only the original was lost. In 1667, a Flemish artist named Remigius van Leemput had made a copy of the Whitehall Mural, and that one is still around today.

A ROCKY RELATIONSHIP

By 1930, Mexican artist (and communist) Diego Rivera had achieved international recognition for his murals, and when the Rockefellers asked him to paint a mural for their new Rockefeller Center in New York City, he readily agreed. Pablo Picasso and Henri Matisse had been offered the commission first, but were unavailable.

The mural was to appear on the interior wall facing the plaza entrance of the RCA Building. Rivera proposed a 63-foot mural called "Man at the Crossroads Looking with Hope and High Vision to the Choosing of a New and Better Future," and he worked feverishly on panels featuring two opposing views of society—capitalism on one side, and socialism on the other.

But in May 1933, Nelson Rockefeller (grandson of John D.) was taken aback by an unexpected addition to the mural: a May Day parade of red-banner-waving socialists led by an unmistakable likeness of Vladimir Lenin. "The piece is beautifully painted," Rockefeller wrote to the artist, "But it seems to me that [Lenin's] portrait appearing in this mural might very seriously offend a great many people . . . As much as I dislike to do so, I am afraid we must ask you to substitute the face of some unknown man where Lenin's face now appears."

Although the figure of Lenin had not appeared in his original sketches, Rivera refused to budge: "Therefore, I wrote, never expecting that a presumably cultured man like Rockefeller would act upon my words so literally and so savagely, 'rather than mutilate the conception, I should prefer the physical destruction of the conception in its entirety, but preserving, at least, its integrity.'"

The Rockefeller Center management team, which never had felt comfortable about Rivera's involvement, reacted swiftly to his dare. He was ordered to stop work and paid his fee in full. Soon, demonstrations and letters of protest poured in, blaming the Rockefellers for an act of "cultural vandalism," as Diego Rivera put it.

Official whistle of NFL referees: The Acme Tornado 2000.

Then, one night in February 1934, two of Rivera's assistants noticed a dozen 50-gallon oil drums near the entrance to the RCA building. When they looked inside, they recognized the smashed-up shards of Rivera's mural. The piece had been hammered off the walls on orders from the center's management team. Rivera, who had returned home, retaliated by painting a replica of the mural at the Palacio de Bellas Artes in Mexico City—and in it, he included both Lenin and Leon Trotsky.

The incident marked the end of Rivera's career as an international muralist. But over the next 25 years, he created a body of work that established him as one of the most important artists of the 20th century. Artistic integrity: Rivera—1. Rockefellers—0.

*   *   *

TO KISS OR NOT TO KISS

In the early 1990s, even though he was enjoying stardom on the sitcom *The Fresh Prince of Bel-Air*, Will Smith was ready to move into motion pictures. For his movie debut he chose the small flick, *Six Degrees of Separation*. An adaptation of a hit play, the film was based on the true story of a con man who earned the trust of several wealthy New Yorkers in the 1980s by claiming he was the son of actor Sidney Poitier. A talented group of actors, including Stockard Channing, Donald Sutherland, and Ian McKellan, starred in the movie. Smith played Paul, a young gay man who deceived his targets by displaying a vast knowledge about art, film, books, and culture.

Smith had a problem with one of the scenes in the script: he didn't want to kiss Anthony Michael Hall onscreen. His reluctance came from a conversation with Denzel Washington, who told him, "Don't be kissing no man." Smith took the advice.

Even without the kiss, the film was a critical success—Channing received an Oscar nomination. Smith has done all right since then, too, but he recently said that he regretted not doing the kiss. In 2004, he told *Biography* magazine, "My eyes weren't open enough to see that this is a piece of work. This is not me, this is Paul Poitier. I think that I'm more mature now. I wish I had another shot at it."

There is eight times as much ice in the Antarctic as there is in the Arctic.

THE ICE MAN COMETH AWARD

Lewis Gordon Pugh

He only began long-distance swimming at the age of 17, but Lewis Gordon Pugh didn't waste any time breaking old records and setting new ones by plunging into some of the world's chilliest waters.

A REFRESHING DIP

Pugh was born in England in 1969, but he grew up in South Africa, the scene of some of his earliest long-distance swimming feats. In May 1987, he was the first person to swim from Robben Island, South Africa, to Cape Town, a distance of 7.46 miles. In 1991, he broke the record for the fastest swimming time around Robben Island—the 6.21-mile swim took him only 3 hours and 42 minutes. Still, he was just warming up. Pugh returned to England to complete a maritime law degree and, while there, found time to swim the English Channel.

Some of Pugh's other swimming accomplishments include:

- First person to swim the entire length of the River Thames in England (201 miles) in 21 days.

- First person to swim across Africa's Lake Malawi. According to Pugh, there were hippos and crocodiles on the lake's edge, so he swam especially fast at the beginning and the end.

- First person to swim around the Cape of Good Hope—one of the world's roughest stretches of water—as well as the Cape Peninsula.

- First person to swim the length of the world's second-largest fjord, Sognefjord in Norway. (The world's largest fjord is permanently frozen.)

- Recordholder for the most southern swim (off of Petermann

Island in Antarctica) and the most northern swim (off the island of Spitsbergen 600 miles from the North Pole).

- First person to complete the "Holy Grail of Swimming"—long-distance swims in all five of the world's oceans (Atlantic, Indian, Pacific, Arctic, and Southern).

THE HUMAN POLAR BEAR

It was his focus on cold-water swimming that brought Pugh the most attention—and earned him the nickname the "Human Polar Bear." In July 2007, he became the first person to complete a long-distance swim at the North Pole. He swam almost a mile (actually 0.62 mile) in 18 minutes and 50 seconds in the coldest water a human being has ever dived into on purpose—the temperatures ranged from just 29° to 32° F.

The average person has a 50 percent chance of surviving a 50-yard swim in 50° F water. Hypothermia will set in almost immediately, and after just minutes, the person's hands and feet should lose circulation and become virtually useless. So, during his North Pole dip, Pugh should've been incapacitated almost immediately—especially since he followed the Channel Swimming Association regulations (for swimming the English Channel). Those rules dictate what a swimmer can wear for his immersion in the water to be registered: a swimsuit, goggles, ear plugs, a nose clip, and a cap. That's it.

So how does Pugh do it? How can he immerse himself in such cold water for such long periods of time and survive? No one's sure exactly how, but scientists who have studied him know that his body definitely prepares for the swims. In fact, they coined a new term for what Pugh's body is capable of: "anticipatory thermogenesis."

A SWIMMING STUDY

Actually, Tim Noakes, a professor of exercise and sports science at the University of Cape Town, is the one who coined the term anticipatory thermogenesis, which means the body creates heat prior to an event. Pugh seems to elevate his body temperature mentally—by standing near the water and getting himself ready for a swim. Pugh won't put even a toe in the water first, because the extreme cold will make him not want to go in. Instead, when he's ready, he dives in and tells himself that the only way to get out of the water is to reach his goal.

In 2005, Pugh swam in Antarctica and allowed scientists to study his internal body temperature. Before getting in the water, his body prepared for the shock of it by rising to 101°F, a temperature most people experience only when they have a fever. He began to sweat, despite the cold outside. Then he dove in, and when he ended the swim, his internal temperature had dropped to 96.8°F.

The body's natural reaction to extreme cold is to protect vital organs by collecting blood in key areas (around the heart and lungs, for example). When Pugh got out of the water, his body started to send blood back throughout his extremities. The result was that within seconds of leaving the water, Pugh's body temperature had plummeted to 91.4°F. And the temperature of his muscles was measured at 86°F—life-threatening for most people.

For Pugh, though, it was no problem. He just took a long, hot shower—his typical post-swim routine. After the shower, he put on shorts and a T-shirt and was back to normal.

In fact, it seems that only one thing really worries Pugh: leopard seals. Although he's swum in waters with sharks, hippos, jellyfish, and polar bears, Pugh really watches out for leopard seals. In 2006, he told *National Geographic*, "They're killers. If my team spots one, they'll pull me out of the water."

DIVING INTO CLIMATE CHANGE

Pugh is famous for being a long-distance swimmer, but he's also a maritime lawyer and avid environmentalist. He typically uses his swims to show the world what goes on at the extreme reaches of the planet. He said,

> Through my swims, I have had a unique perspective on climate change. I have witnessed retreating glaciers, decreasing sea ice, coral bleaching, severe droughts, and the migration of animals to colder climates. It's as a result of these experiences that I am determined to do my bit to raise awareness about the fragility of our environment and to encourage everyone to take action.

THE BRAVE NEW WORLD AWARD

DNA Property Rights

On a cold, northern island country the size of Kentucky lives a population whose genetic makeup has hardly changed since the first explorers set foot on its rocky shores 1,200 years ago. But what seemed like a boon for one researcher and the scientific community was a bust for people's privacy.

VIKING HERITAGE

Iceland's population of about 300,000 people still has the DNA of the Vikings, and the population remains remarkably homogeneous. Iceland is geographically isolated and the country is methodical about record-keeping and genealogy. Detailed medical records have been kept since 1915, and about 80 percent of the Icelanders who ever lived can be traced on family trees.

Considering that Iceland is one of the most developed countries in the world—with a prolific economy, progressive government, and a proud cultural heritage—it's hard to believe that its genetic heritage is more pure than that of many isolated indigenous tribes. Yet because of its relatively slow settlement, the population has remained stable and almost entirely Nordic. (The island was not officially settled until the 9th century.)

TRUE-BLUE GENES

In 1999, Kari Stefansson, a Harvard Medical School professor and native Icelander, founded a corporation called deCODE to collect and study Icelanders' DNA data. Stefansson thought that careful study of Icelanders' genes would give medical science an unprecedented chance to work backward and unravel the roots of illnesses like heart disease and cancer. Syndromes could be chart-

---

Quentin Tarantino's first screenplay was titled *Captain Peachfuzz and the Anchovy Bandit.*

ed back through families and their causes might be more easily identifiable.

To complete his project, Stefansson made a remarkable deal with the Icelandic government: The government promised his company access to the nation's health records and he promised that the population would cooperate in the study, though people who did not want to take part could opt out under a special clause in the contract.

VOLCANO IN A GOLD MINE

The deal quickly started to smell fishy to Icelanders. Giving a single company control of an entire nation's health records seemed suspect to people outside of Iceland, too, who recognized that this deal could have privacy implications for other societies and countries around the globe.

Many people in Iceland did sign up for the study (about 135,000 adults), but they also opted out in large numbers. Stefansson's company tried to bounce back, saying that deCODE would fund drugs for citizens whose DNA indicated predisposition to things like heart disease. However, when a woman named Ragnhildur Gudmundsdottir not only blocked deCODE from her health records but also her deceased father's records, the tempest became more serious. Iceland's supreme court finally ruled that the database Stefansson was trying to create was unconstitutional because it did not adequately protect personal privacy. Eventually, the project was completely scrapped, and in 2004 the Icelandic government finally ruled that the entire deCODE project was a violation of privacy rights.

THE HUMAN LEAGUE

The Icelandic DNA saga may be at a temporary halt, but its narrative has a lot to say about how we are going to obtain, track, store, analyze, and protect genetic information. Deciding to whom DNA belongs is tricky. For example, a parent may donate a tissue sample from a desperately ill child, hoping that a cure will be found, only to discover that that tissue sample is being held hostage by a hospital trying to get more money for its research (as happened in 1998 at Miami Children's Hospital with a gene for Canavan disease).

Because even the smallest snip of DNA contains every bit of information about what makes you . . . well, you, . . . its storage can have widespread implications. As science and technology progress, it may also have even more serious consequences.

Someday, someone—or, more likely, some company—may own your DNA. Patents on genomes will no longer be the stuff of science-fiction novels, but of common court battles. Iceland's pure DNA has given us a glimpse at the implications of both future scientific breakthroughs as well as personal privacy issues..

*   *   *

ICELAND INFO

- According to the Human Development Index—which ranks countries based on qualities like their standard of living, literacy rates, and life expectancy—Iceland is one of the two most developed countries in the world. (Norway is the other.)

- Even though Iceland is about 600 miles from its closest European neighbor (Norway), most people still consider it to be a part of Scandinavia because of its cultural connection to the main Scandinavian countries: Denmark, Sweden, and Norway.

- The record high temperature for Iceland's capital of Reykjavik is 76.6°F, recorded in 2004. The record low: –12.1°F, recorded in 1918.

- The Norsemen from Scandinavia, who arrived on Iceland in the 9th century, are the country's most famous "first" settlers. But the real first settlers were Irish monks who came in the 8th century and left when the Norsemen arrived.

- Only about one fifth of Iceland is inhabited.

- Most famous Icelander: singer Björk.

- Other names you might recognize: bands Sigur Rós and Mezzoforte, Nobel Prize-winning author Halldór Laxness, and explorer Leif Ericsson.

Buffalo milk has 25 percent more protein than cow's milk.

THE LOST AND FOUND AWARD

A Confederacy of Dunces

*John Kennedy Toole lost his battle with depression, but
he left behind two amazing stories: one is his novel,
and the other is the tale of how it got published.*

A WORK IN PROGRESS

After he graduated from college, the future looked bright for Toole. He had earned a master's degree in English literature from Columbia University and then became a professor, first at the University of Southwestern Louisiana and then at Hunter College in New York. After being drafted into the military in 1961 at the age of 23, he even had ample time to work on his novel, which he called *A Confederacy of Dunces* after the line by Jonathan Swift:

> When a true genius appears, you can know him by this sign:
> that all the duncesare in a confederacy against him.

Toole began working on a draft of the book while stationed in Puerto Rico, where he taught English to Spanish-speaking recruits. When his time in the Army was over, he moved back in with his parents and began teaching at St. Mary's Dominican College in New Orleans, completing the novel in his spare time and hoping to get it published.

THE BIG EASY

The book follows New Orleans resident Ignatius J. Reilly—who gets arrested in the first few pages—as he searches for a job, finds one, makes a mess of it, and moves on to another job. Like a series of falling comic dominoes, *A Confederacy of Dunces* sees one outrageous event lead to another. All along, the obese (and gassy) Ignatius works on his own book of comparative history—hilariously drawing conclusions from modern life—and writing letters back and forth to a woman named Myrna, whom Ignatius can't stand (her views are the opposite of his on almost everything) but also can't help but love.

Particularly interesting is the relationship between Ignatius and his doting and long-suffering mother. They spend much of the novel driving each other crazy—but always to comic effect.

CULTURE SHOCK

After his stint in the Army, Toole should have been on top of the world. His writing was going well, he was smart, and his teaching career showed great promise. But something wasn't right.

Although he was a popular teacher at New Orleans's Dominican College, he was still living at home, supporting his parents, and dealing with his domineering mother. He had what he felt was a great unpublished book on his hands, and an editor at Simon & Schuster showed interest in the work but also seemed reluctant to commit to its publication. After two years of revisions and conversations, the editor still thought the book needed work before it could be published. At the same time, Toole was struggling with sexual identity issues. He felt trapped in the closet and repressed by his family and the views of society at large. He was becoming further removed from the world around him.

In early 1969, Toole and his mother had a huge fight. This time Toole left town. He drove to California, then to Georgia to visit the home of one of his literary heroes, the late author Flannery O'Connor. He'd been away from New Orleans for just two months but had gotten progressively more depressed. Then, on March 26, 1969, in Biloxi, Mississippi, Toole stopped on an isolated road, ran a garden hose from his car's tailpipe into the driver's side window, and sat back. It was the end for Toole, but it was just the beginning for A Confederacy of Dunces.

DUNCE CAPPER

Thelma Toole waited until after her husband died in 1974 to continue her son's attempts to get A Confederacy of Dunces published. From that point on, she worked tirelessly in her mission, taking it to publisher after publisher and racking up rejection notices.

When she noticed that Southern author Walker Percy was giving a writing seminar in town, Thelma took the manuscript and thrust it at him. Percy had published three novels by then, and he was used to reading bad manuscripts from people who thought they deserved to be published. In this case, however, the manuscript was good, and he was hooked almost immediately. Percy's help got the novel published in 1980 by Louisiana State University Press. At the end of his foreword to the book, Percy wrote:

> It is a pity that John Kennedy Toole is not alive and well and writing. But he is not, and there is nothing we can do about it but make sure that this gargantuan, tumultuous human comedy is at least made available to a world of readers.

Almost immediately, the novel received massive acclaim. Critics praised it with fervor, in particular because of the heart-tugging story behind its publication: a mother who fought desperately for years to get her deceased son's legacy into print.

MOMMIE DEAREST?

Years later, Joel Fletcher, a friend of both Toole and his mother, wrote about the story behind the publication of *A Confederacy of Dunces* in his own book, *Ken & Thelma*. ("Ken" was a familiar nickname for John Kennedy Toole.) He noted that Thelma loved the spotlight and had her own desire for fame and acclaim. While she always maintained that her work to get the book published was done out of love for her son, Fletcher's work suggests there was far more to it. Perhaps the domineering mother still wanted control.

It's hard to say what the truth is behind the troubled and complex dynamic of this mother and son. What can be said, though, is that Thelma Toole, who died in 1984, lived long enough to see two milestones pass after her son's death: the publication of his master work and its receiving the Pulitzer Prize in 1981. Today, there are over 1.5 millions copies in print in more than 18 languages. An executive at 20th Century Fox has spent 27 years attempting to get a movie version made. Even Ignatius J. Reilly would be proud of those accomplishments.

THE I SPY AWARD

Benedict Arnold

The walls of the Old Cadet Chapel in the West Point Cemetery are covered with plaques and medallions that highlight the brave deeds of America's early military heroes. But one plaque close to the altar is different from the others. The name once etched there—Benedict Arnold— has been scratched out. But if that wall is for heroes, why was a traitor like Arnold included there at all?

ONCE, TWICE, THREE TIMES A HERO

At the start of the Revolutionary War in 1775, apothecary Benedict Arnold of New Haven, Connecticut, was a captain of the colonial militia and devoted to the cause of America's freedom. Between 1775 and 1777, he managed to accomplish some astonishing feats: He fought at the Battle of Lexington and Concord, attacked and secured Fort Ticonderoga, made the first amphibious assault in American history, and so brilliantly planned the Battle of Saratoga that a contemporary called him "the very genius of war." Even more, Arnold fought and led his men through some of the most treacherous terrain in North America, scaling cliffs, negotiating rapids, and enduring famine so terrible that some soldiers ate their leather moccasins.

Yet of each of Arnold's victories was tinged with failure, and his intelligence and bravery were matched by impulsive, self-serving behavior: Arnold raced Ethan Allen's Green Mountain Boys to Ticonderoga in 1775, for example, so that he could claim that victory, but then he submitted an inflated expense report for the venture.

A LEG UP

In the middle of the struggle at Saratoga, American commander

---

Scattered showers, according to weather forecasters, means a one in ten chance of rain.

General Horatio Gates relieved Arnold of his command, partly for insubordination and partly because Gates considered him a "pompous little fellow." Arnold charged into battle anyway, "conveniently ignoring the fact that he had no official command," wrote one historian. The sight of Arnold on horseback reinvigorated the troops, who fought back so hard that the British collapsed.

Arnold's actions also directly led to securing French aid that helped speed the infant United States to victory. There's even a memorial to Benedict Arnold's . . . er, leg at the Saratoga battle-field. It is a sculpted left leg, elegantly booted, standing by itself on what appears to be a cannon, with a brief inscription: "In memory of the most brilliant soldier of the Continental Army who was desperately wounded on this spot . . . winning for his countrymen the Decisive Battle of the American Revolution and for himself the rank of Major General."

In spite of his insubordination, General George Washington, who thought of Arnold almost as a son, rewarded the man and appointed him commandant at Philadelphia in July 1778. However, in Arnold's triumph were the seeds of discontent and deceit. He'd been wounded at Saratoga (in the leg . . . the reason for that odd monument), and that fueled his self-pity and anger.

THE ONE-LEGGED PERSPECTIVE

Arnold had become bitter, especially toward Congress: he felt he should have been promoted higher and faster. In Philadelphia, he also became a social butterfly, and met the woman who became his second wife and was a catalyst in his downfall.

Margaret "Peggy" Shippen was half Arnold's age and a member of a staunchly Loyalist (pro-England) family. While Arnold fell deeper into debt with extravagances and financial schemes that led Congress to investigate him and recommend a court-martial, Shippen encouraged him to throw parties and keep up with other Loyalists. One of them, British officer John Andre, goaded Arnold into switching sides. (Shippen introduced the men and may have had an affair with Andre; no one knows for sure.) Arnold, who was facing financial ruin and was uncertain of future promotion, made a fateful decision to throw in his lot with the British.

BIRTH OF A TRAITOR

First, he wrote to Henry Clinton, the British commander, promising to deliver West Point and its 3,000 defenders for 20,000 pounds sterling (about $1 million today). Playing on George Washington's continued affection, Arnold also convinced the general to give him the post of West Point commander.

In September 1780, Arnold tried to execute his plan, sending Andre with maps and plans to the British forces. But Andre was captured, and the patriot soldiers—not knowing their commander was in on the scheme—sent a message to Arnold, who immediately fled West Point. However, George Washington had decided to visit West Point that day. When he found that Arnold was away, he sat down to wait—and when the soldiers brought him the plans that had been captured with Andre, Washington recognized his friend's handwriting.

ESCAPE

As Andre was being hanged as a spy, Arnold was escaping on a British warship down the Hudson River. For his dirty deeds, Arnold received 6,000 pounds and an appointment in the British Army as a brigadier general. He moved to England and, despite his previous battlefield heroics, was condemned as a traitor in the United States. George Washington wrote to a friend,

> I am mistaken if at this time Arnold is undergoing the torments of a mental hell. From some traits of his character which have lately come to my knowledge, he seems to have been so hackneyed in crime—so lost to all sense of honor and shame —that while his faculties still enable him to continue his sordid pursuits, there will be no time for remorse.

In Philadelphia, patriots built a life-sized effigy of Arnold—seated in a cart with a figure of the devil next to him holding a lantern up to his face so that everyone could see the traitor. They paraded the cart through the city, with a fife-and-drum corps playing "The Rogue's March," before they hanged the effigy and set it on fire. The name Benedict Arnold is now synonymous with "traitor."

THE PRODUCT PLACEMENT AWARD

Human Billboards

If you thought fresh eggs sporting ads for sitcoms was bad, imagine seeing a pregnant belly emblazoned with an ad for a casino.

THE MEDIUM IS THE MESSAGE

Advertising is everywhere, and advertisers will try any space at least once in order to promote a product. Some of the efforts are truly inventive, even if irritatingly intrusive—CBS once tried having fresh eggs stamped with ads for its fall programming lineup. Ads are sprouting up on airline tray tables, on city sewer covers, and on bendable straws. And many of us have seen Volkswagen Beetles tricked out to look like rodents to advertise extermination services. How about adult diaper samples delivered with the newspaper?

Human billboards have been around for centuries with people wearing sandwich boards, carrying signs, pointing customers in the right direction, and barking promotional slogans. But the worst ad placement we've seen has to be one on the human body. Read on . . . and weep—as long as you don't have any promotional logos inked on your cheeks.

ADVERTISING, TO THE FORE

In 2005, Oklahoma college student Andrew Fischer decided to try something different to raise tuition money. He placed a listing on the popular online auction site, eBay, offering to "wear" a company's ad on his forehead.

Fischer had two rules about what he would and wouldn't do:

1. He wouldn't promote anything socially unacceptable such as adult Web sites or stores.

2. He'd accept any brand or logo as long as it was not racially or morally offensive (e.g., a swastika): "I wouldn't go around with 666, the mark of the beast," he told the BBC News.

The winner: SnoreStop (a company that sells snoring prevention products) ponied up just over $37,000 to place a temporary, 30-day tattoo on Fischer's forehead.

BELLY BASICS

While Fischer and SnoreStop got a lot of attention, their "head-vertising" attempt was not the first. In 2003, after answering an eBay listing, C I Host, a web-hosting firm, paid 22-year-old Jim Nelson $7,000 to wear the company's logo permanently tattooed on the back of his shaved head for five years. Nelson's duties include traveling on behalf of C I Host, handing out flyers and business cards, and delivering sales pitches. Within six months of Nelson's debut, the company had 500 new customers.

Other companies have tried to head-butt the competition, too. In 2003, Dunlop Tires hired six men to roam the streets of Boston with their heads shaved in a zig-zag tire pattern. Even Homer Simpson tried to get in on the action during a 2006 episode in which he has "Buy Blue Pants" emblazoned on his head in an attempt to increase demand for his favorite product.

And since all that was working so well, why not advertise on a pregnant belly? Amber Rainey said she got the idea from Andrew Fischer and thought: "I have a really big stomach, you know. Hey, and you can't help but to look at." In 2005 the 24-year-old auctioned off her acreage, and Las Vegas's Golden Palace bought it for $4,042. (A paltry price, perhaps, but foreheads are forever—a third-trimester tummy could go any time.)

A SHOT IN THE ARM

There are lots of print and video ads that feature different kinds of tattoos, including a Brazilian shoe campaign with supermodel Gisele Buendchen "wearing" nothing but a full-body tattoo. (Temporary tattoos, of course.)

Joe Tamargo of Huntington, New York, tried something a little more permanent in 2005, selling advertising space on his body with permanent tattoos. A pharmaceutical company bought an ad on his right arm for $500. Another group, SaveMartha.com, paid $510 for a multicolored ad supporting Martha Stewart during her incarceration for fraud.

The worst deal has to be Kari Smith's permanent forehead tattoo advertising Las Vegas's Golden Palace. (Again!) She settled for $10,000, but even the Golden Palace must have realized that was ridiculous. The casino kicked in $5,000 more.

OH, BABY

However, the worst advertising idea ever has nothing to do with tattoos. In 2006, a Canadian couple, Jonathan and Leanne (they declined to give out their last name, with good reason), put a listing on eBay offering ad space on their newborn daughter's clothing for a year.

After the public decried the couple for including their baby as part of the scheme, the parents pulled the listing. But Jonathan said he thought it was completely all right because the advertising would just be on clothing and would not harm the baby.

Where did he get the idea? "From that guy in the United States who has advertising space on his forehead."

*　　*　　*

SIGNS O' THE TIMES

During the 1978 Academy Awards, singer Debby Boone performed her Oscar-nominated song, "You Light Up My Life." Surrounding Boone on stage were hearing impaired children translating the song into sign language. The Academy was embarrassed the next day when reports surfaced that the kids weren't hearing impaired at all—they were actually local fifth graders who were directed to *pretend* they were deaf. How did the ruse get found out? Actual hearing impaired people couldn't understand their incomprehensible sign language.

In the 1960s *Batman* TV series, it was 14 miles from the Bat Cave to Gotham City.

THE HIDE AND SEEK AWARD

Movie Easter Eggs

When the movie lays an egg, fans can go hunting for something extra. Join us as we crack some shells and celebrate the incredible playable Easter egg of the digital age.

EGG IN YOUR FACE

In the late 20th century, "Easter eggs" took on new meaning for video gamers and movie watchers. No longer just treats left by the Easter Bunny, they now were encrypted treats hidden by wily computer programmers. These digital Easter eggs contained additional content, fun asides, new material, and more.

The history of the digital Easter egg is fuzzy. The most often-told version goes like this: In the 1978 Atari 2600 video game "Adventure," computer programmer Warren Robinett hid his signature in a hidden room. Why? Apparently, Atari didn't give its programmers credit in the early days, and Robinett wanted to secretly "sign" his work. His employers didn't know about it, but when players found it, they thought it was part of the game.

But some people say that they found an earlier Easter egg in a 1977 video game called "Demo Cart." It was played on the Fairchild Channel F, a console that preceded Atari, and supposedly featured a hidden message containing the programmer's name.

INCREDIBLE EVOLVING EGGS

Whatever their origin, Easter eggs in video games became commonplace throughout the 1980s, as software programmers and designers hid their names in credit files for people to stumble upon. From there, the eggs evolved and started showing up on DVDs, where they're usually hidden on menu screens. To open them, people have to know where to look or how to find them.

Lifespan of a U.S. patent: 17 years.

You may have to move the cursor to a specific spot on the screen. If something that doesn't look like a menu option (in other words, if it isn't labeled with anything) is highlighted, chances are you've found an Easter egg. For people who don't enjoy the hunt, many Web sites have sprung up that list where Easter eggs are hidden in popular movies and games.

ON THE HUNT

We went hunting for Easter eggs in our favorite movies. Here is some of what we found (most are in the standard DVD editions):

The Godfather Collection. On the bonus disc, go to "Galleries," click on "DVD Credits," and hit "Next" on your remote four times. You'll find the cast of the TV show *The Sopranos* watching . . . *The Godfather.*

T2: Judgment Day. The DVD for the sequel to *The Terminator* features an extended version of the film with an alternate ending. In the "Special Edition" menu, highlight "Play Special Edition" but don't hit enter. Instead, type in 82997 (a significant date in the film) on your remote. You'll then see "Play Extended Special Edition" highlighted. Press Enter.

The Fellowship of the Ring (Four-Disc Extended Edition). An MTV Movie Awards spoof is included. On the final page of the Scene Selection menu, highlight the "Council of Elrond" scene and press the down arrow on your remote. You'll highlight the ring. Press Enter.

Seinfeld Season 5. On the fourth disc, click on Setup. Go to Subtitles, and then press the right arrow to highlight the heart. Press Enter, and a behind-the-scenes look at a popular episode will play.

Fight Club (2-disc edition). On the second disc, click on "Advertising." Press the down arrow three times and a smiley face will appear. Press enter to go to a gallery of merchandise related to the movie.

Donnie Darko. Go to "Special Features" and choose "The Philosophy of Time Travel." Go to "Appendix A" and hit the up arrow. A circle will appear. Click on it to see a deleted scene.

The Matrix. Nine eggs in one can be found here. Under "Special Features," choose "Making the Matrix." Then select "The Dreamworld." Then select "Continue," followed by a click on "Follow the White Rabbit." Go back and watch the movie, and, periodically, a white rabbit will appear onscreen. When it does, hit enter to see a short feature about the scene. When it finishes, the movie will resume playing, and you can keep looking for more white rabbits. (They're in chapters 1, 10, 15, 23, 24, 29, 30, 32, and 33.)

Citizen Kane (Two-Disc Special Edition). Choose "Production Notes" and then "On the Set." Advance through 10 pages and then hit the up button, which will highlight a sled. Hit enter to see an interview with the film's editor.

Finding Nemo. Under "Bonus Features," click on "Mr. Ray's Encyclopedia." Highlight the curved arrow and press the down button to bring up a fish. Highlight it and press enter to see a short bonus scene between Dory and Marlin.

The Star Wars Trilogy. On the bonus disc, select "Video Games and Still Galleries" from the main menu. On the new menu, press 11, then 3, then 8 on your remote. This plays a five-minute gag reel.

Titanic: Special Edition. Choose "Deleted Scenes" and then select "Scene Selection." Go to scene 29 ("Extended Carpathia Sequence") and hit the down arrow. The people in the bottom left of the screen will be highlighted. Hit enter, and you'll see a *Saturday Night Live* skit related to the movie.

X-Men: The Last Stand. Go to "Deleted Scenes" (from the "Join the Brotherhood" screen, choose "Features" to get there). Go to the fourth page in (hit "More" on three separate screens), and then highlight "Hank Warns Trash of Magneto's Plan." Press the left arrow on your remote, and you'll highlight an X. Press enter to see an alternate ending.

Memento (Limited Edition 2-Disc Set). From the main menu, select the clock. You'll get a quiz. Choose answer "C" for the first five questions. The sixth question involves putting pictures in a certain order; don't worry about the correct order. Instead, put them in this order: 3, 4, 1, 2. The movie (which normally runs backward in time) will now play in chronological order.

Count 'em yourself: In the 1962 hit song "Duke of Earl," the word "Duke" is sung 125 times.

THE LANGUAGE POLICE AWARD

Words That Changed Their Meanings

*We make our living with words, so Uncle John takes them seriously.
We strive for precision, but it's almost impossible when there are
so many commonly misused words and phrases. Even worse?
When the incorrect meaning has become the accepted
meaning. We're calling the language police!*

LANGUAGE LOVE

By most estimates, the English language includes about one
million words, yet native speakers regularly use only about
5,000. And they don't always get the ones they do use correct.
Like all languages, English is constantly changing—new words are
added, old words are phased out, and new word combinations are
formed all the time.

But the following examples of language changes cause trouble
for people who like to use their words correctly because these
words and phrases have pretty much lost their original meanings.

BEG THE QUESTION

If an event or happening raises a question for someone, it's almost
certain he or she will say, "This begs the question . . ." But it does-
n't. Begging the question is a verbal trick speakers use to avoid a
question, not bring one up. The original definition of begging the
question meant to assume that what is being questioned had
already been proven to be true, so the answer sidestepped the
thing in question. Say you were asked a question that just required
a simple yes or no answer. But instead of saying yes, you answer
with a statement that assumes the thing in question is already
true. That's begging the question.

For example, if the question is, "Senator, will this new crime bill be effective?" and he or she answers with a statement that doesn't answer it—"I've been fighting crime my entire career, and this crime bill is the latest example of that"—then the speaker has begged the question.

It's a common practice in formal debate, and it's especially prevalent in politics. In the example above, the speaker is acting as though the crime bill is definitely effective, even though he or she never answered the basic question with a yes or no. Assuming the question is true is not evidence that it is.

From that, beg the question evolved in the language to mean that the statement invites another obvious question. Anytime you run verbal circles around the question without answering it can be called begging the question in this sense (although strict grammarians frown upon it; they like to keep the original meaning).

DECIMATE

It's hard to believe that such a simple word hides such a horrific history. The original definition of "decimate" was "to kill one in ten." The brutal practice was used by the Roman army beginning around the 5th century B.C. and was implemented as a way to inspire fear and loyalty. Lots were drawn, and one out of every 10 soldiers would be killed—by their own comrades. If one member of a squad acted up, anybody could pay the ultimate price. Captured armies sometimes fell victim to this practice as well.

Today, "decimate" has lost that meaning, but some grammarians still like to preserve it . . . at least in the sense of "to reduce by 10 percent." The "dec" prefix means "ten"—it's the same Latin root that gives us decade, for example. So to use "decimate" to mean just "destroy" contradicts the meaning of that prefix. (Note: Language snobs really get up in arms when someone says "totally decimate." Totally reduce by ten? We don't get it, either.)

COULD CARE LESS

This is an easy mistake to make. The correct phrase, of course, is "couldn't care less"—as in, "I don't care at all, so it wouldn't be possible for me to care any less about this." But over the years, that's morphed into a new phrase (with the same meaning), and even though the *Harper Dictionary of Contemporary Usage* criticized the change in 1975, saying it was "an ignorant debasement of language," "could care less" seems to be around to stay.

Language historians say "couldn't care less" was originally a British phrase that became popular in the United States in the 1950s. "Could care less" appeared about a decade later. No one knows exactly why the incorrect form came into being, since it doesn't make sense. But the phrase has stuck, and a lot of grammarians care very much that it's not being used correctly. (Regular people, of course, couldn't care less.)

CARD SHARP

No, that's not a misspelling. Sure it sounds weird to the ear, but people who know the term's history and meaning prefer the original. "Card sharp" first appeared in the 1880s and meant a card player who tricked or scammed others. "Card shark" appeared much later, in the 1940s.

Many people assume that the mix-up simply comes from speakers who either thought "shark" sounded better or misheard the word originally. But that may not be the case. Linguists have traced the history of both "sharp" and "shark" to their original usages, and though it doesn't appear that either word derived from the other, there are a lot of similarities in meaning. "Shark" comes from a 17th-century German word *schurke*, which meant "someone who cheats." "Sharping" came about around the same time and meant "swindling or cheating." The words "loan shark" and "sharp practice" come from these words as well.

So technically, "card shark" could be correct. But because "card sharp" appeared first, many linguists want to preserve it. Whether they'll succeed is anyone's guess, but it's a sharp point of contention for many.

SPIT AND IMAGE

If you think you're the spitting image of your parents, you're forgiven. People have been messing this one up for decades. "Spit and image" was the original term, used from about 1825 on. *The Oxford English Dictionary* defined it as "the very spit of, the exact image, likeness, or counterpart of." "Spitting image" came about some 80 years later and was followed by a few other variations, including "spitten image" and "splitting image" (neither of which really caught on). In this case, "spitting image" has overtaken the use of "spit and image" for most English speakers. But when you're spitting out this phrase, take a moment to remember its original use and think about the image you're trying to project.

IRONIC

Few words cause as much confusion or are used incorrectly as often as "ironic." Not that it's hard to understand why—the definition is not simple: "a pretense of ignorance and of willingness to learn from another assumed in order to make the other's false conceptions conspicuous by adroit questioning . . . the use of words to express something other than and especially the opposite of the literal meaning." What?

In 1996, Alanis Morissette wrote an entire song titled "Ironic," which consistently used the word incorrectly. And even the people who are supposed to know what it means get it wrong. *The American Heritage Dictionary* gave the word "irony" to its distinguished panel of experts (the ones who help ensure the accuracy of all the words the dictionary defines) and asked them if either of the following sentences used the word correctly:

1. "In 1969, Susie moved from Ithaca to California, where she met her husband-to-be, who, ironically, also came from upstate New York." Seventy-eight percent of the panel's members agreed that this was an incorrect use of the word.

2. "Ironically, even as the government was fulminating against American policy, American jeans and videocassettes were the hottest items in the stalls of the market." In contrast, though, 73 percent agreed that this sentence used it properly.

How "ironic" came to be defined as "coincidence" is anybody's guess, but for our purposes, we like to refer to the following quote from the 1994 film *Reality Bites*. When Ethan Hawke's character is asked to define "ironic," he says, "It's when the actual meaning is the complete opposite from the literal meaning." Thank goodness for Hollywood.

THE TOP OF THE WORLD AWARD

The Chrysler Building

Thanks to its creators' drive for perfection and a little conniving, this landmark had a smooth ride to Uncle John's award for the ultimate skyscraper.

REACHING FOR THE SKY

New York City, with its impressive skyline, was a natural home for some of the tallest buildings ever made. Until the late 19th century, erecting a skyscraper was a feat, and buildings higher than six stories were rare—even getting supplies to the higher floors was extremely difficult because of all the stairs. But the invention of the passenger elevator in the mid-1800s and improvements in steel production and other technologies ensured that, by the 20th century, developers around the country (and the globe) had the tools to make buildings that could reach for the sky.

In 1930, a determined group of businessmen and architects constructed a building that redefined New York City's skyline. Twenty-one thousand tons of steel, limestone, and brick along with other exotic materials went into the Chrysler Building, and when it was completed, its beautiful blend of Americana and art deco established it as the city's—and the world's—most elegant skyscraper. Today, other buildings are taller, but none is as intricately embellished and ornamented. In 2005, New York's Skyscraper Museum polled 100 architects, builders, engineers, and others, asking them to choose their 10 favorite city skyscrapers. The Chrysler Building captured first place, with 90 percent of respondents putting it in their top 10.

SWITCHING GEARS

Walter Chrysler worked in the railroad business at the turn of the

---

Plastic bottles were first used for soft drinks in 1970.

20th century, but made a name for himself in the automobile industry after he went to work for Buick in 1912. He had an excellent sense for business and raised Buick's output from 45 cars a day when he started to 600 by 1920.

In 1921, Chrysler purchased the Maxwell Motor Company, which was millions of dollars in debt. He renamed the company after himself and put his business sense to good use again—within seven years, the company was more than $85 million ahead. In 1928, Chrysler introduced two of its most famous makes: the DeSoto and the Plymouth. A year later, *Time* magazine recognized Walter Chrysler's success in the automotive industry by naming him Man of the Year (the first automotive leader to receive that honor). But the magazine was also recognizing another of Chrysler's accomplishments: the September 19, 1929, groundbreaking of the building that still bears his name.

NEXT YEAR'S MODEL

In the 1920s, New York City was in a race to erect the world's tallest building. Several design and construction teams had plans in the works, and Chrysler wanted his building to be the best . . . and the tallest. He found the perfect project in the form of a venture belonging to former New York State Senator William J. Reynolds. Reynolds had hired architect William Van Alen, who was riding a wave of success for designing several decorative buildings around the city, to design a skyscraper in Midtown. Chrysler bought out Reynolds but kept the architect.

Van Alen's design called for 77 stories of bold art deco (a style that, as its name implies, uses art as decoration), mostly with geometric shapes. Chrysler didn't make many changes to Van Alen's original plans, but he did suggest a now-famous detail: the eight stainless steel eagles that jut out from the 61st floor were modeled after hood ornaments on Chrysler cars.

BAIT AND SWITCH

The competition to create the world's largest building was fierce. Van Alen was eager to win the title not just for posterity, but because his former partner (now rival), H. Craig Severance, was designing a skyscraper in the Financial District for the Bank of Manhattan. Chrysler and Van Alen announced the plans for their building and declared it would rise a record-setting 925 feet, making it taller than Severance's planned construction. Shortly thereafter, Severance and the Bank of Manhattan announced that their new building would include a flagpole, increasing the height to 927 feet.

So Van Alen and Chrysler went back to the drawing board, but they did so in secret. Inside the construction site for the Chrysler Building, a 185-foot-long spire was assembled. After the Bank of Manhattan building was completed in early 1930—when it was too late to make any changes—Chrysler and Van Alen unveiled their spire, raising their building's official height to 1,046 feet. Chrysler and Van Alen had their record-breaking building, which not only dwarfed the Bank of Manhattan but also the former tallest structure in the world: the Eiffel Tower. Their bragging rights didn't last long, though. Less than a year after the Chrysler Building's May 27, 1930, opening, the Empire State Building was completed in New York. It opened on May 1, 1931, and was 1,454 feet tall.

GRAND BY DESIGN

But no matter. The Chrysler Building still has some of the most impressive architectural designs of any skyscraper in the world: Its most memorable and recognizable feature is its stepped dome, whose pattern of parabolic curves and many triangular windows form a series of radiant sunbursts. The Chrysler Building was also one of the first buildings to use stainless steel over a large area of a structure's surface.

The building's lobby impressed visitors with its three-story-high red Moroccan marble walls complemented by granite and chrome. It was shaped like a triangle and featured photos of the building itself, taken while it was under construction. The 32 elevators came in five different designs, each one set in art deco geometric patterns and featuring different exotic woods from all over the world.

In addition to housing the headquarters for Chrysler's car company and several other corporations, the building was home to a speakeasy and restaurant known as the Cloud Club. The club filled three floors—the 66th, 67th, and 68th—and featured sparkling pink marble bathrooms with lockers so that, during Prohibition, members would have a place to stash their alcohol if a

---

How about you? The average American eats approximately 67 pickles per year.

raid occurred. The club was a popular members–only attraction until it closed in 1979.

The building's exterior boasted the spire and eagles all made from a new chrome-nickel alloy. The metal has never corroded. Aside from its record-setting height and glamorous look, another of the Chrysler Building's greatest accomplishments was its safety record. No one died during the construction process.

PUTTING ON THE BRAKES

Shortly after the building's completion, Chrysler accused Van Alen of taking bribes from subcontractors and refused to pay the balance of what he owed. The feud was tough for Van Alen to live down, and with the onset of the Great Depression, he had trouble finding work. The Chrysler Building remains his most lasting accomplishment.

Today, the Chrysler Corporation no longer owns the building that bears its name; it leases a portion of it as office space. In 1976, the building became a National Historic Landmark. The Chrysler Building now ranks as the 24th tallest in the world, but in terms of style and elegance, it's still the Top of the World. (You can visit the it at 405 Lexington Avenue at 42nd Street.)

*   *   *

THE TALLEST BUILDINGS IN THE WORLD, 2008

Taipei 101 (Taipei, Taiwan): 1,671 feet
Shanghai World Financial Center (Shanghai, China): 1,614 feet
Petronas Towers (Kuala Lumpur, Malaysia): 1,483 feet (each)
Sears Tower (Chicago): 1,451 feet
Jin Mao Tower (Shanghai, China): 1,380 feet
Two International Finance Centre (Hong Kong): 1,362 feet
CITIC Plaza (Guangzhou, China): 1,283 feet
Shun Hing Square (Shengzhen, China): 1,260 feet
Empire State Building (New York City): 1,250 feet
Central Plaza (Hong Kong): 1,227 feet

Human DNA is closer to a rat's than a cat's.

THE FAVORITE FLAVOR AWARD

Vanilla

We're fed up with it being called plain. Vanilla rocks, and we agree with the rock band the Barenaked Ladies who, in their 1998 hit "One Week," praise vanilla as "the finest of the flavors."

PURE VANILLA

Without vanilla, cakes, cookies, brownies, ice cream, and just about everything else that's good for dessert just wouldn't be worth the calories. And before you say chocolate is better, consider where chocolate would be without vanilla—bitter and tough to swallow. Whether dark, milk, or white chocolate, vanilla is added to complement the flavor, and even unsweetened baking chocolate is rarely used in a recipe that doesn't also call for vanilla. More than 250 components make up pure vanilla's natural flavor, which is why imitation vanilla doesn't taste as good. And vanilla is the second-most expensive spice in the world. (Saffron is first.) It's also a time-consuming process to cultivate this complex flavor. So for all these reasons, vanilla wins our award for the finest of flavors—hands down.

ALL WORK AND NO PLAY

Vanilla is actually a type of orchid, and although there are some 20,000 known orchid specimens, only one type of vanilla plant—*Vanilla planifolia*—produces anything edible. The vanilla bean is the fruit or seed of this plant that opens for just a day and can be pollinated only during the morning of that day. That's not enough time for bees to do their job to produce all of the vanilla that the world craves, so a hand-pollination method was developed in 1841. This gave growers the ability to produce vanilla economically for the first time.

In the 13th century, quality standards for pasta were set by the Pope.

But it's still a laborious process. Vanilla beans have to grow on the plant's vines for nine months before they can be harvested. After that, the flower's vegetative tissue is killed to prevent it from ruining the bean, followed by a hot and humid process called "sweating," which allows enzymes to start producing the many flavors that make up vanilla. The beans are set in the sun to dry out, and when they reach a high enough temperature, they're wrapped in a blanket and placed in a wooden box to sweat. It takes weeks for the beans to turn dark brown and develop a vanillin crust. The next step, the aging process, can last up to two years. After that, the beans are sorted by quality and then are shipped off to delight the taste buds of people worldwide.

THANKS, MADAGASCAR AND TAHITI!

All told, there are about 150 different types of vanilla, but two dominate the market:

1. **Bourbon-Madagascar vanilla** is the type used for baking. It gets its name not from whiskey but from the Île de Bourbon (now known as Réunion island), near Madagascar. Both locales produce a large amount of vanilla for baking, and even though vanilla doesn't have bourbon in it, real vanilla extract contains more than 35 percent alcohol, most of which burns off during baking. Madagascar actually produces about three-fourths of the world's vanilla output, which is used not only to flavor the sweets we love, but also as an ingredient in fragrances, as a medicinal flavoring, and even as a treatment for minor burns.

2. **Tahitian vanilla** is not as flavorful, so its use in food is limited. But because it gives off a strong vanilla scent, it works well in perfumes and other aromatic products.

THE FLAVOR OF LIFE

Americans consume more than 1,200 tons of vanilla beans per year, much of it in ice cream. In spite of the enormous variety of ice cream flavors available, vanilla remains the most popular. And it's all just "vanilla," too. French vanilla isn't a different flavor. Its name comes from the French method of using vanilla to make custard, which in turn can be used as an ice cream base.

One legend says that, after serving as the French ambassador, Thomas Jefferson returned home with 200 vanilla beans and introduced the flavor to the United States. That probably didn't happen, but Jefferson did develop a tasty recipe for vanilla ice cream, and his support of the flavor may have contributed to its (and the ice cream's) popularity.

Note: Ice cream connoisseurs should keep vanilla ice cream at a frosty 8°F for maximum flavor and texture. Keep that in mind if you decide to make Mr. Jefferson's recipe quoted below:

Ice Cream
2 bottles of good cream
6 yolks of eggs
1/2 lb. sugar

1. Mix the yolks & sugar put the cream on a fire in a casserole, first putting in a stick of Vanilla. When near boiling take it off & pour it gently into the mixture of eggs & sugar.

2. Stir it well. Put it on the fire again stirring it thoroughly with a spoon to prevent its sticking to the casserole. When near boiling, take it off and strain it thro' a towel. Put it in the Sabottiere [the inner canister of the ice cream maker] then set it in ice an hour before it is to be served. Put into the ice a handful of salt. Put salt on the coverlid of the Sabottiere & cover the whole with ice.

3. Leave it still half a quarter of an hour. Then turn the Sabottiere in the ice 10 minutes open it to loosen with a spatula the ice from the inner sides of the Sabottiere.

4. Shut it & replace it in the ice open it from time to time to detach the ice from the sides when well taken (prise) stir it well with the Spatula. Put it in moulds, justling it well down on the knee. Then put the mould into the same bucket of ice. Leave it there to the moment of serving it. To withdraw it, immerse the mould in warm water, turning it well till it will come out & turn it into a plate.

(From *American Treasures of the Library of Congress*, Library of Congress. "Jefferson's Recipe for Vanilla Ice Cream." 1780s.)

In Russia, people give flowers in odd numbers for romance and in even numbers for funerals.

THE ACT II AWARD

Three Former Child Stars

F. Scott Fitzgerald said, "There are no second acts in American lives." These performers proved him wrong and get an award for reinventing themselves with second acts that are more interesting than their first ones.

TAKE TWO

Some performers spend their entire lives fighting for their moment in the spotlight, while others step into it effortlessly. But childhood television and movie stars usually find that fame is fleeting, and many are ill equipped to cope with the sudden downturn in their popularity. Many quietly fade from view, but a few surprise their fans by achieving greater fame or success.

THE RIST FACTOR: OLIVER FROM *THE BRADY BUNCH*

When it was introduced to television audiences in 1969, *The Brady Bunch* demonstrated to an increasingly divorce-laden society how wonderful a second marriage could be. But the perfect television family couldn't stay that way forever, at least not without a time machine. In 1974, the Brady kids started to outgrow their roles, and ratings declined.

In an effort to recapture some of the show's youthful chemistry, producers added clumsy, tow-headed Cousin Oliver, played by Robbie Rist, to the show. Instead of boosting ratings, though, Oliver and his ridiculous antics annoyed audiences for the last three episodes of *The Brady Bunch* before it was canceled.

Although it was the end of the line for Cousin Oliver, Robbie Rist went on to rack up countless credits in television, music, and film. Rist's numerous post-Brady television roles included appearances on *The Mary Tyler Moore Show*, *CHiPs*, *Knight Rider*, and

The Bionic Woman. In addition, he was the voice of Michelangelo in 1990's *Teenage Mutant Ninja Turtles* movie.

His most significant, though perhaps lesser-known, contributions are to the music industry. Rist is a musical jack of all trades. He's played guitar, base, keyboards, drums, mandolin—you name it—in countless bands over the years. He's also a producer, an award-winning composer, and founder of Spidercrab West (recording) Studios.

In 2006, Rist showcased his versatility in a satisfyingly cheesy indie horror film he produced called *Stump the Band*, which won several film festival awards, including Best Music Score. What saved Rist from going the way of many fallen child stars before him? He credits good parenting . . . how very Brady.

LOOKS + TALENT + BRAINS = A WINNIE COMBINATION: WINNIE FROM *THE WONDER YEARS*

The 1980s delivered a host of improvements in the lives of teenage boys: arcade video games, *Miami Vice*, MTV . . . and Gwendolyn "Winnie" Cooper, the attractive "girl next door" character on the Emmy-winning series *The Wonder Years*. Played by Danica McKellar, shy, overly dramatic Winnie kept a vice grip on the heart of the show's main character, Kevin Arnold, the quintessential awkward teenager trying to find his way through adolescence in the 1960s and '70s. For the six seasons that it aired on ABC, *The Wonder Years* was a smash hit that made stars out of the cast. But after the show ended in 1993, McKellar put her career on hold to pursue a higher education. As it turned out, acting represented only a fraction of her true potential.

McKellar graduated from UCLA in 1998 with a bachelor of science in mathematics. While she was there, she coauthored a groundbreaking math proof titled "Percolation and Gibbs states multiplicity for ferromagnetic Ashkin-Teller models on $Z2$"—whatever that means. In 2007, her book *Math Doesn't Suck: How to Survive Middle-School Math Without Losing Your Mind or Breaking a Nail* was a national best-seller. It made Amazon's 100 Best Books of 2007 list, and McKellar was praised for her efforts to encourage girls to enjoy and excel at math.

All this and she still had time to build her acting resume, making regular appearances in films, on stage, and on hit television series like *The West Wing*, *NYPD Blue*, and *How I Met Your Mother*. But to most people, McKellar will always be that sweet yet sexy girl next door. In 2005, she was chosen by *Stuff* magazine readers as the 1990s star they would most like to see in lingerie. Not one to disappoint her fans, McKellar did a not-so-girl-next-door lingerie pictorial in the July 2005 issue.

GROWING WORRIES: BEN FROM *GROWING PAINS*

Pretty much everyone can relate to the tumultuous times of adolescence, career changes, spousal conflicts, and sibling rivalries. When ABC aired a new sitcom in 1985 that dealt with all of those issues, it was both relevant and well received. The Seaver family on *Growing Pains* mimicked a then-growing societal trend of dads looking after the household while moms pursued their career goals. But like many sitcoms, ratings eventually began to slide. So producers introduced new, young characters (a baby daughter and a precocious homeless teenager played by then virtually unknown Leonardo DiCaprio) in an attempt to save the show. It didn't work, and *Growing Pains* was canceled in 1992.

Most people still recognize the show's child stars Kirk Cameron and Tracey Gold, but few people would express much enthusiasm over "an evening of Hollywood glitz and glam" with Jeremy Miller, who played youngest son Ben Seaver. Unless, that is, the event was held in China. *Growing Pains* (translated as *Growing Worries* in Chinese) was one of the few American sitcoms approved for syndication in China. Its immediate popularity, more as a "how-to" parenting guide than as a comedy, earned Miller an enormous fan base and a role in the Chinese indie film *Milk and Fashion*. But just how long could one TV child actor ride the wave of a show popular nearly 20 years ago? Thanks to the 2006 DVD release of *Growing Pains*, it seems there's no shore in sight.

In a 2006 interview with Larry King, Miller said he was planning to display his culinary skills as the host of an American-style cooking show in China (no, he doesn't speak Chinese), and he was even considering moving there. Let's see: stay in the U.S. to run a catering company and play yourself in the occasional child star-themed program, or move to China, where your face will guarantee you hordes of screaming fans and great tables in the finest restaurants? Seems like a no-brainer.

After bacteria and viruses, the dominant life form on Earth is insects.

THE CLASSIC COVER AWARD

Sgt. Pepper's Lonely Hearts Club Band

With Sgt. Pepper's Lonely Hearts Club Band, the Beatles gave the world a picture no one could forget.

AN INFLUENTIAL COLLECTION

Before 1967, pop music album covers were staid images of the artists who recorded them—head shots, body shots, and band portraits were the order of the day—and, if someone were *really* creative, perhaps an abstract image. *Sgt. Pepper's Lonely Hearts Club Band* changed that.

The album epitomized the psychedelic rock era, and it remains an essential album for a music lover's collection—in 2003, *Rolling Stone* ranked it the best album of all time. *Sgt. Pepper's* is credited with several milestones: the first album to be tracked sequentially, meaning each song blends into the next, and one of the first concept albums. But the cover was a first, too—it was the first to print the lyrics to the songs on the back.

Sixty-two people populated *Sgt. Pepper's* cover—everyone from psychologist Carl Jung to child star Shirley Temple. There was little or no explanation as to why the different people were depicted or what it all meant. But it proved to be one of the Beatles most (if not *the* most) influential album.

WITH A LITTLE HELP FROM MY FRIENDS

Art gallery owner Robert Fraser, a friend of Paul McCartney's and a major influence in the British art world in the 1960s, came up with the idea for the cover. Originally, the Beatles planned to use a red and white psychedelic painting, but Fraser talked them out of it. (That painting, by a Dutch artists' group called The Fool, showed up in the inner sleeve for the first round of pressings.) English pop artist Peter Blake executed Fraser's idea.

The cover is supposed to depict a party that has gathered after a concert by the fictional Sgt. Pepper's Lonely Hearts Club Band. As would be expected of such an important gathering, the event is memorialized with a photo of the band surrounded by the celebrity concertgoers. All of the Beatles—except Ringo Starr, who didn't want to participate—chose the famous and infamous fake guest list, which included cultural icons like writer Edgar Allen Poe, occult practitioner Aleister Crowley, comedians Laurel and Hardy, scientist Albert Einstein, and socialist Karl Marx. At one time the picture was going to include Jesus and Adolf Hitler, but both were ultimately considered too controversial and were omitted.

Each Beatle appears on the cover twice: once as a member of Sgt. Pepper's Lonely Hearts Club Band and once as a Madame Tussaud's wax figure. The only other person to appear on the cover twice is Shirley Temple—her photo is in the front row, and there's a cloth replica of Temple wearing a "Welcome the Rolling Stones" shirt. (The Temple doll was designed by Jann Haworth, Peter Blake's wife, who helped him with the creation of the cover.)

The drum at the center of the album was attributed to an artist named Joe Ephgrave, but since 1967, people have speculated that Ephgrave didn't actually exist. Many thought the surname was made up and stood for "epitaph grave," which would play into the "Paul is dead" myth. (An urban legend says that McCartney died in 1966 and a look-alike imposter took his place in the band.) But others insist that he did exist and was a visual artist in England.

FIXING A HOLE

Several versions of the famous cover collage exist—from the original album released in 1967 to the current image used for CD pressings, which is missing Indian leader Mohandas Ghandi and actor Leo Gorcey. Gandhi was on the album cover for the original pressings, but the Beatles' record company EMI (which had an office in India) was afraid that people there would be offended, so he was painted out of the portrait in later versions.

Gorcey, a member of the Bowery Boys (a group of actors who played ruffians in several movies during the 1940s and 1950s),

---

Highest note on a piano keyboard: C. Lowest note: A.

asked for money for the use of his image, so EMI removed him. (Fellow Bowery Boy Huntz Hall remains on the album cover). Judy Garland also asked for a fee to use her image, and she didn't make it onto the cover, either.

All the other celebrities, though, gave EMI permission to use their likenesses. Actress Mae West took a little coaxing—initially she responded to the request with a question: "What would I be doing in a lonely hearts club?" But after the Beatles wrote her a letter and asked her to reconsider, she changed her mind.

Peter Blake spent two weeks assembling all the pieces for the famous photograph. Each image was a life-sized cardboard cutout, and he first put the back row of subjects up on a wall in Fraser's gallery. Then he layered each successive row about six inches in front of the one behind it. He added other elements—from a hair-dresser's dummy to a tuba—to give the image more effect.

WHO'S WHO ON THE COVER

Front Row: Wax dummy of boxer Sonny Liston; "The Petty Girl" by artist George Petty; wax dummy of George Harrison; wax dummy of John Lennon; actress Shirley Temple; wax dummy of Ringo Starr; wax dummy of Paul McCartney; Albert Einstein; John Lennon; Ringo Starr; Paul McCartney; George Harrison; singer Bobby Breen; actress Marlene Dietrich; actress Diana Dorrs; actress Shirley Temple

Second Row: Former member of the Beatles Stuart Sutcliff; a wax hairdresser's dummy; comedian Max Miller; "The Petty Girl" by artist George Petty (different from the image in the front row); Marlon Brando; actor Tom Mix; writer Oscar Wilde; actor Tyrone Power; artist Larry Bell; explorer Dr. David Livingstone; swimmer Johnny Weismuller; author Stephen Crane; comedian Issy Bonn; playwright George Bernard Shaw; sculptor H. C. Westermann; soccer player Albert Stubbins; guru Sri Lahiri Mahasaya; author Lewis Carroll; Lawrence of Arabia

Third Row: Illustrator Aubrey Beardsley; former Prime Minister Sir Robert Peel; writer Aldous Huxley; poet Dylan Thomas; writer Terry Southern; singer Dion (singer); actor Tony Curtis; actor Wallace Berman; comedian Tommy Handley; Marilyn Monroe;

author William Burroughs; guru Sri Mahavatara Babaji; actor Stan Laurel; artist Richard Lindner; actor Oliver Hardy; Karl Marx; author H. G. Wells; guru Sri Paramahansa Yagananda; a wax hairdresser's dummy

Back Row: Guru Sri Yukteswar Giri; Aleister Crowley; actress Mae West; comedian Lenny Bruce; composer Karlheinz Stockhausen; comedian W. C. Fields; psychologist Carl Jung; Edgar Allan Poe; dancer Fred Astaire; artist Richard Merkin; "The Varga Girl" by artist Alberto Vargas; actor Huntz Hall; architect Simon Rodia; musician Bob Dylan

Nonhuman items pictured: Two cloth figures (one is Shirley Temple), a candlestick, a television set, four figurines (one of Snow White), a bust from John Lennon's home, a trophy, a doll from India, a hookah pipe, a velvet snake, a garden gnome, and a drum with the Sgt. Pepper's Lonely Hearts Club Band logo

*   *   *

PARODIES OF THE *SGT. PEPPER'S* COVER

If imitation is the sincerest form of flattery, the creators of *Sgt. Pepper's Lonely Hearts Club Band* should feel pretty flattered. Since the album's release, the cover has been parodied many times (mostly lovingly, but sometimes with sarcasm, as in Frank Zappa's case). Here are five famous examples.

- A season five episode of *The Simpsons* featured the Be Sharps band. The back of their album cover parodies *Sgt. Pepper's*.

- Frank Zappa released an album in 1968 called *We're Only in It for the Money*. Its cover is a takeoff on *Sgt. Pepper's*.

- The 1,000th issue of *Rolling Stone* magazine (published in 2006) was a giant tribute to the cover.

- *Mad* magazine took it on in 2002 in a story called "The 50 Worst Things About Music."

- The Rutles, a parody group featuring Monty Python comedian Eric Idle, released their own album called *Sgt. Rutter's Only Darts Club Band* in 1975.

The "Big Dipper" is a portion of a much larger constellation—Ursa Major (the Great Bear).

THE THREE LITTLE PIGS AWARD, #3

Sweden's Icehotel

*It's not built of bricks, straw, or hay, but it gets our award
for the most unique—and temporary—building.*

BRRR! Cocooned in a heavyweight sleeping bag, you lie on top of reindeer pelts that cover a queen-sized bed fashioned completely from blocks of ice. In fact, the walls, artwork, and furniture in your room are all made of pure ice. Moonlight streams in through a glacial skylight. You're a guest at Sweden's famed Icehotel, found in the village of Jukkäsjarvi, about 125 miles north of the Arctic Circle. Before an attendant brings you a morning mug of hot lingonberry juice and invites you to warm up with a sauna, let's look around a bit.

COLD HANDS, WARM ART

The heart of the Icehotel is its design. The hotel melts with each spring thaw, so every year, a carefully selected group of international artists, sculptors, and architects have been trekking to Jukkäsjarvi to participate in the annual creation of a new Icehotel.

Winter 2007–2008 was the 18th season of the Icehotel. For that season, 19 design teams from 16 different countries created rooms that reflected their unique visions. Some are whimsically named, such as "Mind the Gap" for a hotel corridor, or "Meander" for a bedroom suite with a motif of watery twists and turns. The "Kristall" Church pays homage to the hotel's basic building block—the snowflake. And it's no surprise that the drinking hole is—what else?—the Absolut Bar, where vodka is served in specially formed ice tumblers. The hotel's Web site and books showcase the glorious but temporary creations.

A high fever can cause brain damage—but only if it goes above 107.6° F.

Planning starts to rebuild a hotel in the spring, and each November, construction begins anew, using approximately 3,300 tons of ice cut from the pure waters of Sweden's Torne River. Water is sprayed on steel skeletons, and when it hardens, the skeletons are removed. A room's walls don't contain anything except frozen water.

THE FROZEN CHOSEN

Local delicacies are served on ice plates in the Icehotel's restaurant, but that structure, like a nearby inn for the less hardy, is heated. A visit to the Icehotel isn't just remarkable; it's truly a once-in-a-lifetime experience, since you can never stay in the same room or—for that matter—hotel twice. Interestingly, that temporary quality seems to have inspired a trend that's about long-lasting things: Icehotel weddings. Along with the hotel and the Icebar, each year the design team creates an Ice Chapel, complete with fur-covered pews and frosty flying buttresses.

THE COLD, HARD TRUTH

The Icehotel is open from early December to mid-April, depending on the weather. If you just happen to be in Jukkäsjarvi, you can tour the hotel each day from 10 a.m. to 6 p.m. After 6 p.m., the hotel is reserved for guests. Prices start at around $250 a night for doubles, with single rooms costing significantly more.

The number of rooms varies but typically includes about 80 rooms, including 22 bedroom suites. The night-time temperature is around 23°F, so guests need to be sure to follow instructions about what to wear and how to get ready for bed. (With all the long underwear, sleep hats, socks, mittens, and separate sleeping bags, a night in the Icehotel is not necessarily one for love.) The hotel provides guests with free outerwear—snowmobile overalls, hats, mittens, and boots. You can't keep your luggage with you—if you left it in your room, it would freeze—so the hotel's porters lock it up in a special luggage area. But not everywhere at the hotel is cold: there are saunas to help you wake up in the morning, and the hotel's toilets are heated. (Uncle John's readers, rejoice!)

For the other Three Little Pigs Awards,
turn to pages 7 and 52.

Average lifespan of a rural oak tree: 150 years. Average lifespan of an urban oak tree: 13 years.

THE FIRST AMENDMENT AWARD

The Pentagon Validates Wicca

We're pleased to report that when faced with choosing between supporting religious freedom and oppressing part of its ranks, the U.S. military chose to side with the First Amendment . . . sort of.

IT TAKES ALL KINDS

There are about 1.4 million men and women currently serving in the U.S. military, and within that group, all types of religions are represented. Christians make up the largest portion, but Jews, Muslims, Buddhists, Mormons, Russian Orthodox, and even Unitarians are included. And each of those religions also has a chaplain and an approved symbol to appear on a fallen soldier's grave. (Deceased Christian soldiers have crosses on their tombstones, Jews have Stars of David, Unitarians have a Flaming Chalice, and so on.) But when the military's Wiccan contingent asked that its religion be recognized equally by the military, they hit some roadblocks.

ARE YOU A GOOD WITCH OR A BAD WITCH?

The controversy started at Fort Hood in Texas. With about 75,000 soldiers, Fort Hood is the largest U.S. military post; it's also home to the Fort Hood Open Circle, a Wicca congregation of less than two-dozen military personnel. The group's members gathered monthly for worship and had been doing so for years. But in 1999, press coverage of their services enraged locals who believed that Wiccan practices verged on the satanic. Photos of the Open Circle's rites (including some members dancing bare-chested around a fire) were published in the *Killeen Daily Herald* and the *Austin American-States-*

Cotton swabs cause 2.5 times more injuries than razor blades.

man, and in response, one minister was quoted as saying, "We need to stop them . . . God says, 'Suffer not a witch to live.'" Ouch!

COMPASSIONATE CAMOUFLAGE

The group's champion turned out to be none other than the U.S. military. Military regulations protect religious freedom for all, so Fort Hood's Wiccans got the same treatment as everyone else—a place to worship, clearance for a clergyperson, and access to military support (including a mention in Fort Hood's weekly newsletter that lists all worship services.)

Not only that, but the *U.S. Army Military Chaplain Handbook* also included Wicca as a legitimate religion, noting that even though some people consider its beliefs to be witchcraft, Wicca's origins are rooted in nature worship. The handbook also emphasized that "it is very important to be aware that Wiccans do not in any way worship or believe in 'Satan,' 'the Devil,' or any similar entities." This victory, of course, led to other military Wiccan groups coming out of the closet . . . and to more condemnation from the establishment.

FREEDOM IN DEATH

Wiccans and the military seemed to coexist peacefully in life, but in death, things were initially a little thornier. Army Sergeant Patrick D. Stewart died in 2005 while serving in Afghanistan with the Nevada National Guard. He was awarded a Purple Heart and the Bronze Star posthumously. But when his widow, Roberta Stewart, asked to have his religious affiliation as a Wiccan acknowledged on his memorial stone, the VA (U.S. Department of Veterans Affairs) refused. Why? According to Stewart, it was because the Wiccan pentacle—an upright five-pointed star surrounded by a circle—offended Christian sensibilities. An upturned star (one with a single point facing down and two points facing up) is often used as a symbol of Satanism, but the Wiccan pentacle actually represents the religion's five elements: earth, fire, water, air, and spirit.

According to the military, however, the reason the pentacle couldn't be approved was the lack of a "central hierarchy" in the Wiccan religion. Because there is no one group of clergy or laypeople who make decisions about the religion's practices, there was no one for the VA to write to and have acknowledge the pentacle's religious significance.

Roberta Stewart kept pushing, though, and finally in late 2007, the five-pointed Wiccan star was added to the military's list of emblems allowed on veterans' grave markers. As of 2007, 11 families nationwide were waiting to have their loved ones' markers modified with pentacles. (Changes to military headstones often take time because the markers must be identical, and the 11 are spread across the country.)

RECOGNITION

That wasn't the end of it, though. Don Larsen had joined the Army as a Pentecostal Christian, and his reputation as a chaplain was one of the "best," according to his superior officer. But Larsen had a crisis of faith and he decided to become a Wiccan because its beliefs about feminism, equality, and nature were more aligned with his vows. But in 2006, when Larsen applied to change his religious affiliation and become the first Wiccan chaplain in the U.S. Armed Forces, he ran into obstacles from paperwork bungles to emails pleading with him to confirm that his request was an error. Eventually, he was relieved of active duty.

Many believe Larsen was the victim of outright religious discrimination. The superior officer who spoke so highly of him said, "I think it's political. A lot of people think Wiccans are un-American because they are ignorant about what Wiccans do." The Army offered little explanation for Larsen's dismissal but stated that there are simply too few Wiccans in the military to justify a full-time chaplain. However, according to Pentagon figures cited in a *Washington Post* article about Larsen's case, there are several faiths with small numbers that do have their own chaplains: "Among the nearly 2,900 clergy on active duty are 41 Mormon chaplains for 17,513 Mormons in uniform, 22 rabbis for 4,038 Jews, 11 imams for 3,386 Muslims, six teachers for 636 Christian Scientists, and one Buddhist chaplain for 4,546 Buddhists."

Thanks to the efforts of Larsen, Roberta Stewart, and others—even the Pentagon itself—there are now recognized Wiccan groups at Fort Polk, Louisiana; Fort Wainwright, Alaska; and Fort Barrancas, Florida. But there is still no official Wiccan chaplain in any branch of the U.S. military.

Like flowers, children grow faster in the springtime.

THE HENRY DAVID THOREAU AWARD

Going off the Grid

Power to the people! Uncle John thinks this is an empowering trend.

RESISTANCE ISN'T FUTILE
Henry David Thoreau was a 19th-century rebel—an avid abolitionist, a tax resister, and the writer of *Civil Disobedience,* a book that advocated resisting government interference in daily life. He was also one of the first environmentalists, and he retreated to nature for a two-year experiment to escape what he saw as an encroaching and messy modern society. He documented his experience and what he saw as a need for self-reliance in the book *Walden.*

Today, people still take to heart Thoreau's insistence on the importance of preserving nature and being self-reliant. And one of the ways they're heeding his call is by "going off the grid."

BURN BABY BURN
The United States began to get juiced on electricity around the turn of the 20th century, when homes started getting wired. Only 10 percent of rural homes had electricity (compared to 90 percent of urban ones) when President Franklin D. Roosevelt signed the Rural Electrification Administration law in 1935. Over the next 30 years, almost every home, farm, and business in the country got electricity via power lines and a place on the public utility's power grid.

Today, a growing number of people are "going off the grid"— meaning living their lives without taxing traditional water and power supplies. Why? According to the Department of Energy, electricity usage is growing about 1.3 percent each year. That's about one-third of the growth the United States saw in the 1970s, and about half of what it was in the 1980s and 1990s. Yet today's

---

Every year in the United States, 17 tons of gold are used to make wedding rings.

average American uses seven times more electricity than his or her counterpart in the 1940s. And electricity suppliers haven't been able to match the increase in use, which has led to a series of blackouts (total loss of power to a region), brownouts (partial loss of power), and rolling blackouts (series of planned successive power losses) in major cities over the past several years.

Other concerns are the environmentally damaging emissions that come with generating electricity and the inefficiencies of the process. In 2000, 40 quadrillion BTUs of energy were used by the electrical sector, but only 12 quadrillion actually went to consumers. The rest were lost (mostly emitted as heat) during production.

AND THEY'RE OFF

Somewhere between 180,000 and 250,000 people in the United States live off the grid, with more going for it every day. Off-gridders don't have as much power as those on the grid, so they have to conserve—an off-gridder wouldn't watch television while doing laundry, for example. To get their power, they rely on the sun, water, or wind. By far, solar is the energy generator of choice for most off-gridders. With solar panels, sunlight is converted to usable energy and then stored in batteries. Plus, solar power is clean and doesn't add pollutants to the atmosphere.

For its part, the U.S. government encourages people to go off the grid by offering federal tax credits. (Some states pony up tax credits and rebates.) Those credits help to make up for the initial investment. Installing solar power can run from $10,000 to $25,000 for a house.

Water and wind power are also options, but they can be more restrictive. Relying on water power requires that you live near a running water source, though hydro power is more efficient than solar because it collects energy all of the time (solar panels can only collect energy during the day). The equipment is also substantially cheaper: often under $10,000. To harness the power of the wind, you'll need a rotor—one about 50 feet in diameter will work for most houses—and a stand to support it.

Off-grid power living is growing by 33 percent, and sales of renewable energy sources like solar panels are seeing similar growth. We think Henry David Thoreau would be proud.

THE IT'S EASY BEING GREEN AWARD

Fluorescent Light Bulbs

These light bulbs created their own buzz before they got a prize-worthy upgrade (and went small in the process).

TURN ON THE LIGHTS

Most people associate fluorescent light bulbs—used primarily in business and industrial settings—with giant tubes that emit a persistent hum and sometimes flicker annoyingly. When fluorescent lights were reconfigured as regular screw-in light bulbs for lamps and other home lighting, they didn't work as well as traditional incandescent bulbs, and they cost a lot more. But now, they light up our lives, and all it took was a little retooling to show consumers how a compact fluorescent lamp (CFL) could deliver five times more power than an incandescent bulb.

LET THERE BE LIGHT

The principle of a traditional incandescent light bulb is relatively simple: The bulb gets its energy from the electrical outlet, and that energy heats up the filament (a small metal wire) inside the bulb. When it gets hot enough, it glows. Voila . . . light! On the other hand, fluorescent light bulbs (the old ones and the new CFLs) have two filaments, one at each end of a tube. There's also mercury vapor inside the tube. As the filaments heat up, atoms bounce around, knock into the mercury, and move between the filaments. All that activity makes light.

OUT WITH THE OLD

Currently, Americans buy one billion incandescent light bulbs every year. CFLs have only 6 percent of the market, but their

Artificial waves can make a goldfish seasick.

share is growing—in 2001, it was only 1 percent. Other countries have adopted CFLs at a much faster pace: in Germany, the share is 50 percent, and in Japan, it's 80 percent.

CFLs use drastically less power than incandescent bulbs, which are remarkably inefficient because most of their energy is wasted in the form of heat (from the filament). Plus, the amount of light incandescent bulbs produce is small compared to the amount of energy they consume (15 lumens per watt used).

CFLs produce 50 to 100 lumens per watt used. In fact, the CFL is so much more efficient that it will produce the same light as an incandescent bulb with four or five times more wattage. Since roughly half the country's energy supply comes from coal-burning power plants, cutting down on the energy used to produce light can significantly reduce the emission of greenhouse gases, which also make CFLs better for the environment.

There's more to the story. CFLs not only save money by using less energy. They last longer, too. They have a lifespan lasting years, so they don't need to be replaced that often. Fewer light bulbs used means fewer spent bulbs in the trash—yet another environmental benefit.

RATTLE AND HUM

CFL technology began to take off in the early 1980s, after the rising price of energy in the 1970s led people to look for less expensive options. Still, while the technology was there, the initial savings weren't. CFLs were a lot more expensive than incandescent bulbs (as much as $25 each). And although the energy savings meant that they paid for themselves over time, consumer demand wasn't high enough compared to industrial usage.

The ballasts of the bulbs (the electrical part that supplies electricity to the bulb) were sometimes slow to conduct electricity and kept the bulbs from illuminating immediately, which is why old fluorescents often took a few seconds to fully light up. And the electrical current charging through the mercury gas emitted a distinct hum. It was easy enough to ignore in an office setting, where other background noise drowned it out, but much more difficult to overlook on a quiet night at home.

As the technology of fluorescent lighting evolved, both of those problems were fixed. What hasn't been fixed entirely is the type of light the bulbs emit. Typically, incandescent bulbs emitted a warmer, softer light that was easier on the human eye, while many people complained that the old fluorescent bulbs were too harsh. Even though testing among consumers has shown that CFL light is now as warm as incandescent, some people remain unconvinced. And it's true that CFLs are brighter and stronger and, therefore, can be more off-putting when used in multiple places in the same room. To counteract that effect, most people use a mix of both CFLs and incandescents.

GO GREEN

Over its entire life, one CFL will prevent a half-ton of CO_2 from being pumped into the atmosphere compared to its incandescent counterpart. If Americans replaced just 100 million incandescent light bulbs with CFLs in their homes, they'd offset the greenhouse gas emissions of one million cars. That's a change worthy of an award.

* * *

SHINE A LIGHT

In Livermore, California, a light bulb screwed in sometime in the early 20th century is still burning—the longest-lasting light bulb on record. The exact date the bulb was screwed in is in question, but it was somewhere between 1901 and 1905. Ever since, it's been burning in a fire station . . . one of three stations, actually; it was moved from one to another, until it found its current home in Fire Station #6 in Livermore. The bulb has rarely been turned off in its history, which is one of the reasons for its longevity. (The stress of being turned on is what most commonly burns out light bulbs.)

When Livermore celebrated the bulb's 100th (give or take) anniversary in 2001, a Web site was established—BulbCam—so people everywhere can see the still-burning light bulb in all its glory.

THE PAPER CHASE AWARD

Ticker-Tape Parade Cleanup

We like to celebrate our heroes in style, but the people who clean up afterward deserve praise, too.

A HERO'S WELCOME

There is no better way to celebrate a victory than with a ticker-tape parade. This time-honored tradition began in New York City on October 29, 1886, during a parade honoring the dedication of the Statue of Liberty. Viewers high up in office buildings along the parade route threw out shredded pieces of paper, which rained down on thousands of celebrants below, and an American tradition was born.

Historically, ticker-tape parades were held in New York's Financial District. They ran along lower Broadway from Bowling Green and Battery Park up to City Hall, roughly a mile-long route nicknamed the "Canyon of Heroes." Tall office buildings line both sides for most of the route and provide good vantage points for office workers and viewers, as well as for dumping a blizzard of paper onto the parade itself.

CONFETTI BY ANY OTHER NAME

Ticker tape, a leftover product of the stock exchange at the time, was used to create just the right effect for a day of celebration. Fluttering down like snowflakes, ticker tape—now made from any shredded paper, but mostly newspapers—glimmers and shimmers in the wind and creates a storm of confetti in the street. As much as 50 tons of ticker tape are typically dumped into city streets during a parade. And that much paper requires some serious cleanup. So the city of New York's Department of Sanitation employs hundreds of people to clean up after parades and other major events.

First city to have street addresses: Paris (1463). London was the second, 300 years later.

THE PAPER TRAIL

New York isn't the only city to host ticker-tape parades. In 1969, for example, Chicago, Houston, and Los Angeles threw ticker-tape parades for returning astronauts Neil Armstrong, Michael Collins, and Edwin "Buzz" Aldrin Jr. But the events remain primarily a New York institution, and the city takes them seriously.

In 2004, the Alliance for Downtown New York spent $22 million to rebuild the famous Canyon of the Heroes path, repaving sidewalks and putting in new lampposts, signs, and wastebaskets. The group also commemorated every ticker-tape parade ever thrown on the Canyon of Heroes by installing more than 200 black granite plaques, each about 20 feet apart, to explain when and why each previous parade had taken place.

GREEN GIANTS

The victory of the New York Giants over the New England Patriots in 2008's Super Bowl XLII was a surprise to many; but New York's City Hall was ready. Officials had begun planning a ticker-tape parade for the Giants in secret, calling it Operation Haystack, but they didn't let anyone know because they didn't want to jinx the sports team.

When the Giants won (in the upset heard 'round the NFL), the city threw the champions a proper ticker-tape parade on February 5, 2008. With 36.5 tons of ticker tape thrown, it wasn't the biggest parade shower—that distinction goes to the parade that celebrated the Allies' victory in Japan in 1945 and accumulated 5,438 tons of paper. There is one reason for less paper in 2008—modern office buildings have windows that don't open.

But the Giants victory parade was unique for two reasons: it was the first in New York in the 21st century, and it was the most eco-friendly in history. About 6 percent of the paper used in the parade was recycled, according to the New York City Sanitation Department. Sure, 6 percent doesn't seem like a whole lot, but we did the math, and that's 2.19 tons of recycled paper.

FROM GREEN TO CLEAN

A city as big as New York can't afford to shut down major streets for very long to clean up such a mess, particularly in the Financial Dis-

---

In Tajikistan, state employees are banned from having gold teeth.

trict, home to the New York Stock Exchange and the center of the global economy. So immediately after the Giants' parade ended, 350 Sanitation Department and 50 Alliance for Downtown New York workers hit the street with hand brooms, leaf blowers, and mechanical street sweepers to clear up the debris, which was placed in 12 collection trucks. They finished before the evening rush hour.

TICKER TAPE TRIVIA

- Admiral George Dewey, hero of the Battle of Manila Bay, was the first living person to be honored with a ticker-tape parade on September 30, 1899.

- One of New York's most famous ticker-tape parades (and its 21st) occurred on June 13, 1927, in honor of Charles Lindbergh's successful transatlantic flight.

- Aviators—like Amelia Earhart, Wiley Post, and "Wrong-Way" Corrigan—and then astronauts were popular recipients.

- So were sports figures and teams: golfer Bobby Jones (twice), Jesse Owens, the 1928 and 1950s American Olympic teams, Connie Mack, the New York Yankees (8), the New York Mets (3), the New York Giants (baseball) (1), the New York Rangers (1), and the New York Giants (football) (1).

- Some fairly forgettable people were honored as well—Jack Binns, Joseph Joffre, and the Order of the Knights of Pythias. Who?

- The following people (outside of sports teams) have been honored more than once: explorer Rear Admiral Richard E. Byrd (3), Captain George Fried (2), golfer Bobby Jones (2), Amelia Earhart (2), pilot Wiley Post (2), Dwight D. Eisenhower (2), Charles de Gaulle (2), Ethiopian emperor Haile Selassie (2), John Glenn (2), and Italian politician Alcide De Gasperi (2).

* * *

A DUBIOUS HONOR

Each year, the *Boston Phoenix* releases a list of the unsexiest men on Earth. 2008's Top Five: baseball player Roger Clemens, Spencer Pratt (of the reality show *The Hills*), Senator Larry Craig, Tom Cruise, and CNN's Lou Dobbs.

THE POP, POP, FIZZ, FIZZ AWARD

Galco's Soda-Pop Stop

If you're bored with the same old soda choices, take a drive to this tasty relic from Hollywood's golden age.

TEMPTING TREATS

Diet Coke, Sprite, and Sunkist Orange sodas are so . . . common. You can find them anywhere. If you're ready for something different in a soft drink—a new taste, a bolder flavor, a different kind of carbonation—you need to head to Galco's Soda-Pop Stop in Los Angeles. The small, 100-year-old sandwich shop carries 400 varieties of soft drinks to tempt you.

Galco's started life as an Italian grocery, and John Nese and his family still make their famous overstuffed sandwiches in the back. But the front room is dedicated to Nese's passion for pop.

EGG CREAM OF THE CROP

Galco's carries common and classic sodas, like Coca-Cola and Faygo, but it also stocks more unique products like bottled New York egg creams. Those egg creams were a New York-area craze for decades, consisting of nothing except chocolate syrup (usually Fox's U-Bet), whole milk, and fresh seltzer.

Some of the other products Galco stocks are among the champagnes of soda pop: Fentiman's Mandarin and Seville Orange Jigger, Almdudler Krauterlimonade (herbal lemon–lime soda), and Blenheim's HOT HOT Ginger Ale. These sodas—with unusual recipes and high-quality, all-natural ingredients—qualify for gourmet status. And Galco's doesn't view soda pop as just an American institution; Nese recognizes that people all over the world enjoy soft drinks, so his store carries imports from Europe, Asia, Latin America, and the Caribbean.

Every year, approximately 1 billion seabirds and mammals die from ingesting plastic bags.

Along with colas, ginger ales, and cream sodas, you'll also find rose-petal pop, sorrel soda, and bubble-gum bubbly. There are plenty of brewed choices, too; after all, "root beer" got its name from the process by which it's manufactured. Birch beers and sarsaparillas will take senior family members right back to the good old days.

Whenever possible, Nese tries to stock all-natural sodas. You'll find Coke products, but they come from Mexico, where the sweetener is still sugar cane and not high-fructose corn syrup. Plantation Mint Julep soda has real mint in it, and some of the citrus sodas contain real zest.

THE PAUSE THAT REFRESHES

Nese originally decided to devote his shelf space to boutique brands of soda pop as a mini-revolt against the big bottlers, whose products dominated grocery store aisles around the country. At first, his customers were older people looking for a taste of the past, but Web and other media coverage has brought him many new customers.

Perhaps the younger crowd is drawn to shelves filled only with glass bottles—there's not an aluminum can or plastic bottle in sight. Nese believes that, because plastic leaks, modern beverage makers overcarbonate soda and as a result ruin its natural flavor and feel. In creating his collection of soft drinks, Nese has been a blessing for small manufacturers, both in the United States and overseas. When he hears about a new soda, he tracks it down— and often orders enough stock to keep the manufacturer in business for a while.

DRINK UP

In fact, Nese has actually revived five sodas, including one that used to be known as Delaware Punch (now called Pennsylvania Punch). Delaware Punch was never made in Delaware; it was invented and sold in San Antonio, Texas. But its flavor came from Delaware grapes, hence the name. Delaware Punch was a soft drink without carbonation (in the 1920s it was billed as "America's SOFT Soft Drink"). Today, the Coca-Cola Company owns the name Delaware Punch and sells versions of it in Texas and

---

In Finland, speeding ticket fines are based on income.

Louisiana. But when Nese tried to track Delaware Punch down for a customer who wanted it, he found someone who had the original recipe. Nese took the original formula (complete with real sugar instead of high-fructose corn syrup), rather than the one Coca-Cola uses, and had a small bottling company in Pennsylvania re-create it.

Although tracking down and reviving old sodas has an element of nostalgia, Nese doesn't see his store as being a nostalgic enterprise. He believes that by offering customers a large variety of high-quality products, he's simply serving their needs. Considering how many people from the Los Angeles area and around the country flock to Galco's Soda-Pop Stop now, it seems that they find Nese's approach a refreshing alternative.

*   *   *

FAILED SODAS

- **Pepsi AM (1985):** After research showed that some people drink cola instead of coffee for breakfast, Pepsi introduced this, which had more caffeine and less carbonation than regular Pepsi. Morning Pepsi drinkers continued to just drink regular Pepsi.

- **Orbitz (1996):** A clear, fruit-flavored soda with round bits of gelatin floating in it.

- **Pepsi Blue (2002):** A highly sugared "berry cola fusion"—and it was blue.

- **C2 and Pepsi Edge (2004):** To cash in on the low-carb diet fad, both Coke and Pepsi released sodas with half the sugar of their regular versions. Both bombed in under a year.

- **Mountain Dew Black (2004):** Same flavor as regular Mountain Dew—only it was black.

- **Coke Blak (2006):** A combination of Coca-Cola Classic . . . and ice-cold, imitation coffee.

Misnomer: Horny toads are not toads—they are lizards.

THE MISSED MANNERS AWARD

Forgotten Etiquette

Uncle John may have forgotten which fork to use first, but he's certain that these customs are a little behind the times. While many of the rules sound absolutely ridiculous now, they were rooted in practicality, or at least in logical thought.

HERE'S MY CARD

Today, people exchange business cards all the time with little thought, but there was a time in Western society (particularly British society) when giving a card with business information to a social acquaintance would have been terribly rude. During the 19th century, every gentleman and lady had engraved calling cards—some were made of thick paperboard, others from copper. The cards served as an introduction, and there were many rules to govern their use and contents:

- A married woman's card was larger than her husband's; his had to fit in his breast pocket. A young girl could have a calling card, but only after she'd been in "proper" society for a year and only one that included her full and proper name.

- Cards were always presented (by a servant) to the mistress of the house. If the mistress wasn't at home, the caller wasn't welcome.

- Servants collected the cards on silver trays (or in glass bowls for the less-well-to-do) and presented the cards to the lady of the house with the most important caller on top.

- After moving to a new neighborhood, it was polite to wait until your neighbors left their cards before you went over to meet them.

- A proper lady or gentleman never wrote "regrets" or "accepts" on a card as a reply to an invitation. Those required a hand-written note.

There was also an elaborate system of card protocol when leaving a community. Some people used special "P.P.C." cards, or simply wrote these initials at the bottom of their usual cards. "P.P.C." meant "Pour Prendre Conge," or "To Take Leave." In other words—so long! Accompanying the initials was an even more elaborate system of corners turned up or down that showed whether you were leaving on a short trip, a long trip, or moving away permanently.

SEAT-SIDE RINGS

These days, napkin rings are more likely to hold paper napkins than cloth ones, if a host even uses them at all. But in the 19th century, cloth was the rule, and napkin rings were as common to a table as forks . . . they were as practical, too. Before washing machines, all clothes, bedding, and other cloth items had to be washed by hand. That was a lot of washing, either for a servant or for the lady of the house. So people were always looking for ways to cut down on the laundry.

Enter napkin rings. Made of wood or silver, napkin rings, monogrammed with each person's initials, kept track of whose napkin was whose. The same person used the same napkin for several meals and would only wash it when it got really dirty. Of course, over the years, napkin rings became widely used and were put into service at formal occasions, when no one would be reusing a napkin afterward.

BRIDAL BESTS

Have you ever gone to a wedding and enthusiastically said "Congratulations!" to the bride, only to have a relative correct you? That's because, as Emily Post reminded us in 1922, "it is a breach of good manners to congratulate a bride on having secured a husband."

There are probably people who still abide by this bit of forgotten etiquette, but the reason behind it is so outmoded that it bears mentioning. You're supposed to say "Congratulations!" to the groom and "Best wishes!" to the bride. That's because a long,

long time ago, in a world of etiquette far, far away, two things were true:

First, throughout history, women were not always willing participants at their own weddings. Marriages were often arranged to bring together warring clans or to join financial forces. The bride was the prize ("Congrats, old man!"), and the poor young woman could only be encouraged with good wishes as she left for a life she might detest.

Second, by the 18th century, if not before, securing a marriage proposal and wedding had become the goal most women's lives. But to congratulate her would be unseemly because one wouldn't want to imply that a genteel lady had been involved in any intrigues, snares, and machinations to snag her man. So "Best Wishes" it was.

HATS ON OR OFF?

Maybe the rule requiring men to doff their headgear inside a building has faded in the face of so many guys wearing billed caps, but real cowboys still know and practice the increasingly forgotten art of hat etiquette. Historically, tipping a hat was practiced mostly by cowboys. Removing one's hat dates back to the days of chivalry when knights would raise their helmet shields as a sign of respect.

But no matter, gentlemen. According to the John B. Stetson Hat Company, founded in 1868, there are very specific rules that dictate when to tip your hat and when to remove it:

Tip Your Hat . . .

If a woman thanks you.

After receiving directions from a stranger.

If you excuse yourself to a woman.

When walking with a friend and he greets a woman you don't know.

Remove Your Hat . . .

During the playing of the national anthem.

On entering a building (one exception: you may keep it on in an elevator).

During an introduction.

When attending a funeral.

When initiating a conversation.

Disposable diapers are five times more likely to cause diaper rash than cotton diapers.

THE SANDWICH MAKER AWARD

Mayonnaise

Anyone asked to name a favorite condiment might quickly reply "ketchup" or "mustard," and sure—those are good. But we're going to tell you why mayonnaise is the real culinary star.

YOU SAY MAHONNAISE, I SAY AIOLI

Mayonnaise is the bedrock ingredient of numerous condiments and sauces worldwide (rouille, remoulade, tartar sauce, and Thousand Island dressing, for example). Mix a jar of ketchup with mayo and you've got Russian dressing. Mix mustard with mayo, and you've got Hellman's Dijonnaise. The list just goes on and on.

There is no definitive source for the origin of the word "mayonnaise," but there are several theories:

- One is that the word derives from the Old French word *moyeu* for the yolk of an egg, which is an essential ingredient.

- Another is that the French made mayonnaise from a popular Spanish recipe for allioli, an egg-based sauce flavored with lots of garlic.

- A third story says it's from the French verb *manier*, meaning "to mix or blend."

- "Mahonnaise" may be an honorific after the Spanish port of Mahon, where the French Duke de Richelieu defeated the British in a 1756 naval battle.

OLD, BUT NOT SPOILED

If mayonnaise comes from Mahon, it's more than 250 years old now—and as popular as ever. The first recorded English use of "mayonnaise" appears in an 1841 cookbook. The British renamed it "salad cream" in 1914 and kept this term after an attempt to return to mayonnaise in 1999 resulted in a public outcry.

AMERICAN FLAIR

The first commercially manufactured mayo was born in a New York City delicatessen—Richard Hellman's Columbus Avenue storefront—in 1905. Hellman sold his wife's homemade salads, which used mayonnaise as a dressing, and soon people were asking to buy it on its own. The condiment became so popular that in 1912 Hellman built a factory to produce it in large quantities.

Originally, there were two versions of the creamy spread, and to tell them apart, Hellman tied a blue ribbon around one jar, which was consistently more popular. He called that one Hellman's Blue Ribbon Mayonnaise.

Meanwhile, across the country, Best Foods introduced Californian consumers to a slightly tangier version of mayonnaise. No one outside the conglomerate knows for sure, but gourmands suspect that the Best Foods formula contains more lemon juice. (Today, Best Foods owns Hellman's, but maintains both brands and their distinct recipes.)

Hellman's and Best Foods split the coasts, but there's one more brand in the American mayo lineup, beloved by Southerners past and present: Duke's. Still made to Mrs. Eugenia Duke's original formula in Greenville, South Carolina, Duke's Mayonnaise ("The Secret of Great Southern Cooks") contains more egg yolks than the other commercial brands and no added sugar.

IT'S ALL IN THE WHISK

True mayonnaise eggheads, however, swear by homemade, even though it's made less often now due to the fear of contracting salmonella from raw eggs. Making mayo isn't difficult—just slow and steady.

The essential ingredients are an egg yolk and oil. Additions may include mustard, vinegar, lemon juice, and different oils and seasonings. Mayonnaise making is all in the whisk (or blender or food processor), because the oil has to be added drop by drop to emulsify with the yolk and then is beaten until a thick cream forms.

It takes about 10 gallons of crude oil to make one gallon of jet fuel.

MAYONN-AIZING FACTS

- The world record for eating mayonnaise is held by Russia's Oleg Zhornitskiy; he ate four 32-ounce bowls in eight minutes.

- In Hispanic markets, Mayonesa con Jugo de Limon (mayonnaise with lime juice) is so popular that, in 2002, Hellman's began marketing it as a separate brand.

- Of the Spanish-speaking countries, Chile is the largest mayonnaise consumer.

- Residents of New Orleans, Louisiana, eat 2.4 times as much mayonnaise as citizens of any other U.S. city; people in Omaha, Nebraska, eat the least.

- The Midwest remains loyal to Miracle Whip, a Depression-era concoction that replaced some of mayonnaise's more expensive fat with starch.

- Mayonnaise can be used in baking to produce moist cakes.

- Mayonnaise is touted for many nonfood uses, including lice removal, hair conditioning, and facial masks. It's even said to be effective for bumper sticker and tar removal from cars. And professional florists swear by it to produce clean and shiny leaves.

*   *   *

THE MOUNT HOREB MUSTARD MUSEUM

In downtown Mount Horeb, Wisconsin, Barry Levenson's World-Famous Mustard Museum opened in 1986 when Levenson started collecting bottles of the spicy yellow stuff. Mustard Museum lore says that, distraught from the Red Sox' World Series loss to the Mets, Levenson drove to his local supermarket and wandered the aisles, eventually picking up 11 bottles.

Those 11 bottles have swollen to 4,800 bottles—and jars, tubes, and packets—from all over the world. The Museum also hosts its annual National Mustard Day on the first Saturday in August and publishes a newsletter. Levenson judges the World-Wide Mustard Competition, whose finals are held at the Napa Valley Mustard Festival.

Scientist Nicola Tesla found pearls revolting—and didn't allow his female employees to wear them.

THE WORLD'S LONGEST STORY AWARD

Peanuts

The trials and tribulations of Charlie Brown and friends played out in 18,250 strips—day by day—for 50 years.

LI'L FOLKS

Creator Charles Schulz wrote *Peanuts* from 1950 until 2000, making it, as one scholar put it, the "longest story ever told by one human being." Actually, the story began even earlier, in Schulz's comic strip *Li'l Folks*, which ran in Minnesota's *St. Paul Pioneer Press* in 1947. That strip included some of the same characters who later showed up in *Peanuts*: a dog that was a lot like Snoopy and a kid named Charlie Brown. *Li'l Folks* was retired in 1950, and Schulz moved on to the strip that made him famous.

GOOD OL' CHARLIE BROWN

When United Features Syndicate picked up *Peanuts* in 1950, it ran in seven newspapers around the United States. (Eventually, more than 2,000 picked it up.) The strip got more elaborate over the years—Schulz added color and more detail—but it was always notable for its simple look and approach to life. The drawings are characterized by spare lines and little background, and the comic's themes and dialogue match that simplicity. In the first *Peanuts* strip on October 2, 1950, two children sat on the sidewalk. One said, "'Well, here comes ol' Charlie Brown!' . . . 'Good ol' Charlie Brown' . . . 'Yes, sir! Good ol' Charlie Brown.'" And then, as Charlie Brown passed them, "How I hate him!"

The characters were always honest, too, in the ways that most children are: they said what they thought and didn't couch their

---

Since 1959, more than 105 million yards of fabric have been used to create Barbie clothes.

opinions in euphemisms. And they were funny. As one critic said, the *Peanuts* gang "brought . . . humor to taboo themes such as faith, intolerance, depression, loneliness, cruelty and despair. [The] characters were contemplative. They spoke with simplicity and force. They made smart observations about literature, art, classical music, theology, medicine, psychiatry, sports and the law."

Peanuts had other unique and endearing aspects, too. In particular, the strip featured a whole cast of characters—rather than just one or two. And the group included types of people most readers could relate to: the nerd, the grouch, the philosopher, the slacker, the jock, the insecure thumbsucker, and the dreamer.

THE PEANUTS GALLERY

Unlike many comic strip artists who collaborated with a number of writers, storyboard artists, and colorists, Schulz produced all aspects of *Peanuts* himself. He worked on the strip everyday, and each of the characters was his own creation. Schulz once told an interviewer that the entire *Peanuts* gang was based on people he knew—his fussy daughter, Meredith, was the inspiration for Lucy, and Charlie Brown's "little red-haired girl" mirrored an unrequited love named Donna Johnson who rejected Schulz's marriage proposal in 1950. Some characters even portrayed aspects of Schulz's personality—he said more than once that Linus represented his spiritual side.

The core cast included the following:

- Charlie Brown, the eternal outsider who never managed to kick a football

- Snoopy, the beagle with the wild imagination and the sardonic wit

- Linus Van Pelt, thumb sucking philosopher king and Charlie Brown's best friend

- Lucy Van Pelt, professional grouch and Linus's older sister

- Sally Brown, Charlie's sunny-tempered little sister

- Woodstock, Snoopy's avian sidekick, prone to mishaps

- Schroeder, the piano prodigy with a Beethoven fixation

- Peppermint Patty, sandal-sporting tomboy

The airline industry purchases six million pounds of peanuts per year.

- Marcie, archetypal best friend and confused sort
- Pigpen, the outcast surrounded by a cloud of dust
- Violet, the snob
- Franklin, scrappy new kid introduced in 1968 and the strip's first African American character
- Rerun, Linus's little brother

Over the years, more kids came and went, but adults remained out of the picture, likely because the philosophical musings and often progressive ideas the characters had were less threatening coming from children. Plus the lack of adults gave the *Peanuts* kids a great deal of self-sufficiency: they had to rely on themselves and each to solve problems.

THE DOCTOR IS IN

Writing the strip also gave Charles Schulz a way to confront his own anxiety. When Lucy set up her counseling stand with a sign reading "The Doctor Is In—5 cents," Schulz was consoling himself as much as Charlie Brown. Depression plagued the artist his entire life. "You can't create humor out of happiness," he wrote in *Charlie Brown, Snoopy and Me*.

Schulz's friend Lynn Johnston, creator of the comic strip *For Better or Worse*, said that Schulz told her in the last year of his life, "You control all these characters and the lives they live. You decide when they get up in the morning, when they're going to fight with their friends, when they're going to lose the game. Isn't it amazing how you have no control over your real life?" Johnston reflected, "[But] I think, in a way, he did." In fact, Schulz spent every day doing what he loved best: drawing.

THE RED BARON

Charlie Brown was the longest-running *Peanuts* character, but the most beloved had to be Snoopy. The beagle was based on Schulz's own childhood pet—a black-and-white-headed hunting dog named Spike. *Ripley's Believe It or Not!* published one of Schultz's illustrations of Spike when Schulz was just 15. Spike also appeared from time to time as Snoopy's brother.

People tend to eat less when food is served on a blue plate.

If any character in the **Peanuts** universe was a revolutionary who did his own thing, it was Snoopy. He was a writer, a thinker, and even a fighter pilot called the World War I Flying Ace who flew his plane . . . ahem, his doghouse . . . in some serious battles trying to shoot down the Red Baron. The dog spent his first two years in the strip quietly going about his canine business, but in 1952, Schulz gave Snoopy a voice via thought balloons. Suddenly, the reader was privy to what the rebellious dog was thinking—and he had a lot of "wise" things to say:

- "Yesterday I was a dog. Today I'm a dog. Tomorrow I'll probably still be a dog. Sigh! There's so little hope for advancement."

- "Sometimes when I get up in the morning, I feel very peculiar. I feel like I've just got to bite a cat! I feel like if I don't bite a cat before sundown, I'll go crazy! But then I just take a deep breath and forget about it. That's what is known as real maturity."

- "My life has no purpose, no direction, no aim, no meaning, and yet I'm happy. I can't figure it out. What am I doing right?"

- "Dear IRS, Please remove me from your mailing list."

- "My life is full of unsuffered consequences . . ."

GOOD GRIEF

"Good grief!" wrote Sally Brown in a school report on night and day: "Daytime is so you can see where you're going. Nighttime is so you can lie in bed worrying." Schulz's obituary mentions that Schulz woke up one night and thought, "Good grief, who are all these little people? Must I live with them for the rest of my life?"

Thankfully for us, he did. The last *Peanuts* daily strip appeared on January 3, 2000. Schulz died at home of colon cancer on February 12, and his last Sunday panel appeared the next day. It included a farewell that read "Charlie Brown, Snoopy, Linus, Lucy . . . how can I ever forget them."

*   *   *

"In the book of life, the answers aren't in the back."

—Charlie Brown

Boxer Gene Tunney made more money in one match than Babe Ruth made in 14 seasons.

THE TROJAN HORSE AWARD

Songs That Don't Say What They Mean

Musicians usually write songs to communicate, but sometimes what they're trying to say gets completely confused.

BABA O'RILEY" BY THE WHO
You think it's about . . . kids getting drunk.
It's really about . . . a futuristic England where the landscape is a wasteland. In 1971, as a follow-up to their rock opera *Tommy*, the Who (well . . . mostly Pete Townshend) penned another play—*Lifehouse*—about a futuristic, severely polluted English society that the government keeps under control with "the Grid," an Internet-like means of surveillance. The term "teenage wasteland" refers to the scrappy kids crossing the polluted countryside, heading for a huge music festival where the story's climax takes place. And the song's name? It has nothing to do with the lyrics. "Baba" comes from Townshend's spiritual guru, Meher Baba, and "O'Riley" from minimalist composer Terry Riley, whom Townshend counted as one of the inspirations for the song's instrumentals.

"SHINY HAPPY PEOPLE" BY R.E.M.
You think it's about . . . shiny, happy people.
It's really about . . . oppression. The song was based on a propaganda poster from Communist China that proclaimed the country full of "shiny, happy people holding hands." Then, in 1989, Stipe was horrified by the Tiananmen Square uprising, when the Chinese government killed hundreds of student protesters. The song was the band's response to both events, but people in the United

States took it as a fun, upbeat tune. The song even appeared on a 1999 episode of *Sesame Street*, in which the "shiny happy people" line was changed to "furry happy monsters" and the band performed with the Muppets.

"THE ONE I LOVE" BY R.E.M.

You think it's . . . a love song.

It's really about . . . using people. This song's meaning has been misinterpreted so many times that lyricist and singer Michael Stipe finally said, "It's probably better that they just think it's a love song at this point." But the line "A simple prop to occupy my time" makes it clear that the song is really about using people and not appreciating a significant other.

"EVERY BREATH YOU TAKE" BY THE POLICE

You think it's . . . a love song.

It's really about . . . obsession and control. Sting wrote the song just after his first marriage fell apart and says, "It sounds like a comforting love song. I didn't realize at the time how sinister it is. I think I was thinking of Big Brother, surveillance, and control."

"WHAT'S THE FREQUENCY, KENNETH?" BY R.E.M.

You think it's about . . . who knows!

It's really about . . . the 1986 attack on CBS news anchor Dan Rather, who was mugged on a New York City sidewalk by a man who shouted, "Kenneth, what's the frequency?" The man, William Tager, thought the media was beaming radio signals into his brain to test their frequencies. He also thought that by attacking Rather (or at least asking the question) he could figure out the frequencies and block the signals from his brain. (Tager proved even crazier nine years later when he shot a stagehand outside the *Today Show*'s studios. He's still in jail for that crime.)

"IN THE AIR TONIGHT" BY PHIL COLLINS

You think it's about . . . the time Phil Collins's friend (or father or someone else) drowned and a bystander did nothing about it.

It's really about . . . how angry Collins was after his 1979 divorce. The urban legends surrounding this song's meaning sprung up in

End to end, the corks from all the wine bottled in France in a year would circle the world 3 times.

the 1980s, and no one knows for sure how they got started. But there were several variations—in some stories, "In the Air Tonight" was about the time Collins's father drowned; in others, it was about his wife being raped and the attacker drowning; still others said it was about a young Collins and a bystander witnessing a drowning but doing nothing to help. All of the stories ended with the bystander being sent a free, front-row ticket to one of Collins's concerts and being serenaded with the dark song. None of it was true. Collins said, "When I was writing this I was going through a divorce. And the only thing I can say about it is that it's obviously [written] in anger. It's the angry side, or the bitter side of a separation."

"WONDERFUL TONIGHT" BY ERIC CLAPTON

You think it's about . . . how beautiful his girlfriend looks.

It's really about . . . waiting impatiently for a girlfriend to get ready so he can leave the house—Eric Clapton was waiting for his girlfriend Pattie Boyd (who later became his wife). The year was 1976, and they were heading for a party thrown by Paul McCartney as a tribute to Buddy Holly. While Boyd kept trying on different outfits, Clapton waited—and came up with the idea for the song. (This was not the only song Boyd inspired. She was also behind Clapton's hit "Layla" and George Harrison's "Something.")

"MARTHA MY DEAR" BY THE BEATLES

You think it's about . . . convincing a lover to stick around.

It's really about . . . well, there are three theories. Paul McCartney wrote the song in 1968 and said that it was about his muse, whom he nicknamed Martha ("Martha my dear, you have always been my inspiration"). But it turns out McCartney had a dog named Martha, so it could be about her. (McCartney has also said he named his dog after his muse.) Finally, McCartney's longtime girlfriend at the time, Jane Asher, could have been the inspiration. She allegedly walked in on him in bed with another woman and broke off their relationship. (Apparently, she wasn't won back by the lyric "Help yourself to a bit of what is all around you.")

THE "IT TAKES TWO" AWARD

The Tango

*In its heyday, the tango was considered more
subversive than rock 'n' roll. Saucy!*

DANCE SOLO
There are many theories about how the tango got started
in Argentina: Some say it came over with African slaves.
Others claim it evolved from a flamenco-like dance women performed alone. Both of these probably did influence the early
tango, but the dance as we know it today was born in the mid- to
late 1800s in the tenement blocks of Buenos Aires, where residents gathered in the evenings to play music. The communities
were melting pots of people—from Africa, Europe, and so on—
who blended styles to form a new kind of "street" dance."

The tango got a reputation for being a favorite in the city's
brothels likely because the madams hired tango musicians to
entertain clients while they waited for their dates. Argentina, in
the 1850s, had many more men than women, the result of an
influx of European immigrants who arrived to build the country's
railroad. When the men arrived at the city's brothels, they usually
had to wait their turn. So they listened to music and they danced,
often alone or with other men for partners.

And what of the name—"tango"? There are many theories
about its origin as well, but most likely, the word came from Spanish . . . tango was a type of Spanish music, even though the music
we now consider "tango" is different from the original.

PARIS IS BURNING
In the early 20th century, the tango traveled to Europe, reaching
France via the port town of Marseille courtesy of visiting Argen-

tinean sailors. By 1909, a couple had performed the tango on a stage in Montmartre, and by 1912, the dance was embraced by all classes of Parisians. Fashions began to change as a result, as Parisian women stopped wearing constraining corsets so they could dance more easily. Shops sold new styles of skirts (with openings in the front), new hats (with a feather pointing up instead of across a woman's face, so it wouldn't get in her tango partner's way) stockings, and shoes. And orange became the most popular color in dancehalls all over the city. Of course, Parisians' tastes soon set the standard for the rest of the world.

Just a year later, people were dancing the tango all over the Western world. In 1913, the Waldorf Hotel in London began holding Tango Teas to cater to the people who were enjoying this new dance. Professional dance couples demonstrated the dance in fashionable restaurants. Tango was equally popular in New York City and was embraced famously by Hollywood actor Rudolf Valentino, who danced it in 1921's *Four Horsemen of the Apocalypse*.

With all this international success, the tango returned to Argentina a new dance: no longer hidden away in the tenements and brothels of Buenos Aires, it was suddenly popular with the upper classes in its hometown. In the 1930s, Argentina's status in the world grew—it became one of the richest nations. And the tango was seen internationally as a fun and exciting expression of Argentinean culture.

THE GOLDEN AGE

It was the rise to power of one of the country's most infamous couples, though, that really brought the tango into its own. Socialists Juan and Eva Peron became the president and first lady of Argentina in 1946, and they ushered in the tango's Golden Age. The tango has always been a dance of the people, and the Perons (who billed themselves as the rulers of the people) promoted it in order to appeal to the middle and lower classes who'd elected them. The couple also supported tango artists and even hired them to work in Peron's administration.

But when Peron was overthrown by a military coup (supported by the upper classes) in 1955, the tango went underground. The upper class of Argentina was now in charge, and they frowned on the dance. They also didn't want to support anything Peron had supported. Although not forbidden by law, the suppression of certain songs and the enforcement of curfews made it difficult for clubs to attract customers who'd previously gone out on the town to dance the tango. Also, the new military government imprisoned many of the tango artists Peron had hired.

Argentina's ruling class even began to enforce laws that kept minors out of dance clubs . . . but only clubs where the tango was danced. Minors in Argentina were free to frequent rock 'n' roll clubs, which were considered less dangerous and less likely to promote unrest. It wasn't until 1983, when the military government was overthrown in Argentina, that the tango regained its proper place in the country's culture. Free to learn and practice the dance, Argentineans once again took to the dance floor. As for the rest of the world, they'd continued dancing the tango all along.

THE BASIC STEPS

Many variations of the tango exist around the world, and the American tango is different from the Argentinean tango. But if you want to do a basic tango, here are the steps you need to know:

- The tango has five steps performed over eight counts. Basically, it's a slow walk followed by a quick one. The five steps are counted out: "Slow, Slow, Quick, Quick, Slow." Some people like to spell out the dance: "T-A-N-G-O." (Whatever helps.)

- For the first three steps, the man moves his left, right, and then left food forward. The fourth is a shuffle of the right foot to the right, followed by bringing the left foot into the right. The woman mirrors these movements.

(And please, remember: Uncle John bears no responsibility for awkward tangos performed as a result of reading these instructions.)

*   *   *

"The forms of tango are like stages of a marriage. The American tango is like the beginning of a love affair . . . The Argentine tango is when you're in the heat of things . . . The International tango is like the end of the marriage, when you're staying together for the sake of the children."

—Barbara Garvey, *Smithsonian* magazine

Potatoes were the first vegetables grown in space, in 1995.

THE SHOE-BIZ AWARD

Crocs

*Distinctive and ugly, Crocs clogs haven't
worn out their welcome . . . yet.*

NOT JUST FOR THE OUTDOORS ANYMORE
Love them or hate them, Crocs are everywhere. After becoming standard professional footwear among medical staffers and kitchen pros, Crocs leapt into the fashion mainstream. From Hollywood to high schools to the White House, these clunky, colorful, clown-like clogs are a sensation.

In 2007, Crocs (the company) claimed a 138 percent leap in sales with annual revenues surging from $354 million to $847 million. Analysts predict that demand will continue to be strong with estimated 2008 sales of a whopping $1.16 billion. The manufacturers' recent expansion into foreign markets is credited with fueling Crocs' amazing growth. And to think, Crocs creators designed the shoes solely with boating and outdoors activities in mind.

CROCS CRAWL OUT OF THE WATER
Back in 2002, three fishing buddies from Boulder, Colorado— George Boedecker, Scott Seamans, and Duke Hanson—happened on a new breed of slip-resistant, nonmarking footwear made by a Canadian company called Foam Creations, Inc. The enterprising threesome licensed the clever clog, added a strap to the shoe's design, and dumped the utilitarian name in the process. They introduced the now-classic Croc Beach Model at that year's Florida Boat Show—it sold out in two days. From that moment on, their venture took off like wild . . . rubber.

But contrary to popular opinion, Crocs are not made from rubber. According to the company, their clogs are made from a proprietary closed-cell resin called Croslite. It is Croslite that accounts for the shoe's legendary comfort, softness, super gripping power, and odor resistance.

What Croslite doesn't account for is the polarizing opinions about Crocs. We're talking fierce convictions on both sides of the fence.

LOVE IS A MANY JIBBITZED THING

In one corner are the Crocs fans, which have been known to liken the experience of wearing a pair to "walking on air," they adhere to the company's advertisements, which promote that "ugly can be beautiful." In fact, part of the shoes' appeal seems to be their unattractive character, with enthusiasts zealously focusing on comfort and function over looks.

That said, devotees have tried to doll up their Crocs, spawning a whole new fashion fad. Enter Jibbitz, a company that makes charms created to decorate Crocs of all shapes, sizes, and colors. Like Crocs, Jibbitz was founded in Boulder, Colorado. In 2005, Sheri Schmelzer, a stay-at-home mom, was inspired to decorate her kids' Crocs with clay and rhinestone charms that she fit in the clogs' aerating holes. Thinking she was on to something, her husband encouraged her to craft an entire collection.

The couple set up shop in their basement, selling their charms via the Web under the name Jibbitz, which came from Mrs. Schmelzer's nickname, "Flibberty-Jibbit." A year later, Jibbitz weren't just available on the Internet—they were also stocked in thousands of stores across the country. Then, in 2006, Crocs bought the Schmelzers' company. Now, Crocs fans can decorate their shoes with 11,000 Jibbitz designs—everything from peace signs to butterflies to smiley faces.

CROC CONTEMPT

In the other corner are the Croc-haters, and they are a vehement bunch. Two detractors in particular, Kate Leth and Vincenzo Ravina, launched a Web site called IHateCrocs.com, "dedicated to the elimination of Crocs and those who think their excuses for wearing them are viable." The pair also began a Croc-hating group on Facebook. And just to take their social media anti-Crocs cam-

---

According to NASA, the foods astronauts miss the most are pizza, ice cream, and soda.

paign one step further, Leth and Ravina posted a Croc-burning video on YouTube.

The media doesn't help, either. Not long ago, the Crocs company got some negative press when reports surfaced in the blogosphere about Croc-wearing kids being harmed on escalators because of the shoes. Then a Swedish hospital considered asking its staff to stop wearing Crocs clogs, saying that static electricity from the shoes was to blame for knocking out medical equipment on three different occasions.

Luckily for Crocs, the shoes seemed to beat the bad press for the time being, with sales continuing to skyrocket. And only time will tell if Crocs are enduring statements of style or simply a crock.

CROCOPHILES

- Jack Nicholson has been seen sporting a baby blue pair.
- Rosie O'Donnell appears to prefer them in hot pink or sunshine yellow.
- President George W. Bush likes to wear his black Crocs with black socks and shorts.
- Country crossover music artist Faith Hill is faithful to subdued beige.
- Celebrity Chef Mario Batali never seems to take his bright orange pair off, even deigning to wear them at red-carpet events.

*   *   *

TWO TRENDSETTING UGLY SHOES

Earth Shoes: The "Negative Heel Technology" just means that the heel sits lower than the toe. Supposedly Earth Shoes mimic the action of walking in beach sand. They've been a favorite of the hippie set since the 1960s and are currently enjoying a renaissance.

Uggs: Skin-out, shearling-in shoes have long worked for sheep shearers and other folks who need to keep their feet warm, but they've always been known as "ugh," "fug," or "ug" boots. In the first millennial decade, these shapeless beige booties became a celeb must-have.

THE BRIGHT STAR AWARD

Marilyn Monroe

Beautiful, sexy, glamorous, legendary, and never out of style—Marilyn Monroe gets Uncle John's vote for being Hollywood's most enduring icon.

HEY, MARILYN

Most people know that Marilyn Monroe was born Norma Jeane Mortenson (later Baker) in Los Angeles in 1926, and that her early life was, as her *New York Times* obituary states, "Oliver Twist in girl's clothing." No wonder she married as soon as she could (at age 16 in 1942, to her 21-year-old neighbor Jimmy Dougherty). Four years later, she divorced Dougherty, changed her name to Marilyn Monroe, and launched her acting career. She became an inspiration for the likes of Madonna, Elton John, and Norman Mailer, who wrote a 1986 play about her called *Strawhead.*

Her career was brief but prolific: she made *All About Eve* in 1950, gained stardom with *Niagara* in 1953, and appeared in 28 other films before she died in 1962. Yet, Marilyn Monroe's image still appears in magazines and television commercials. She got her own postage stamp in 1995. And in 1999, *People* magazine voted her "Sexiest Woman of the Century." In 2004, her estate earned $8 million, and she was sixth on the Forbes list of top-earning dead celebrities. (Elvis was first at $40 million.) Not bad for someone who's been dead for almost 50 years.

MISS GOLDEN DREAMS

She was, of course, also an incredibly pretty face and often used that, along with her feisty sense of humor, to bolster her image. In 1952, Marilyn got her first chance to solidify that sassy "sex symbol" image when photographer Tom Kelley sold a series of nude photographs of her to Hugh Hefner, who had a new magazine in the works: *Playboy*. The pictures had been taken in 1949, during a period when she was unemployed—Kelley paid her $50 for the photo session—and they were published first as a pin-up calendar called "Miss Golden Dreams." In 1952, the photos resurfaced, and an anonymous blackmailer threatened to expose her as Miss Golden Dreams. Rather than deny the story or even ignore it, Marilyn took questions on the subject: When asked about being nude at the photo shoot, she said, "It's not true I had nothing on. I had the radio on." When asked why she posed for the pictures, she said, "I was hungry."

Hefner then bought the photos and published them in 1953, in the first issue of his new magazine. One of the images—Marilyn Monroe lying on a wrinkled velvet sheet—became the first *Playboy* "Sweetheart of the Month," the precursor to the magazine's centerfold. Marilyn was on the cover, too.

MORE THAN JUST A BOMBSHELL

But she wasn't content just to be just a pretty face. She once said, "Being a sex symbol is a heavy load to carry, especially when one is tired, hurt, and bewildered." Monroe wanted to be considered a good actress too, and for the most part, she was. She was nominated for four Golden Globe Awards and won three times: Best Actress in a Musical or Comedy for *Some Like It Hot* (1960) and World Female Film Favorite (1953 and 1962). Sir Lawrence Olivier once remarked that she was "a brilliant comedienne, which to me means she is also an extremely skilled actress."

"BYE, BYE MISS AMERICAN PIE"

Marilyn Monroe died on August 5, 1962, and though her death was ruled a probable suicide, rumors that she was murdered abound. But we like to remember her as a tough, talented, enduring star who, as Darryl Zanuck, the former president of 20th Century Fox said, "earned her own way to stardom."

And of course it's Hollywood, so with all that notoriety comes myth and the occasional truth. Here are some of the most incredible legends about the legend:

- **Monroe had six toes:** Supposedly a 1946 photograph seems to show that she had a sixth toe on her right foot, and the rumor is that she had the extra digit surgically removed before she became a star. Her first husband Jimmy Dougherty, however, always said that was absolutely false—both of her feet just had the regular five toes.

- **She was the inspiration for** "Miss American Pie" in Don McLean's song, "American Pie": Maybe. Many people believe that McLean's blockbuster hit mentions Monroe in its chorus: "Bye, Bye Miss American Pie . . ." It seems plausible, since the song references other nostalgic icons of the 1950s and 1960s (Buddy Holly, Ritchie Valens, and so on). But we couldn't find any evidence that McLean himself ever confirmed the rumor.

- **She took 20 capsules of Nembutal every day:** This is true. In 1961, while working on her last film *The Misfits*, Monroe took 20 of these pills every day. She even pricked them with a pin before swallowing them so they'd work more quickly.

- **After she died,** second husband Joe DiMaggio had fresh roses delivered to Monroe's crypt three times a week until 1982. He also never spoke about her publicly, never wrote a tell-all book, and never remarried.

- **Tinker Bell in the 1953 Disney version of *Peter Pan*** was modeled after Marilyn Monroe: Not true. Actress Margaret Kerry was the model for blond, sassy Tink.

- **Marilyn Monroe** wore a size 16 dress: Well . . . kind of. Dress sizes were different in the 1950s, so she might have worn a size 16 dress at one time, but given her measurements—37-23-36 (studio's claim), 35-22-35 (dressmaker's claim)—she was more likely a modern size 12.

*   *   *

"I knew I belonged to the public and to the world, not because I was talented or even beautiful, but because I had never belonged to anything or anyone else."

—Marilyn Monroe

All-time bestselling lunch box: The Walt Disney School Bus (9 million sold from 1961–73).

THE FUN IN A CAN AWARD

Play-Doh

The smell of Play-Doh is a staple in classrooms, playrooms, and nurseries around the country. It's also worthy of a Golden Plunger.

A FUN DISCOVERY

The story of Play-Doh is quintessentially American, from invention to patent to market success. When her husband Cleo died in 1949, Irma McVicker hired son Joseph to run his company, Kutol Products, which specialized in the manufacture of soap and wallpaper cleaner. On May 17, 1960, a patent was granted to Noah McVicker (a relative and company manager) and Joseph McVicker for a "plastic modeling composition of a soft, playable working consistency." They got the patent, but they hadn't been searching for modeling clay at all. Joseph was investigating wallpaper cleaner and stumbled onto an alternate use for the substance.

Joseph's sister-in-law Kay was a teacher in New Jersey. After seeing an article in a magazine about making Christmas tree ornaments out of wallpaper cleaner, she drove to the nearest hardware store and bought their only can (which happened to be Kutol's . . . small world). Her nursery class had a great time playing with the "dough."

When word about the success of the cleaner with the school children reached Joseph, he and Noah proceeded to test the product in numerous nursery and elementary schools around the country. Once its properties as a toy had been established (it was clean, easy to model, and could be reused), Noah and Joseph founded Rainbow Crafts to start manufacturing the new product. Play-Doh made its official debut in 1956 at the Woodward & Lothrop department store in Washington, D.C. The white compound came in a 1½-pound cardboard can. By 1965, Joseph and Noah McVicker were millionaires.

A LOT OF DOH

For nearly 20 years, Play-Doh came in just four colors: white, red, yellow, and blue. White, of course, was introduced in 1956, and the three primary colors—red, blue, and yellow—appeared a year later. It wasn't until 1983 that four more colors were introduced. Now the kiddie modeling compound is available in 50 colors (including gold and silver), and more than 900 million pounds have been sold in the past 50 years. Factories produce about 95 million cans of Play-Doh annually for 6,000 U.S. stores and 75 different countries.

SECRET RECIPE

No one has ever revealed Play-Doh's exact formula, but Hasbro (the company that now manufactures it) does let people know that the dough contains water, salt, and flour—and no peanuts, peanut oil, or milk, all well-known allergens. (It does contain wheat, though.) According to its current patent, the stuff also is made with water, a starch-based binder, retrogradation inhibitor, salt, lubricant, surfactant, preservative, hardener, humectant, fragrance, and color. Not exactly a wholesome snack—but ultimately harmless.

PLAY-DOH FACTS

- Play-Doh was put into plastic cans in 1986, which kept the tightly capped dough soft and pliable for longer periods of time.

- In 1960, the first Play-Doh Fun Factory was introduced. Basically just a souped-up pasta maker made out of plastic, the lever-based device allowed kids to make different kinds of ropes and discs of Doh.

- For years, Play-Doh cans and labels were graced with the impish cartoon of Play-Doh Pete, who morphed from an elf to a beret-wearing boy in 1960 and then traded his headgear for a baseball cap in the 1970s.

- One of the most popular sets ever made was 1977's Fuzzy Pumper Barber and Beauty Shop Playset (known from the start simply as the Play-Doh Barber Shop). The barbershop exists today in a new incarnation—the Fuzzy Pumper Pet Parlor.

One cubic foot of gold weighs 1,206 pounds. (A cubic foot of lead weighs 708 pounds.)

THE "THAT'S THE WAY THE BALL BOUNCES" AWARD

Bill Buckner's Error in Game 6

It was the roll heard 'round the world . . . or at least 'round the country.

The setting: Game 6 of the World Series, October 25, 1986. The location: Shea Stadium, New York City.

The opponents: The New York Mets and the Boston Red Sox, long thought to be suffering under the dreaded "Curse of the Bambino."

AH, THE CURSE

Back in 1919, the Boston Red Sox were a force to be reckoned with in baseball. They had won the first World Series in 1903 (when they were called the Americans) and they did it again in 1912, '15, '16, and '18—that last one due in large part to their star player, Babe Ruth.

Ruth was, and remains, the ultimate baseball player. He started with the Red Sox as a pitcher in 1914 but moved on to play first base and the outfield. Over his career, he hit a total of 714 home runs. Despite Ruth's accomplishments, the Red Sox's owner, Harry Frazee, sold him to the New York Yankees on January 2, 1920. (Frazee needed the money to finance a play his girlfriend was writing.) Things would never be the same again for the Red Sox. The smashing successes they'd enjoyed all those years came to an end, and the team didn't win another World Series until 2004—eighty-six years later!

Fans started calling the event the "Curse of the Bambino" because the losing streak started with Ruth's departure, and the

Great Bambino was one of his nicknames. Whether or not the curse was real, the Red Sox did make it to the World Series four times, losing each time. But on October 25, 1986, the outcome could have been very different. But unbeknownst to Red Sox fans, their team was battling not only their own bad luck but that of the Chicago Cubs. That's right—if you're a superstitious sports fan (and is there any other kind?), Game 6 was the night of the double curse.

BATTER UP

After a tough but triumphant season, the 1986 Red Sox were back in the World Series. Their opponents were the New York Mets. Spirits in Boston were riding high, and they only got higher when the team won the first two games of the seven-game series. Boston's hopes diminished when the Mets won the following two games. But a Red Sox win in Game 5 put the team back on track. Just one more victory was all they needed to banish the curse forever.

Game 6 was a hard-fought battle that saw the teams tied at the end of nine innings. In the top of the tenth, Boston scored two runs, taking the lead at 5–3. When the Mets stepped to the plate in the bottom of the tenth and recorded two outs relatively quickly, millions of baseball fans were already preparing for a Red Sox victory.

But that third out would prove elusive. Three consecutive hits produced one run. Then Mets' left fielder Mookie Wilson took his turn—an at-bat that would live on in baseball history forever. First came a toss from pitcher Bob Stanley that went wild, passed catcher Rich Gedman, and allowed one more Met to score. The game was now tied, and a runner was in scoring position.

The scene was intense: More pitches were thrown. The count was full. Then came the pitch that Wilson connected with—an easy grounder to Red Sox first baseman Bill Buckner, 36 years old and an 18-year Major League veteran. Inexplicably, Buckner, who had made easy plays like this thousands of times, missed the ball. It rolled into the outfield. The Mets scored and history was made—the hearts of millions of Red Sox fans were broken.

TWO CURSES IN ONE

It was 17 years before anyone noticed an oddity about Buckner during the infamous play. While the play itself had been dissected more times than anyone could count, 12-year-old Kevin Mahon, the son of a sports reporter for the *Philadelphia Daily News*, noticed what no one else had. Buckner was wearing a Chicago Cubs batting glove. Mahon's father wrote about the astonishing discovery in his October 2003 sports column.

Buckner had formerly played for the Chicago Cubs, so it's not shocking that he had one of their batting gloves. What's shocking is that he would wear it at such a pivotal moment in baseball history. Sports fans know that the Cubs have their own curse to contend with. According to legend, Chicago tavern owner William "Billy Goat" Sianis tried to bring his pet goat to Game 4 of the 1945 World Series, when the Cubs were playing the Detroit Tigers. Attendants stopped Sianis and the goat before they could enter Wrigley Field, saying the man could come in, but the goat wasn't welcome because "he stinks!" Angry and offended, Sianis cursed Wrigley Field (and the Cubs) with the infamous Billy Goat Curse. The Cubs haven't been back to the World Series since.

To make matters even worse for Buckner, he wasn't wearing the Cubs batting glove earlier in the evening. Pictures of his at-bats show dark batting gloves. He put the Cubs batting glove on later.

The Curse of the Bambino combined with the Billy Goat Curse? For superstitious sports fans, the pairing was just too much.

AN UNFORTUNATE PREDICTION

Now hear this: On October 7, 1986, just two weeks prior to Game 6, Buckner gave an interview to a local Boston news program and provided what can only be described as a strange and sadly prophetic quote:

> The dreams are that you are going to have a great series and win, and the nightmares are that you are going to let the winning run score on a ground ball through your legs. Those things happen, and I think a lot of it is just fate.

Speculation as to why Buckner missed the ball ranges from Buckner having bad ankles and arthritis in his knees (preventing him from easily bending over to scoop the ball) to the chilly weather of that late autumn evening. But speculation aside, Buckner later said the slip was simply the result of a bad bounce the ball took. Even if Bucker had managed to scoop the ball, there was still the chance that Wilson could have made it to first before

Buckner. And the score was already tied due to two errors from right fielder Dwight Evans and catcher Gedman. But the lasting legacy of Game 6 is still Buckner's mistake.

THINGS GET OUT OF HAND

The next season, the Red Sox released Buckner. He went on to play with the California Angels and the Kansas City Royals before returning to Boston for a final year in 1990. After that, he retired to Idaho, where he didn't have to deal with irate Red Sox fans anymore.

Despite having 2,715 career hits, Buckner is still best (and maybe only) remembered for the infamous error that helped keep the Curse of the Bambino alive until 2004, when the Red Sox finally won another World Series.

For years, Buckner refused to sign anything related to Game 6, but that outlook has changed: Interested sports collectors can now own a picture of the infamous event signed by both Buckner and Mookie Wilson. And in 1992, actor Charlie Sheen scooped up the historic ball for the price of $93,000. He auctioned it off, along with his other baseball memorabilia, in 2000. The ball now resides with songwriter Seth Swirsky.

The memory of Buckner's great mistake still resides in the minds of Red Sox fans. All may have been forgiven when the team won the 2004 World Series, but the fateful night of October 25, 1986, has definitely not been forgotten. It stands as a lesson that one curse might be broken, but when you put two together, you just don't have a chance.

*   *   *

WHOOPS!

In the 1984 NBA draft, Portland had the #2 pick, and guard Michael Jordan of North Carolina was available. Instead, Portland took Kentucky center Sam Bowie, passing on Jordan because they already had a star guard, Clyde Drexler. Jordan went as the #3 pick to the Chicago Bulls and became one of the best basketball players ever. Bowie was a reserve player for the next decade for several teams, averaging 10 points per game.

THE WISH YOU WEREN'T HERE AWARD

Pop-Ups

Pop-up ads shake, dance, and flash seizure-incuding pink letters at you. (Other than that, they're great.)

INTERNET IRRITANTS

So many things about the Internet experience are irritating. Everyone hates spam, and the creators of those e-mails are always finding new ways to get around spam-blockers. But you don't have to open those spam e-mails, and they're easy to delete.

Pop-up windows, though, are almost universally reviled and show no signs of disappearing. They appear when you least expect them, sometimes slowing down the bandwidth of your computer, sometimes using voices and sounds to announce their presence, and often using lots of flashing lights and colors to get your attention.

Let's include pop-unders, too. Those are the windows that open behind a Web page, so you don't notice them until you close or minimize the window. They can sit there unnoticed on your computer for a long time—lurking, waiting.

In theory, pop-unders were created to be less intrusive. So many users had complained about pop-ups appearing and covering up their Web pages that Internet designers tried to hide them down below. It may sound good, but let's face it: people like to see what's going on with their computers.

NOW YOU SEE IT

Dr. Jakob Nielsen, a Web-design expert who founded the online research company Nielsen Norman Group, has done some studies

---

on how people act online. Most importantly, he wanted to know how a computer-user's eyes react. Overwhelmingly, people don't look at static ads. In fact, they don't even look at regular Web site content that looks like an ad.

This is why pop-ups are so popular. Advertisers know they're ticking off their potential customers by using pop-ups, but studies have found that pop-ups work. Advertising.com reported in 2003 that users clicked on pop-up ads 13 percent more often than they did with banner ads. And Web sites that allow them can earn four times as much for a pop-up ad than for a banner ad.

NEW TRICKS

As users become savvier to the ways of the pop-up, advertisers, too, have become slyer. The most successful pop-up ads, according to Nielsen, are the ones that look like dialog boxes. They look harmless enough, but if you try to click the "close" button, they take you to another page. Deception is the name of the game. Crawling pop-ups, sometimes featuring cute animated characters, are here to stay. Hiding the way to close a pop-up is a new method, too. The longer it takes a user to shut down the pop-up, the longer the ad has the person's attention.

By far, though, the worst offender in the pop-up world is a spyware program, one of the many reasons some people are afraid to go online. If you download a file or program, you could be getting more than you intended because when spyware gets loaded onto your computer, you're in trouble. Spyware can clog up your computer with unwanted programs that monitor your Internet usage and generate unwanted pop-up ads. It's enough to make people fear they will never be free of the ads. But don't give up hope just yet.

STOPPING THE POP

As recently as 2002, Forrester Research, which focuses on the technology sector, reported that only one percent of American Web users had pop-up blockers installed on their computers. But by 2006, Forrester noted that more than half of all users in the United States were using them. Pop-ups are starting to decline as more and more users install pop-up blockers. Advertising.com noted in 2006 that, for the first time in years, pop-up ads were not expected to be profitable for advertisers. Finally!

Actor William H. Macy once told a reporter that he believes he was a golden retriever in a past life.

THE GANDER AWARD

Female-Inspired Men's Wear

Murses, utilikilts, and mirdles—what's good for the goose is getting tried out on the gander. Uncle John applauds the fashion industry for its open-mindedness.

A LOT OF BAGGAGE

Men have long been known for flexing their muscles, but nowadays they're just as likely to be found flexing their fashion sense. We're not talking just about men wearing colorful clothes or designer jeans. The most current men's wear trend involves borrowing from the ladies. Metrosexuals—those style-conscious heterosexual men—helped break the ice. And these latest looks for men may be based on personal appearance perfection, but they're also focused on practicality.

American men have been laughing at European "man-purses" for decades. (Remember the *Seinfeld* episode when Jerry carried one?) The small, square leather bags with shoulder straps reminded late 20th-century guys too much of the handbags the women in their life carried. To be a real man meant you couldn't leave the house with anything but a simple wallet. (Briefcases were OK for the deskbound, and male students were allowed backpacks.)

In recent years, though, the trend toward bags for both sexes has spilled over into urban chic. After all, it's a lot easier to tote your cell phone, work files, energy bars, and bottle of water if you've got a bag instead of just a back pocket.

For their part, designers have come out with all manner of "murses" (i.e., man purses), from the clean-lined Jack Spade flap bag to the high-end Louis Vuitton Geronimo bag to ubiquitous

---

The *New Yorker* magazine has more subscribers in California than in New York.

(and vegan-friendly) nylon laptop bags. Many designers are also now creating rectangular or square bags with shoulder straps. Nowadays, you can find a man bag that's suitable for any taste, style, or use.

TOO SEXY FOR YOUR SKIRT
There are kilts for Scotsmen, sarongs for Sri Lankans, cassocks for priests, djellabahs for Moroccans, and dashikis . . . Wait! Men have been wearing skirts and dresses for how long? Plenty of native and ethnic costume variations include skirts for men, but over the centuries, Western culture developed a definite pants-for-boys and skirts-for-girls mentality—and impressed it on other cultures around the globe.

One group advocating a change in this mentality is the Bravehearts, "an international band of men who enjoy the freedom, comfort, pleasure, and masculine appearance of kilts or other male unbifurcated (skirt-like) garments, and who reject the absurd notion that males must always be confined to trousers." The Bravehearts call their man-skirts "unbifurcated garments," MUGs for short.

The best-known U.S. purveyor of MUGs is the Utilitkilt Company, which makes kilt-like pleated skirts for men with many of the same features of men's cargo and work pants. (Their "Survival Model" claims to accommodate up to 20 bottles of water or energy drinks.) These man-skirts aren't cheap; they start at about $140 for a basic model, and the all-leather version is well over $600. Like its Scottish predecessor, the Utilikilt derives its comfort and versatility from its pleats, which require many more yards of fabric than the typical women's straight short skirt would . . . hence the cost.

MIDDLESEX
Modern women felt oppressed by the girdle, so now they're compressed instead by stretchy bodyshapers. Why shouldn't guys be able to take advantage of more comfortable shapewear, too?

As the *Wall Street Journal* pointed out, the latest "mirdles" (man girdles) aren't really anything new. Nineteenth-century men could choose from gender-specific items at the local corsetiere, and Go Softwear, a company that now is having great success with men's shapewear, was basically laughed out of the market in the late 1990s when it first attempted to sell its male paunch-slimmers. Now that men in their twenties and thirties have gotten used to the idea of holding it all together with a little help from some Lycra, they're looking for specific garments.

WHAT'S NEXT, GUYS? "MAN-TY HOSE?"

In a word . . . yes. Activskin, a Missouri-based company, sells what they call "NOT your mother's pantyhose!" These full-cover tights are made specifically for men. As the company's ads say, "Think of it as invisible underwear and socks for men!" (Although you needn't shave your legs like the male models in their ads.)

Activskin isn't a novelty—there are a couple of dozen companies around the world that make men's pantyhose, stockings, and knee-high hosiery. The items are marketed to improve athletic performance, to energize muscles, and to improve circulation (compression from hose or tights can help reduce swelling and decrease the dangers of circulatory problems). Of course, there also just may be some men who like the soft, smooth feeling of hose beneath slacks . . . like the ladies do.

*   *   *

FRANK COSTANZA'S FINEST MOMENT

In Season 6, Episode 17 of *Seinfeld*, Frank Costanza was living with his son George. When he took off his shirt, George and Kramer saw that Frank had developed the dreaded "man boobs," and Kramer decided to invent an undergarment to solve the problem. The duo wanted to market a garment for "older men who have excess flab in the upper chest area that gives the appearance of having breasts."

Of course, solving a problem on *Seinfeld* just means creating another problem. When they pitched the idea to a lingerie company, the trio couldn't decide on a name. Kramer wanted to call their new undergarment the "bro," but Frank deemed that name "too ethnic" and proposed that it be the "manziere."

THE PLAIN AND SIMPLE AWARD

The Golf Tee

*Sometimes the simplest things aren't just
the best—they're one of a kind.*

YOU SAY TIGH, I SAY TEE

We know golf originated in Scotland, even if we don't know exactly when: a game called "gowf" was being played in the 15th century, but it may have been more like modern field hockey than golf. However, by the 17th century, the precursor of modern golf was definitely being played on the "auld sod."

In early golf, the area in which the ball could be played was known as the "tigh," or "house," which referred to the circle around the ball. The first "appliance" for the tigh area wasn't invented until 1882, when Scottish golfers William Bloxsom and Arthur Douglas patented a device made from rubber that had three vertical rubber prongs to keep it upright. However, this "tee" did not pierce the ground, so it was unsteady.

A few others tried to make a moveable golf tee: Percy Ellis's 1892 "Perfectum" tee did pierce the ground, and Scotsman P. M. Matthews' was the first American to patent a tee device.

A PATENT GRANT-ED

However, it took a dentist (perhaps owing to familiarity with rooting teeth in gums) to devise a golf tee worthy of future generations. Dr. George Grant graduated from Harvard Dental School in 1870, one of the first two African Americans to do so, and was an avid golfer. In 1899, Grant applied for (and received) a patent for his golf tee design. Like many golfers before him, Grant had grown frustrated trying to keep the ball from rolling away in his tee-off attempts. He didn't want to take a swing at a moving ball and

---

First non-human to be *Time* magazine's "Person of the Year": the Personal Computer (1983).

send off a wild shot. So he came up with a device that held the ball (then made of rubber) in place and raised it just enough off of the ground so that a player could control the direction and speed of his drive.

TEE'D OFF

Grant's innovation didn't catch on in golf circles. No one is sure why, but for at least two decades, most golfers continued to use small piles of sand to tee off. The golf club provided the sand, which is why many golfers still refer to the "teeing ground"—the place where they tee off—as "tee boxes." (The sand also proved useful for filling in divots on the course.)

It wasn't until 1922 when Dr. William Lowell, Sr. (interestingly enough, also a dentist) patented and began marketing his "Reddy Tee"—a simple (red, so it was easy to see) wooden peg like Grant's, but with a flared top—that the golf tee became the sport's must-have accessory. And although there have been some minor innovations since 1922, Lowell's flared wooden peg is still the basic, must-have golf tee: about two and one-eighth inches long and now available in a variety of colors so that groups can identify each other's tee-off points.

TEE TIME

The last few years brought one major design change to golf tees—also developed by a dentist. (At this point, we have to wonder whether or not all this dental golf inventiveness had more to do with technical expertise or time spent on the green.) Dr. Arnold DiLaura invented the Sof-Tee which allowed the tee to sit on top of the ground rather than burrow into it.

Others updated traditional flared tees. There's a metal, zero-friction tee; flavored tees (yes, wooden tees that can be sucked on like toothpicks); and high-performance FlexTees.

Of course, the magic of any golf tee—old, new, metal, plastic, plain or grape-flavored—is that it just might promise a great shot. No wonder it took golfers nearly 300 years to change from sandy tee boxes to a wooden peg, and another 70 or 80 years to try something different. There's no tee like a tried-and-true tee.

THE MEDIEVAL MEDICINE AWARD

Maggots and Leeches

*This might sting a little bit—and maybe make
you squirm—but it's for your own good.*

EWWW!
A few hundred years ago, leeches seemed like the answer to everything that ailed a person. Whether it be fever, flu, headaches, hemorrhoids, or something else—a little bloodletting would clear the problem right up. The first documented use of leeches was by Hippocrates in the 5th century B.C., but the worms' medicinal use is believed to predate even that.

Although maggots have not been used medicinally as long, they have been used for hundreds of years to clean out wounds and prevent infection. They were especially in vogue in the 19th century, before the development of antibiotics. In the 1920s, maggots were often used by U.S. doctors to treat tuberculosis and bone marrow bacterial infections. By the 1940s, the medical community had abandoned them in favor or surgical and medicinal treatments.

Now, both leeches and maggots have staged comebacks and are rising stars in the medical community. In July 2005, the FDA classified them as medical devices, which—like a stethoscope or a defibrillator—means that maggots and leeches can now be used for diagnostic or therapeutic purposes, and doctors across the country are now ordering maggots to the tune of up to 5,000 per week.

FLY BY NIGHT

Maggots are involved in a process called *debridement*, the removal of dead or diseased tissue to allow healthy tissue to grow or for semihealthy tissue to repair itself. Maggots work so well because they eat only dead tissue—they have no interest in healthy living tissue. Plus, they excrete a substance that includes an antibiotic that helps clean wounds and keeps out bacteria.

A maggot's performance in treating a wound is actually better than a human surgeon's because the insect stops as soon as it comes across healthy tissue. A surgeon doesn't have the ability to be that precise; when a surgeon cuts away dead tissue, he always takes away good tissue, too.

Maggot debridement lasts two or three days on most wounds. The tiny 1 mm-long maggots are put in the affected area, a gauze pad is placed over it to keep them from wandering off, and they get busy doing what they do best—eating. Patients come back at the end of the treatment and the gauze is removed. So people worried about maggots turning into long-term visitors can relax. The maggots are easy to get rid of—after gorging themselves, they become 10 times bigger in size and are eager to leave the wound. The maggots won't stay where they can't eat (or breathe—they need oxygen).

THAT TICKLES!
Medicinal maggots are the larvae of green blowflies, and because they're grown in a laboratory, they're sterile when applied. Patients typically don't feel them wiggling their way around. Instead, patients usually describe the sensation as "tickling." Some patients have reported they do feel it when the maggots eat tissue that's a little too close to healthy tissue or when they move around an exposed nerve.

It's a small price to pay for most patients treated with maggots, who otherwise run the risk of losing valuable limbs or appendages. If an injury or skin lesion gets really bad, amputation may be required, so maggot treatment is usually the last resort to prevent the loss of an appendage. Even though most patients are squeamish at first, they get over it when they consider the alternative.

LEECH PATROL
Leeches were first used for medicinal purposes in Egypt some 2,500 years ago. They've come a long way since then. Today, they serve humans best by getting rid of excess blood left over after surgical

---

Heart to believe: Only 69% of the roses purchased on Valentine's Day are red.

reattachments, skin grafts, and plastic or reconstructive surgery. One long-problematic portion of these surgeries was the complication of reconnecting veins, the vessels that carry blood to the heart. Arteries have thicker walls and cause surgeons fewer problems, but veins often tear and resist suturing. Tears in the vein lead to pools of blood inside the body that form clots and can kill off tissue.

Leeches are designed perfectly for the cleanup job. Their saliva has almost three dozen proteins that, in combination, numb the body to pain, keep swelling down, and provide a remarkably long-lasting anticoagulant so that the blood keeps flowing. A leech may have had his fill after just an hour, but the blood will continue flowing for several hours longer. After the leeches drop off, they are usually too fat to move and are, as far as the medical community is concerned, infectious waste. They're thrown into an alcohol solution to kill them and then disposed of, just like used needles.

MEDICAL LEECH DISTRIBUTOR?
Leeches are medical marvels. Scientists are trying to understand how their anticoagulation works so it can applied to other health problems like heart attacks and strokes, where blood clots cause life-threatening injury to people. And leeches have been used for treating inflammations, arthritis, glaucoma, infertility, tendinitis, embolisms, and a variety of rheumatoid and venal disorders.

The largest distributor of medical leeches in the United States is a New York-based company called Leeches USA, the distributor for a French company that gained FDA approval to sell leeches in the United States in 2004. The company sells the bloodsuckers for about $10 apiece (with volume discounts), selling about 30,000 critters a year to doctors around the country.

BLOOD TIES
Although there's been a resurgence in the use of maggots and leeches, patients and the medical community have been slow to embrace them. Though their benefits and uses are well documented, squeamishness and a general "ick" factor make many turn away.

Coincidence? Every rise in the American divorce rate is matched by a rise in toy sales.

Currently, about 200 hospitals across the United States and Europe prescribe maggots and leeches, but more are coming around. It may not be pretty, but when the alternative is loss of a limb (or death), no one seems to mind. Turns out maggots and leeches aren't just for the Dark Ages anymore.

*   *   *

LEECH LORE...

- Leeches are probably smarter than a fifth grader; they have 32 brains.
- There are 650 species of leeches, and they're found almost anywhere there is water.
- They range in size from 1.2 inches to 10 inches long, with the longest known leech recorded at 18 inches.
- They need to feed every 50 to 70 days.
- Leeches are related to earthworms.
- Their average lifespan is 10 years.

...AND MAGGOT MISCELLANEA

- Forensic entomologists at murder scenes use maggots to pinpoint the time of death.
- Francesco Redi, an Italian poet and physician, demonstrated that maggots do not spontaneously generate but come from eggs laid by flies in putrefying meat.
- Napoleon's surgeon noted that soldiers whose wounds got infested with maggots were less likely to die or need amputation than soldiers whose wounds were "clean."
- Fishermen sometimes grow their own maggots for bait, and some claim that maggots breed better in dead fish than in meat.

THE "IT'S NOT EASY BEING GREEN" AWARD

Carbon Offsetting

No good deed goes unpunished, and the people who practice carbon offsetting are a case in point.

FOOTPRINTS ON THE PLANET

Dire warnings from scientists, the success of the cautionary film *An Inconvenient Truth*, and endless speculative coverage in the media have motivated many people to seek ways to minimize their carbon "footprint"—their impact on the natural world. That impact comes in all sizes: According to the footprint calculator on the Web site Green Progress for a Green Future, every 100 miles of air travel nets a carbon footprint of 44 pounds because of the carbon dioxide (CO_2) pumped into the atmosphere. And driving a regular car 12,000 miles each year leaves behind about 3.5 tons. So to combat that problem, many people and businesses are turning to carbon offsetting.

The companies selling carbon offsets do things to counteract the purchaser's footprint . . . planting trees or investing in renewable energy, for example. They might also pay developing countries to not produce CO_2. Anyone can buy the offsets—from countries to businesses to individuals—and the prices are typically set per metric ton of CO_2.

THE GOOD AND . . . THE BAD?

Carbon offsetting gained prominence after the Kyoto Protocol was ratified on February 16, 2005. Kyoto was an international agreement (backed by more than 140 countries, though not by the United States) that was committed to reducing greenhouse

---

The sounds made by happy ferrets is called *dooking*.

gases and other environmental problems worldwide. One part of the agreement allowed governments and companies to earn carbon offsets as credits that they could sell to each other. When Kyoto began, a ton of CO_2 was worth about 8 euros. Within a year, the price had tripled, but countries kept buying them. Japan and the Netherlands, in particular, bought from markets in Asia and Latin America. London bought more carbon offsets than any other city.

Sounds great, right? But lots of people aren't fans of the process. In particular, the European Union (EU), the largest buyer of carbon offsetting, has suggested that developing nations haven't done enough to offset their carbon footprints. In 2008, the EU announced that it wanted developing nations to cut their CO_2 production. But the developing nations don't think they should shoulder the burden. From their point of view, the developed countries have benefited and profited from environmentally unfriendly practices for years before penalties were in place. Developing nations argue that they shouldn't be forced to comply with the new regulations while they're still up and coming.

HEY! NO WAY!
The resistance doesn't stop there. Environmental groups haven't been quick to embrace carbon offsetting, either. In 2007, a U.K.-based environmental group called Friends of the Earth issued a press release that said, "a number of other organizations [are] becoming increasingly concerned that carbon offsetting is being used as a smoke-screen to ward off legislation and delay the urgent action needed to cut emissions and develop alternative low-carbon solutions." Environmentalists fear that, by allowing countries, businesses, and individuals to offset their carbon footprint by paying someone else to plant trees or invest in renewable energy, the practice encourages people not to take responsibility for their effect on the environment.

Other environmentalists maintain that carbon offsetting doesn't do enough to stop global warming anyway. Even if all the carbon emitted by First World nations were offset by Third World nations, they say, it wouldn't be enough to solve the problem.

Some government agencies are also against it—they worry that the business of carbon trading could easily turn corrupt. In January 2008, California Attorney General Edmund G. Brown Jr. asked the Federal Trade Commission to start regulating the carbon trading business. Attorneys general from nine different states joined him.

One major problem they found was that people were paying for carbon they hadn't even emitted yet. The idea behind carbon trading involves stopping future carbon emission, but there are no clear guidelines about how it should be carried out. Thus, carbon trading could become a shady business with no clear-cut rules. "Currently, the market for these offsets is volatile, largely unregulated, and has serious potential for fraud," Brown said.

WHAT TO DO?

Instead of carbon offsetting, environmentalists recommend changing the way people act so that we all create less CO_2. Most people agree that would be ideal. But in the meantime, carbon trading continues to grow as an industry—a 2007 *New York Times* article noted that carbon trading is now a $30 billion business worldwide and could grow to a $1 trillion industry by 2017.

People want an easy-to-follow solution so they can feel better in the knowledge they're helping to take care of the problem. But carbon offsetting may need to go back to the drawing board before it becomes the answer that environmentalists are calling for.

*   *   *

JUST IN TIME

How do you view time? The way you see it affects how you talk about it. For example, if your boss says he wants to move his meeting with you back, does that mean he wants to schedule it earlier or later in time? Some people think moving something "back" in time means to make it earlier, and some people—these are the ones who have the dictionary on their side—know it means to make the meeting later. Technically, moving something *back* means pushing it farther away from where you are (which is the present).

National treasure? Over 450,000 of Bob Hope's jokes are housed at the Library of Congress.

THE JOHNNY WEISMULLER AWARD

San Alfonso del Mar Lagoon, Chile

He may not have won an Oscar for his starring role as Tarzan, but champion swimmer Johnny Weismuller would award a Golden Plunger to the world's largest swimming pool—and so would we.

BLUE LAGOON
At the San Alfonso del Mar resort in Chile there's a man-made body of water that could fit 6,000 standard-sized eight-meter backyard swimming pools inside it. Called the San Alfonso del Mar Saltwater Lagoon, the pool overlooks the Pacific Ocean and has racked up some impressive stats, according to the *Guinness Book of Records*:

- It's more than 3,323 feet (1,013 meters) or a half-mile long. (The Orthlieb pool in Casablanca, Morocco, previously the world's largest, looks downright puny at 164 yards long and 109 yards wide.)
- The pool had more than 20 acres of surface area.
- It's filled with 66 million gallons (2.5 million liters) of water.
- It's 10 feet (3 meters) deep at most points, and 115 feet (35 meter) deep at its deepest.

San Alfonso del Mar isn't just for swimming, either—you can snorkel, scuba dive, kayak, and sail in it. A water shuttle is available to ferry guests from the hotel to ocean side. Naysayers may question building a huge pool next to an ocean, but Chile's waters often have a fierce undertow, making them inhospitable to swimming.

The lagoon's crystal-clear, bright-blue saltwater is supplied by the nearby ocean and is kept at a constant temperature of 79° F.

It cost $1.5 billion and took 10 years to complete. Fernando Fischmann, founder of Crystal Lagoon, the company that built the pool, developed a specially patented pool-cleaning process called "pulse oxidation," which he claims uses 100 times fewer chemicals than normal swimming pools. But since this pool is 6,000 times larger than a normal pool, maintenance costs are still considerable—estimated at more than $4 million. It takes 211,400 gallons (800,000 liters) every day to replenish the San Alfonso del Mar Saltwater Lagoon, and two days to empty it of water.

IN THE SWIM

With its balmy water temperature and sunny location, the lagoon is open most months of the year, but if the weather turns windy or rainy, visitors need not sacrifice their tropical vacation—they can simply retreat to a temperature-controlled beach inside a glass pyramid adjacent to the lagoon. That oasis not only has warm water and jet massages, but waterfalls, bubble beds, and heated sand, too.

Even the sand surrounding the indoor and outdoor pools gets special treatment; it's washed and filtered to be softer than beach sand. The *Daily Telegraph* reports that the Crystal Lagoon group has plans to open at least six more mega-pools in places like Panama, Argentina, and Dubai.

CRYSTAL-CLEAR HISTORY

Some other interesting aquatic tidbits from our "pool of knowledge":

- The first known swimming pool in human history was the "great bath" at Mohenjo-Daro, which dates from the third millennium BCE and is located in modern-day Pakistan.

- Ancient Romans built the first swimming pools (different from baths); they also created the first heated pools.

- The first municipal outdoor swimming pool in the United States opened on June 24, 1883, in Philadelphia.

- The modern swimming pool made possible several modern sporting events, including women's synchronized swimming, first organized in Canada in the 1920s.

- San Francisco's Fleischhacker Pool, which closed in 1971, was

1,000 feet long and 150 feet wide; lifeguards patrolled it in row-boats.

- Nemo 33, a recreational diving center near Brussels, Belgium, is the deepest pool in the world with two flat-bottomed areas at 16 and 32 feet, and a large circular pit that descends to 108 feet.

- In Iceland, geothermal springs beneath the island's volcanic rock surface allow naturally heated outdoor swimming pools to remain open year round.

- According to *Travel & Leisure* magazine, the best view from a hotel swimming pool can be found at the Hotel du Cap Eden-Roc near Cannes, France, with a stunning panorama of the Mediterranean.

- North America's largest indoor water park and the world's largest indoor wave pool is located at the West Edmonton Mall in Edmonton, Alberta, a five-acre water park.

- Miyazaki, Japan, boasts the world's largest indoor water park—the Ocean Dome, which can hold 10,000 people and includes 450 miles of sandy beach, a fake volcano that flames on the hour, and even mechanical parrots.

- Some Las Vegas hotel pools have gambling tables in them for sun seekers who don't want to miss out on the gaming action.

- Humans produce approximately 25,000 quarts of spit per person in their lifetime—that could fill two swimming pools.

*   *   *

AN AWARD ORIGIN: THE PEABODY

Peabody was a businessman who switched to public service in 1906 at age 54, working for various universities and the Democratic National Committee. After Peabody died in 1941, the University of Georgia, where he'd served on the board, established the George Foster Peabody Award. Officially presented by the college's journalism school, the awards honor excellent radio and TV reporting and socially redeeming programming. Winners in 2006 included *The Office* and *Scrubs*.

About 50 percent of the bacteria in your mouth live on the surface of your tongue.

THE "MAKE MY DECADE" AWARD

Movies of the 1970s

*Do you feel lucky? You did if you were a moviegoer
in the '70s, the golden age of cinema.*

HOORAY FOR HOLLYWOOD

The end of Hollywood's studio system should have spelled disaster for movies in the 1970s. If nothing else, it could have heralded the advent of a long learning period in which actors, directors, producers, and writers all searched for different ways to work together in a new paradigm. But that didn't happen. Instead, creativity exploded. Young directors began exploring bold new visions. Established actors took chances on unlikely projects. And the result was a decade of more unique and groundbreaking movies being made in a shorter period of time than any other in movie history.

The studio system began in the 1920s, when big movie studios like MGM, Warner Bros., and 20th Century Fox owned nearly every part of the business, right down to the theaters themselves. Even famous actors like Bette Davis, Judy Garland, and Clark Gable were controlled by this system, with the stars being bound by contracts to a single studio that decided what movies the actor made. This monopoly was mostly broken up in 1948 by an antitrust lawsuit, but it was another 20 years before studio contracts and controls were completely dissolved. The Hollywood bigwigs had spent a lot of time and money creating the images of their contracted stars, and they wanted to protect that investment.

By the 1970s, actors and actresses were no longer under contract to a single studio, which allowed performers to fight for the roles they wanted. It also allowed the studios (both big and small)

Each letter in the Hollywood sign is 45 feet tall.

to hire the actors they wanted, rather than to rely solely on the ones under contract to them.

GOT ANY BREAD, MAN?

All this freedom didn't automatically create a boon at the box office, though. When the 1970s began, Hollywood was facing serious money shortages. Studios were cutting the number of movies produced (MGM production dropped from 15 movies per year to five between 1973 and 1974). A shrinking pool of moviegoers also worried filmmakers—between 1960 and 1969, weekly attendance had dropped by about 35 percent and it hit an all-time low in 1971. Plus, foreign filmmakers were beginning to break through. In particular, French movies under rule-breaking directors like Jean-Luc Godard and Eric Rohmer were becoming popular, especially with younger audiences . . . movies' target group.

So how were the bedraggled Hollywood studios supposed to make money? They hired their own young, creative crop of new filmmakers. Soon this group included some of the biggest names in movie history. But in the early '70s, no one was sure who they were—or how successful their projects would be. These young mavericks, all in their 30s or younger, included Martin Scorsese, Steven Spielberg, George Lucas, Brian De Palma, David Lynch, William Friedkin, Francis Ford Coppola, and John Carpenter.

Older directors, like Woody Allen and Hal Ashby, stuck around too, and like Hitchcock, Capra, and a few other well-known directors before them, they achieved superstardom and helped to usher in an entirely new approach to filmmaking: the age of the auteur—the director whose single, cohesive vision ruled over the film. Previously, a movie's direction was dictated by the studio; some famous films, like *Gone with the Wind*, even had multiple directors. But now each movie was the director's artistic statement, and the young mavericks adopted this idea wholeheartedly.

BEST OF THE BEST

To see what those directors created, we need only to look at the list of Best Picture Academy Award winners from 1970 to 1979: *Patton, The French Connection, The Godfather, The Sting, The Godfather Part II, One Flew Over the Cuckoo's Nest, Rocky, Annie Hall, The Deer Hunter,* and *Kramer vs. Kramer.* Of those films, *The Sting,*

Patton, and *Kramer vs. Kramer* are the only ones that did not make the American Film Institute's "100 Greatest Movies of All Time" list, a ranking of the 100 best movies of all time. (To be fair, *Patton* made the first list in 1998, but it was dropped when the list was revised in June 2007.) In fact, 20 films from the 1970s made that revised list, more than any other decade:

#2 *The Godfather*	#56 *Jaws*
#13 *Star Wars*	#57 *Rocky*
#21 *Chinatown*	#59 *Nashville*
#30 *Apocalypse Now*	#62 *American Graffiti*
#32 *The Godfather Part II*	#63 *Cabaret*
#33 *One Flew Over the Cuckoo's Nest*	#64 *Network*
#35 *Annie Hall*	#70 *A Clockwork Orange*
#52 *Taxi Driver*	#77 *All the President's Men*
#53 *The Deer Hunter*	#93 *The French Connection*
#54 *MASH*	#95 *The Last Picture Show*

And when totals are adjusted for inflation, more movies from the 1970s make the top 10 list of the highest domestic box-office moneymakers of all time than any other decade: #2 *Star Wars*, #7 *Jaws*, and #9 *The Exorcist*.

LEAVE THE GUN

Perhaps the greatest movie of the 1970s—some argue it's the greatest movie ever—is *The Godfather*. Based on Mario Puzo's best-selling novel, director Francis Ford Coppola gathered some of the most celebrated actors of all time for a masterpiece of American life told through a crime family's eyes. Puzo cowrote the screenplay with Coppola, who fought to maintain his vision of the film, including its stars. If Paramount had gotten its way, Marlon Brando, Al Pacino, Diane Keaton, and Robert Duvall all might have been replaced by Ernest Borgnine, Robert Redford, Mia Farrow, and Paul Newman. But the players believed in Coppola's vision and were willing to make concessions to him. Brando (a bit of a prima donna) even agreed to a pay cut to play Vito Corleone and signed a contract saying he would not hold up production of the movie.

In the end, Coppola's hard-won film was a triumph:

- On its release in 1972, *The Godfather* was the highest-grossing film of its time and the first film in history to make more than $100 million.
- It was nominated for 11 Academy Awards and won three.
- It spawned a sequel, which also won the Academy Award for Best Picture and is the only sequel to make the American Film Institute's list of 100 Greatest Movies of All Time.

THE FORCE IS STILL WITH US

The 1970s will forever be remembered for being *the* classic decade for virtually every genre of film:

Romantic comedy (*Annie Hall, The Goodbye Girl*)

Scary movie (*Jaws, The Exorcist*)

Raucous comedy (*Animal House, Blazing Saddles*)

Thriller (*Chinatown, The French Connection*)

Disaster flick (*Airport, The Towering Inferno*)

Westerns (*The Outlaw Josey Wales, Straw Dogs*)

Political and social commentary (*All the President's Men, The Deer Hunter*)

Tearjerker (*Love Story, The Champ*)

Sci-fi (*Star Wars, Close Encounters of the Third Kind*)

Musical (*Cabaret, Grease, Saturday Night Fever*)

Satire (*MASH, Network*)

Psychological drama (*Taxi Driver, A Clockwork Orange, Apocalypse Now*)

And where would modern movies be without the car chase? Although 1968's *Bullitt* established the modern high-octane car chase scene in movies, *The French Connection* (1971)—the first R-rated movie to win the Best Picture Academy Award—set a new standard with multiple camera angles used on real New York streets, actual collisions, and the movie's star, Gene Hackman,

really driving his car at high speeds . . . all of which translated to
the most thrilling car chase scene ever shown in theaters.

As for the maverick filmmakers of the '70s, they've produced some
of the most important and relevant movies of the last three
decades. But their roots will always be planted in the greatest
decade there ever was for American cinema.

*　　*　　*

TOP 10 CLASSIC '70s MOVIE QUOTES

"Fat, drunk, and stupid is no way to go through life, son."
—*Animal House*

"You've got to ask yourself one question: 'Do I
feel lucky?' Well, do ya, punk?"
—*Dirty Harry*

"I'll make him an offer he can't refuse."
—*The Godfather*

"Keep your friends close but your enemies closer."
—*The Godfather Part II*

"Yo, Adrian! I did it!"
—*Rocky*

"Come up to the lab, and see what's on the slab!
I see you shiver with antici . . . pation!"
—*The Rocky Horror Picture Show*

"You talkin' to me?"
—*Taxi Driver*

"Soylent Green is people!"
—*Soylent Green*

"May the Force be with you."
—*Star Wars*

"I'm as mad as hell, and I'm not going to take this anymore!"
—*Network*

First lunch box character: Hopalong Cassidy. The design sold 600,000 in its first year.

THE LOCAL GRUB AWARD

A Sampling of Favorite Treats

We couldn't pick just one region's signature local snack, so here are a few delicacies from different parts of the United States.

SPAM MUSUBI

Spam became popular in Hawaii when military personnel introduced it there during World War II. One of the most popular takeout and street foods in Hawaii is the Spam musubi. It's sort of like sushi, but with Spam instead of fish. On top of a block of sticky rice is a thick slice of grilled spam. It's all then wrapped and held together with a strip of seaweed. You can even buy a cheap kitchen gadget to make them (essentially a plastic box and a presser) called the Spam Musubi Maker. The food is available in convenience stores, school cafeterias, fast-food restaurants, and snack bars.

HANGTOWN FRY

In 1849, Hangtown (now Placerville), California, was a supply stop for Gold Rush miners. One day, a miner who struck gold went into the El Dorado Hotel and asked for the most expensive meal available. The cook told him his priciest ingredients were eggs (because of how hard they were to transport), bacon (because it had to be shipped from Chicago), and oysters (because they had to be taken on ice live from San Francisco Bay in barrels of salt-water). The cook combined them into the Hangtown fry, which cost $6 (about $140 today). It's still a popular breakfast item on diner menus in California and the Pacific Northwest.

COFFEE MILK

Popular only in Rhode Island, this is similar to chocolate milk, but made with thick, coffee-flavored syrup (nearly impossible to find outside of the state) instead of chocolate syrup. A now-unknown drugstore soda fountain operator in the 1930s was trying to attract new customers with new drinks, so he added milk and sugar to leftover coffee grounds. It created a thick syrup, which the soda jerk thought tasted great in a glass of cold milk. The drink grew in popularity until it became standard soda fountain fare. In 1932, a New England company named Silmo started bottling the syrup. Coffee milk is the official state beverage of Rhode Island.

BOILED PEANUTS

Roadside stands in Georgia, Alabama, Mississippi, and the Carolinas sell boiled peanuts (also known as "bald" peanuts owing to the pronunciation in a Southern drawl). Raw peanuts still in the shell are boiled in saltwater for hours. The shells get soggy, and the peanuts taste like freshly roasted beans. They're hard to open to get to the nut inside, so most people use their teeth. One popular way of eating boiled peanuts: drop the nut into a soda or sweet iced tea and gulp it down. It's traditional to then toss the shells on the ground. No one knows when boiled peanuts started, but they date back at least to the Civil War, when starving Confederate troops had little to eat besides salt and peanuts, which are widely grown in the South.

LOBSTER ROLLS

In the rest of the country, lobster is an expensive delicacy. But in Maine, where most lobster comes from, it's so plentiful that it's just an ingredient in a cheap sandwich at a roadside stand. A lobster roll is a long sandwich, usually made in a grilled hot dog bun or hoagie roll. It's then filled with celery, scallions, a few huge dollops of mayonnaise, and as much lobster meat as will fit.

LUTEFISK

It's a fish dish that originated with the Vikings and came to the United States with Norwegian immigrants, who settled in Minnesota and Wisconsin in large numbers. Lutefisk is dried cod soaked in lye for several days. Then it's baked or boiled and seasoned with butter, salt, and pepper. The final product is a salty fish with the consistency of Jell-O.

HORSESHOE SANDWICH

This originated in Springfield, but is popular throughout Illinois. It's a heart-stopping sandwich that begins with two slices of thickly sliced toast. On top of that is either a ham steak or two hamburger patties. Then, a plate of French fries are dumped on top, followed by a large portion of cheddar cheese sauce. Supposedly, the sandwich suggests a horseshoe: the beef is supposed to resemble an anvil and the fries represent horseshoe nails. It was created in Springfield's Leland Hotel in 1928 by chefs Joe Schweska and Steve Tomko, who went on to work at a number of other restaurants where they cooked up the Horseshoe. (A half portion—one slice of bread with one hamburger patty or small ham steak—is called a "Pony Shoe.")

CINCINNATI-STYLE CHILI

"Real" chili doesn't necessarily come from Texas. Cincinnati has its own chili-making tradition. Whereas Texas chili is slow-cooked until the raw beef gets tender, Cincinnati chili starts with the meat already cooked. It's much thinner than the thick, hearty Texas brand and is spiced differently. Cincinnati chili is savory, not spicy, because it's made with cinnamon, chocolate, allspice, and Worcestershire sauce. The concoction is then served over spaghetti and traditionally topped with onions, shredded cheddar cheese, refried beans, and oyster crackers. (A bowl with all five toppings is called "Five-Way Chili.")

TURDUCKEN

Many of Louisiana's settlers were French Canadian, and they brought with them a dish called galantine, which consisted of veal, poultry, fish, vegetables, and bread crumbs all finely ground and stuffed into a large bird like a turkey, duck, or chicken. Galantine gave way to an invention claimed by Louisiana chef Paul Prudhomme: turducken. The dish—and the name—combine turkey, duck, and chicken. A turkey is stuffed with a duck, and the duck is stuffed with a chicken. In between each bird is a layer of sausage stuffing. Also claiming inventor's rights is Herbert's Specialty Meats in Maurice, Louisiana, which has been making and shipping turduckens since 1985. In recent years, it's caught on nationally as an alternate Thanksgiving entree.

The O' prefix in Irish surnames means "grandson of."

THE POGO FOR PRESIDENT AWARD

Walt Kelly's *Pogo* Comic Strip

Uncle John is voting for Pogo because the little possum is lovable, thought-provoking, and has enough opinions to hold his own against any politician. Silliness, satire, and politics combine in Walt Kelly's Pogo to create a comic that's still making people laugh—and think—more than 50 years after it was first published.

CREATING THE COMIC

Pogo possum lived in the Okeefenokee Swamp, where he and his critter friends commented satirically on American culture and politics. Wonderfully drawn animal characters, great art, slapstick humor, and clever nonsense talk helped creator Walt Kelly tackle serious subjects without alienating readers.

The strip was published between 1948 and 1975, and at its peak in the late 1960s, more than 600 papers carried it (though *Pogo*'s increased political commentary during the 1968 presidential campaign cost it some subscribers). When Walt Kelly passed away in October 1973, his widow, also a cartoonist, kept the strip alive until July 1975. (*Pogo* was revived from 1989 to 1993 with several different creative teams.) In addition, 31 paperbacks were published along with 33 collections (two posthumous) of the strip. Quite a legacy for a bunch of swamp critters.

Pogo had more than 700 individually named characters, along with hundreds of unnamed ones. All were vehicles for Kelly's whimsical wordplay and political views. The major players were:

- Rational Pogo, the "everyman" opossum

- His best friend Porky Pine

- Bombastic straight man Albert Alligator

- Albert's love, Miss Mam'selle Hepzibah (a French-speaking skunk)

U.S. Patent #4,429,685 was granted for a "Method of Growing Unicorns."

- And pals like superstitious turtle "Churchy" La Femme and know-it-all Dr. Howland Owl

PLAYING POSSUM

Kelly began *Pogo* in 1943, after a career that included a stint drawing cells for animated movies like *Snow White* and *Pinocchio*. The Walt Disney work gave him a discipline that he applied to his own finely drawn strip.

Kelly seemed to have an innate knowledge of which frames required shading, which frames could go borderless (one of his innovations), and which scenes needed details like tree stumps and kudzu. He also had an eye for critter caricature—Pogo's nose, Albert's tale, Howland's feathery "ears." Kelly's characters have expressions that range from consternation to confusion to glee with just a curve of an "eyebrow" or a "mouth's" down-turned corners.

SWAMP SPEAK

Reading a *Pogo* strip or book requires that the audience pay attention—not because the dialogue is difficult, but because it's fast paced and full of puns, coined words, dialects from French to Elizabethan English, unusual typefaces, and general wackiness. Swamp speak was richer than Cajun roux and more ambiguous than left-over gumbo, including part real dialect ("Choose yo' weapons"), part made-up patter ("What an ignoram-bumptious youth!"), and part invented words (like Pogo's "Rowrbazzle!").

Kelly's love of made-up language and nonsense talk had a popular culmination in his fractured Christmas carol "Deck Us All with Boston Charlie." He was never afraid to be silly and smart in the same strip, making Pogo a hit with kids and adults alike.

Literary critic Jonathan Yardley of the *Washington Post* remembers one particularly fun Kelly bit: "Howland Owl and Churchy-la-Femme hatch a plot to build 'Adam bombs,' which involves crossing 'a gee-ranium plant an' a li'l baby yew tree,' at the end of which, as the wise owl puts it, 'you gits a yew-ranium bush!'"

POSSUM-BILITIES

Silly as he could be, Kelly had a serious side. Political commentary

---

First fruit eaten on the moon: a peach.

on nuclear weapons was a recurring theme in Kelly's work. His G.O. *Fizzickle Pogo* book was based on the "International Geophysical Year," an international scientific effort that lasted from June 1957 to December 1958 and included discoveries about the deep sea and the launch of the Soviet satellite *Sputnik I*. Chapters in Kelly's book included "The Defense of Utter Space" and "A Mine Shaft to the Moon," and one storyline features the animals trying to explore the world.

In some cases, Kelly's political messages are enduring. Pogo's most famous quote is, "We have met the enemy, and he is us," which originally appeared in a strip Kelly wrote about pollution. Kelly took the line from Naval Captain Oliver Perry's 1813 message to then-U.S. Army General (and future U.S. president) William Henry Harrison after the Battle of Lake Erie: "We have met the enemy, and he is ours." Pogo's version is often resurrected by environmentalists as a rallying cry.

And if that weren't enough to make Pogo and Walk Kelly worthy of a Golden Plunger, many famous cartoonists cite the strip as an influence, particularly in the art of combining comics with satire. From Jim Henson of Muppets fame to Garry Trudeau (*Doonesbury*), Bill Watterson (*Calvin and Hobbes*), and even *Shoe's* Jeff MacNelly, graphic artists bow down before the brilliance of Walt Kelly.

A LOT OF MALARKEY

In 1953, Kelly took his political humor even farther. That year, he introduced a bobcat, Simple J. Malarkey, who was based on right-wing Senator Joseph R. McCarthy. The stand was brave—McCarthy never shied away from accusing creative types of being communists and hauling them before Congress to defend themselves. When media lashed out against Kelly, the cartoonist had Malarkey wear a paper-bag mask. Kelly survived the backlash and was emboldened by it. Over the years, he went on to skewer J. Edgar Hoover, Spiro Agnew, Nikita Khruschev, Fidel Castro, and Richard Nixon. And he didn't quit there.

Kelly the satirist was matched by Kelly the professional. He knew some newspapers would hate his political strips, so he drew comics for those publications that featured white bunnies taking

In ancient Egypt, only high priests were allowed to wear cotton clothing.

part in harmless, apolitical antics. He told readers that if they saw the bunnies they should try to find the "real" strip in a different paper.

In 1952, Kelly decided that having Pogo "run" for president made as much sense as some of the real candidates did. According to the Web site IGoPogo.com, most of Kelly's pretend "Pogo for President" press releases "make more sense than the current presidential candidate statements." And although Kelly remained a liberal who voiced his views through the mouths, maws, and beaks of his creations, with "Pogo for President," he tried to show readers how comical all the human frontrunners were, regardless of party affiliation.

Today, Walt Kelly's daughter, Carolyn Kelly, administers his estate. Not only is there a 2008 "I Go Pogo" campaign, but there's an annual "Pogofest" in Waycross, Georgia, where Pogo was named the state's "ofishul" possum.

*   *   *

TAKING BACK TEXAS

Joining Pogo in the realm of unlikely candidates for public office is Richard S. "Kinky" Friedman, whose unsuccessful but lively 2006 Texas gubernatorial run resulted in lots of extra publicity for the singer, songwriter, novelist, humorist, and former *Texas Monthly* columnist. His original platform was "The Dewussification of Texas," with slogans that included the says-it-all "Why the hell not?"

But Friedman's laissez-faire campaign strategy has some hardcore beliefs behind it. He supports higher pay for teachers, alternative fuel development, and gay marriage. ("I believe they have a right to be as miserable as the rest of us," he told an AP reporter.) He's against illegal immigration, capital punishment, and smoking bans. (He likes to quote Mark Twain: "If smoking is not allowed in heaven, I shall not go.")

Until the next campaign, Friedman remains happily ensconced on his family farm outside Kerrville, Texas, where he writes quirky mystery novels (with a suspiciously Kinky-esque protagonist named Kinky Friedman) and keeps an eye on his animal rescue ranch.

THE GOAT BUSTERS AWARD

Buzkashi

Sports fans—especially fans of hockey and rugby—would really enjoy a buzkashi match. Uncle John hopes that giving this little-known game an award will inspire a major television network to pick it up—it's a lot more interesting than many of the reality shows crowding the airwaves.

KHAN-TACT SPORT

In the organized chaos of this spirited Middle Eastern game, bones will be broken, teams will be mixed up, and sometimes a carcass-bearing team leader will gallop off the field and into the path of oncoming traffic. The players and their mounts keep going, though, in spite of honking horns and swerving cars. Welcome to Afghanistan's national sport . . . buzkashi!

Buzkashi began in the days of Genghis Khan (using a skull as a ball), and not in Afghanistan but on Central Asia's steppes. These wide-open prairies provided the perfect playing fields for the free-wheeling game. It probably started as a hunting method, since chasing goats on horseback was more efficient than trying to run after them on foot, but it certainly derived some of its violent aspects from the mounted warfare of ancient times.

Buzkashi came to Afghanistan in the 1950s as a favorite of King Zahir Shah, the country's last king, who loved the game. His government-hosted tournaments made it the "national game," and when the Soviets invaded Afghanistan in 1979, Shah's buzkashi riders were among the warriors who defended the country. When the communists seized power in 1979, the game's leaders went underground, and it became part of the rebel mujahideen culture. When the Taliban took over in 1996, its leaders banned buzkashi.

Most popular place to burn candles in a house: the living room.

But after that regime's 2001 fall, the game returned and spread nationwide again.

GOATBUSTERS

Buzkashi is played on horseback, like polo, but that's where the similarities end. *Buzkashi* means "goat grabbing" in Afghanistan's Dari language, and the *boz* or goat carcass (often a calf) acts as the ball. The playing field ranges from dry, cracked mud flats to rocky promontories.

The original game was more free-ranging and could last for days or even weeks. Today's version has (roughly) a one-hour limit. Around 60 players are divided into six or more teams. Each player wears a short, padded leather tunic or coat (chapan, hence the riders' name of chapandaz), which makes it almost impossible for spectators and players to figure out who is on what side, adding to the chaotic fun.

A buzkashi match takes some advance preparation. Someone needs to butcher a goat, remove its head and hooves, and soak it overnight in cold water to toughen the carcass. The innards are also removed, and if necessary, the carcass is filled with sand so that it weighs at least 80 pounds. Then, voila—a boz . . . er, ball!

LET THE GAME BEGIN

To begin, the "ball" is placed in a shallow, specially dug pit centered in the starting area, called the "Circle of Justice." From there, the rules and game play of buzkashi range from violent to more violent. Although the rules state that no foul play is allowed, lashing competitors doesn't seem to count. Once a player has snatched up the boz, he will be surrounded by other players on horseback, each clenching a short rawhide whip. The whips are used continuously against the other riders, and few players leave a match without facial slashes and burns. The more scars on a player's face and body, the more respected he is. And it's not just the whips that do damage: if the game is played near a river, riders have sometimes conspired to drown their opponents. But the whips aren't the biggest danger in buzkashi—the horses are. Most horses stop at obstructions by instinct, but a buzkashi horse is trained to keep going and trample over any obstacle, including humans. It's common for players to suffer broken limbs, and sometimes people even die. The horses belong to tribal commanders who organize and sponsor the competitions. The more people who attend a game, the more powerful the commander is, and a buzkashi match is mostly an opportunity to flaunt his authority.

FOXY CHAMPIONS

Chapandaz (or riders) compete only four months per year, but they earn enough prize money to live until the next season. The winner of the match also receives the boz. After all of the hits, the meat is very tender. And winners get prizes like new tunics and turbans. The ultimate prize, though, is having a long enough career to be awarded a fox-trimmed turban (the fox symbolizes cunning). The game-toughened riders who sport this distinctive headgear are revered figures in Afghan society. Eat your heart out, Beckham!

*   *   *

A "BONEHEAD" MISTAKE

The Cubs weren't always unlucky. In 1908, they received one of the luckiest breaks in baseball history. On September 23 of that year, the Cubs were playing the New York Giants. In the bottom of the 9th inning, the score was tied 1–1. Infielder Fred Merkle came up to bat with two outs and one man on base. Merkle hit a single. The next batter went up and hit another single. The runner on second made it to home to score the winning run, and Merkle, thinking the game was over, went to celebrate with his team—without ever touching second base. The Cubs' second baseman grabbed the ball and stepped on second base to force out Merkle, which disqualified the winning run. There was so much confusion (fans had stormed onto the field to celebrate) that the game was ruled a tie. The Cubs ended up winning the National League pennant that year by one game . . . over the second-place Giants. The mistake earned Merkle the nickname "Bonehead."

THE "DON'T MESS WITH ME" AWARD

Civil War Surgeon Mary Walker

To receive an award and lose it must be incredibly painful (which is why Uncle John vows never to revoke a Golden Plunger). But to receive an award, have the government threaten to take it away, and then face down the Feds with a shotgun . . . now that's something to talk about!

BADGE OF HONOR

The Congressional Medal of Honor is the highest award the U.S. government can give to a soldier. It's meant for a member of the military who distinguishes himself "conspicuously by gallantry and intrepidity at the risk of his life above and beyond the call of duty while engaged in an action against an enemy of the United States."

The award was supposed to go just to military personnel for war service, but historically, presidents have given the medals to civilians (Buffalo Bill Cody got one) or to soldiers who distinguished themselves, but not necessarily in war (29 men got Medals of Honor for acting as guards at President Lincoln's funeral).

In 1917, the government reviewed the medals they'd awarded and decided to revoke 911 of them as ineligible because they didn't meet the requirements. (Buffalo Bill and the Lincoln soldiers lost theirs.) And the government didn't just strike the names from its list either; members of the Army went door to door and took the medals back.

One woman, Civil War Assistant Surgeon Mary Walker, refused to give hers up. Despite her valiant service as an Army surgeon, Walker did not technically qualify because she hadn't "engaged in an action against an enemy of the United States." However, when federal marshals arrived at Walker's door to take her Medal of Honor, she met them wearing it around her neck and brandishing

---

In the Victoria era, giving someone red tulips was considered a declaration of love.

a 12-gauge shotgun. Evidently the weapon spoke volumes, because Walker kept her medal and wore it every day until she died two years later.

THE DOCTOR IS IN

Walker had always been feisty. Born into a family of freethinkers in rural New York, she often wore "bloomers" (a scandalous skirt-and-pants outfit designed by feminist Amelia Bloomer) and once declared, "Corsets are coffins!" She also prided herself on being arrested many times for wearing men's clothes in public.

Walker went to college and then medical school, and in 1855, she became the second woman (after Elizabeth Blackwell) to graduate from Syracuse Medical College. Afterward, she married fellow student Albert Miller (and wore pants and a dress coat to the ceremony) but kept her own name (naturally). Mary and Albert set up a medical practice in Rome, New York, but the locals weren't ready to accept a woman physician, so the practice eventually failed. So did the marriage—Mary and Albert divorced in the late 1860s.

WAR!

In 1861, when the Civil War broke out, Mary Walker was just 29 years old. She tried to join the Union Army but was denied a commission because of her gender. So she volunteered instead and became, first, a nurse and then an acting assistant surgeon—the first female surgeon in the U.S. Army. For almost two years, she worked on the Union front lines and then was appointed to the 52nd Ohio Infantry. (She may or may not have acted as a Union spy during this time, too. No one seems to be sure.)

In 1864, dressed in an officer's uniform that she'd modified to fit her, Walker crossed into Confederate territory to treat civilians (or spy on the Confederate soldiers), and she ran right into a group of rebels. Their commanding officer captured her and sent her to jail in Richmond, Virginia. Four months later, Walker was released during a prisoner exchange—and was greatly pleased that she'd been traded "man for man" for a Confederate officer. She served out the rest of the war practicing medicine at a women's prison in Kentucky and at an orphan's home in Tennessee.

The aorta, the largest artery in the human body, is about the diameter of a garden hose.

MEDALS SCHMEDALS

For her wartime service, Mary Walker was paid $766.16 and initially granted a monthly pension of $8.50, less than that of most war widows. (Eventually, her pension increased to a whopping $20 a month.) But President Andrew Johnson recognized her service and awarded her a Medal of Honor. All was well until the marshals knocked on her door in 1917.

When Mary Walker died in 1919, she still had her medal but she'd been removed from the government's list of medal winners. Finally, in 1977, she was vindicated. President Jimmy Carter and an Army board reinstated the award, citing her "distinguished gallantry, self-sacrifice, patriotism, dedication, and unflinching loyalty to her country, despite the apparent discrimination because of her sex." She remains the only woman ever to be so honored.

*   *   *

WAYS TO GO GREEN

There are lots of ways to make small but noticeable differences to help the environment:

- Only run the dishwasher when it's full. Dishwashers use energy and water, but you actually use less water to wash a full load in the washer than to wash them by hand. The average dishwasher uses four gallons per load. Washing the same amount by hand would take almost 24 gallons.

- Wash clothes in cold water. It's cheaper and 90 percent more efficient. Only 10 percent of the energy used to wash with warm water is used to power the washer. The rest goes to increase the water temperature.

- Unplug things you're not using. Leaving appliances plugged in uses up a lot of juice. It's been estimated that 75 percent of household energy usage goes to unused appliances.

- Turn the water off while you're brushing your teeth. Leaving it on wastes about five gallons of water a day.

In 1915 William Wrigley Jr. sent free chewing gum to every person in the Chicago phone book.

THE "AS SEEN ON TV" AWARD

The ThighMaster

*The man who made the ThighMaster a household name
didn't even invent it. This savvy businessman was in the
right place at the right time, and then he squeezed,
squeezed, and squeezed his way to millions.*

ICONIC INFOMERCIAL

Prior to 1984, the FCC limited the amount of airtime broadcasters could give to commercials: 18 minutes an hour. After 1984, when that law changed, it paved the way for infomercials—long blocks of ads that can run half an hour or an hour. Infomercials became staples in the late-night hours, when viewership is low and ad rates are cheap.

The ThighMaster infomercial debuted in 1991, promising better-toned and attractive legs through the use of a remarkably simple contraption that used a steel coil to provide resistance training for the upper legs. The slam-dunk part of the ad was its spokeswoman: leggy, 1970s blonde bombshell Suzanne Somers. The ad opened with a close look at her long gams while an announcer (Somers' husband, Alan Hamel) proclaimed, "Great legs! How'd you get 'em?" It turned out the world wanted to ask that question too—and the answer was available to them for just $19.95 (plus shipping and handling).

Within two years, six million ThighMasters had been sold, and the man behind the infomercial, Peter Bieler, was on his way to making $100 million on the product. Bieler knew that infomercials were the way to advertise and make money. His formula for the right combination of attention-getting elements included: a good product that people wanted, a spokesperson viewers were interested in, and a not-subtle, tongue-in-cheek approach. Bieler

---

Studies show: The scent of rosemary can improve mental performance.

was not the inventor of the ThighMaster, and how he found it is a tale itself.

THE BIRTH OF THE THIGHMASTER

A woman named Anne-Marie Bennstrom invented the device in the 1980s and called it the V-Bar. Bennstrom was a chiropractor and physical medicine therapist from Sweden, as well as a cofounder of The Ashram, a no-holds-barred weigh-loss retreat near Santa Monica, California. The Ashram attracts celebrities and the wealthy for its grueling programs that begin at 6:00 a.m. and involve rigorous weight training, mountain climbing, water exercises, and not very much food. Famous graduates of the course include Oprah Winfrey, Jane Fonda, and Shirley MacLaine.

Initially, the V-Bar was being used less for exercise and more as an aid for injured skiers, who could work their sore muscles with it. It was in that capacity that it came to the attention of Joshua Reynolds, heir to the R. J. Reynolds tobacco company. Reynolds is often mistakenly credited with inventing two things: the Thigh-Master and the mood ring. In reality, he invented neither. He just knew a good product when he saw it. (He correctly predicted the mood ring fad of the 1970s and put them on the market quickly, which is why some people think he invented them.)

Reynolds took the V-Bar design and renamed it the V-Toner. Sales were hardly overwhelming. With very little marketing or word of mouth, the V-Toner was mostly a dud, until Reynolds paired up with Bieler.

THREE'S COMPANY

Bieler had worked his way up in the marketing field for years, becoming an executive with Procter & Gamble. He was also a video producer. He left that behind, though, in 1990 to form Ovation, Inc., a company dedicated to infomercials. He wouldn't have to wait long for his dream product to come to him.

Reynolds approached Bieler about working together to promote the V-Toner, and Bieler was impressed. He knew it had potential. First, he renamed it the ThighMaster, and then he went to work looking for the face—and the legs—that would sell it. He found Suzanne Somers, former *Three's Company* star and Las Vegas lounge act. With her striking figure and beautiful legs, Somers was perfect for the role, and she still had just enough fame to carry the program—but not enough fame to make her too expensive.

Somers' infomercials helped create a media whirlwind around the product, which soon began selling 75,000 units per week. The infomercial was also spoofed on several TV shows, which just added to the frenzy. Ovation, Inc. spent about $9 million on advertising the ThighMaster in 1991. That investment paid off many times over—more than 10 million have been sold.

The craze also rejuvenated Somers' career, leading to further television roles and her status as a fitness guru. She's written several diet, fitness, and anti-aging books since and now owns the ThighMaster World Corporation. Bieler and Reynolds are no longer associated with the product.

*   *   *

AWARD ORIGINS

- **Fields Medal.** Canadian mathematician John Charles Fields died in 1936 and stipulated in his will that a prize be awarded every four years to one or more groundbreaking mathematicians who are under the age of 40. Presented by the International Mathematical Union, the Fields Medal is the highest honor in math. Andrei Okounkov won a Fields Medal in 2006 for "his contributions to bridging probability, representation theory, and algebraic geometry." (Don't worry—we don't know what that means either.)

- **Eisner Awards.** It's named after Will Eisner, a pioneering comic book artist who pioneered the long-form comic or "graphic novel" with his book *The Spirit*. Eisner Awards are given out each year to artists, writers, and publishers for excellence in comic books.

THE SMALL WONDERS AWARD

Nanotechnology

*Smaller . . . smaller . . . smaller . . . nanoscientists
take on the task of making everything mini.*

WELCOME TO THE MINIATURE WORLD
While technology continues to make data smaller and
devices more lightweight (for example, thin laptops),
nanotechnology goes even further into the miniature world—
down to the microscopic level, in fact.

Nanotechnology is the science of designing electronics and
mechanics at the atomic level. To give you an idea of how small
that is, consider this: one nanometer (NM) is one-billionth of a
meter (about a hundred-thousandth of the width of a human
hair), and nanotechnology concentrates on sizes between 0.1 NM
and 100 NMs. Nanotechnology aims to build chips, circuitry, and
other mechanical devices one atom at a time, pushing the limits
of technology to the point where one bit of data could be represented by just an electron.

THE BIBLE ON THE HEAD OF A PIN

In an effort to prove that science is fun (!), researchers in Israel
made headlines in 2007 when they were able to fit the entire text
of the Hebrew Bible (39 books) on an area smaller than the size of
a pinhead—half the size of the pinhead, to be exact. Doctoral student Ohad Zohar supervised the project and proudly pointed out
that the area the 308,428 words were printed on—a tiny piece of
silicon—was the size of a grain of sugar. And it took Zohar and his
band of scientists only about an hour to do it.

The process was surprisingly easy. The scientists first covered
the silicon surface with a tiny layer of gold. Then they put the

---

World's longest hot dog: A 1,996' wiener made by the Sara Lee Corp. for the 1996 Olympics.

words on to that surface by focusing a particle beam at it—this blasted microscopic particles at the silicon and carved away the gold, etching the words into the silicon.

The laser beam they used is called a focused ion beam (FIB). FIB technology grew out of research in the mid-1980s and has been a major breakthrough in nanotechnology. FIB technology uses ions from gallium, a metal that becomes a liquid at room temperature, to make deposits—which in turn created the "etching" for the Bible.

DOWN THE RABBIT HOLE

Nanotechnology originally was devoted to building machines, robotics, and computer technologies at the microscopic level, and it's been around for decades. It began as an idea in 1959 proposed by physicist Richard Feynman, who was speaking at the annual meeting of the American Physical Society. "What I want to talk about is the problem of manipulating and controlling things on a small scale," Feynman said. And he did, in a way that inspired a new movement in science. He continued,

> There is a device on the market, they tell me, by which you can write the Lord's Prayer on the head of a pin. But that's nothing; that's the most primitive, halting step in the direction I intend to discuss. It is a staggeringly small world that is below. In the year 2000, when they look back at this age, they will wonder why it was not until the year 1960 that anybody began seriously to move in this direction. Why cannot we write the entire 24 volumes of the Encyclopedia Britannica on the head of a pin?

The idea was brought further along in the 1970s by K. Eric Drexler, the first person to earn a Ph.D. in Molecular Nanotechnology from M.I.T. Nanotechnology development continued throughout the 1980s, with amazing discoveries on molecular and atomic levels.

In November 1996, U.S. scientists from a variety of agencies began meeting to further the discussion and understanding of nanotechnology. In 1998, they officially became the Interagency Working Group on Nanotechnology, renamed the National Nano-technology Initiative in 2001, when President Bill Clinton declared the science a federal initiative. Americans love to think big, but they don't want to be left behind on the submolecular level either.

As a teenager, author Zane Grey made rural house calls as an unlicensed dentist.

SMALL STEPS

The Center for Responsible Nanotechnology has identified at least 11 risks that the world will face from the development of nanotechnology, ranging from economic problems like price-fixing to its use in terrorist activities. Every submolecular discovery may fill casual observers with wonder, but it's also cause for trepidation—at least a little bit.

Scientists believe that the study of nanotechnology will eventually lead to nanofactories, microscopic production farms that could even create *new* nanofactories. Clearly, this is going to be a big little business. And it will bring about major changes in the structure of everything from your personal computer to the global economy.

*　　*　　*

VIEWERS' CHOICE

In 1999, ESPN asked its viewers to name the top-10 rivalries in sports. Here's what they said:

1. University of Michigan vs. Ohio State University (football)

2. Muhammad Ali vs. Joe Frazier (boxing)

3. University of North Carolina vs. Duke University (basketball)

4. Wilt Chamberlain vs. Bill Russell (basketball)

5. Toronto Maple Leafs vs. Montreal Canadiens (hockey)

6. Arnold Palmer vs. Jack Nicklaus (golf)

7. New York Yankees vs. Boston Red Sox (baseball)

8. Auburn University vs. University of Alabama (football)

9. Dallas Cowboys vs. Washington Redskins (football)

10. Brooklyn Dodgers vs. New York Giants (baseball)

THE NOVEL APPROACH AWARD

Watchmen

This groundbreaking graphic novel series changed the landscape of comics forever with a tale that mixed fantasy and cold, hard reality.

CREATIVE COMICS

Often relegated to the depths of sub-literature, comic books enjoyed a renaissance in the mid-1980s. Cheaper and more efficient printing processes raised the quality of the paper that comic books were printed on. A mini "British Invasion" of talented artists redefined the art form. Independent presses began to grow in the industry, and more mature storylines helped both to retain grown-up collectors as well as to attract new readers.

For the most part, the backbone of comic books remained superheroes, and superheroes have always been larger-than-life figures fighting for truth and justice in landscapes far removed from the reality of American life. Whether they lived in imaginary settings like Metropolis or Gotham City or in actual places like New York, superheroes didn't participate in real-world events. They didn't fight in wars, stop assassinations of world leaders, or prevent millions from starving in third-world countries. The real world was just a backdrop for epic battles fought against archenemies and super villains.

COMICS GET REAL

Watchmen, a comic book series that debuted in 1986, changed that. The brainchild of Brits Alan Moore and Dave Gibbons, *Watchmen* turned all of the previous conventions on their ear. Moore had already made a name for himself in comics by writing

---

Since the United Nations was founded in 1945, there have been an average of 2.2 wars per year.

the acclaimed series *Saga of the Swamp Thing*, as well as a famous 1985 *Superman* story called "For the Man Who Has Everything," in which Batman, Robin, and Wonder Woman come to celebrate Superman's birthday, only to find him under the control of a monstrous alien. Gibbons was a talented artist who had drawn several comics series in the United Kingdom before being hired in America to draw *Green Lantern*.

THE PLOT THICKENS

In the mid-1980s, DC Comics bought the properties of Charlton, a defunct publisher that had produced superhero comics like *Captain Atom* and *The Peacemaker* in the 1940s. DC Comics hired Moore and Gibbons to relaunch those Charlton characters for a modern audience, but Moore envisioned a story far beyond the scope of what DC wanted. Instead, Moore and Gibbons created *Watchmen*, a monthly series that spanned 12 comic-book issues and was based loosely on the Charlton characters. For them, the pages of *Watchmen* became a canvas on which to mix the troubles of the real world with the optimism of superheroes.

That's not to say that *Watchmen* was entirely realistic. In its pages, Richard Nixon is still president in 1985, the United States won the Vietnam War, and the world has a nuclear doomsday clock that's sitting at five minutes to midnight. Superheroes exist in this world, too, but they've mostly gone into hiding. The very first superheroes, masked adventurers from the 1940s who banded together as the Minutemen, had enjoyed decades of adoration from the public for their exploits. But their successors are not so lucky. Times have changed, and now the public is suspicious of people who hide behind masks.

Worse still, a killer is hunting America's retired superheroes.

THE STORY

The story opens with a narrative from the journal of the superhero Rorschach, a demented and violent psychopath with a twisted hatred toward almost all of humanity (although he claims to protect it). The Comedian, a former superhero whose brutal methods and tactics have earned him a place working for the government, is dead. Although the Comedian's death appears to the police to be an isolated homicide, Rorschach believes it's a case of someone hunting down heroes.

Rorschach begins his investigation by checking in on the retired superheroes who, in the 1960s, had formed a group named the Crimebusters. He finds . . .

- Dan Dreiberg (Nite Owl), an indecisive and impotent middle-aged man;

- John Osterman (Dr. Manhattan), formerly a human scientist and now the only person in the world with superhuman powers (he can teleport, read minds, etc.). Osterman was caught in a nuclear physics experiment and transformed into someone who can manipulate molecular structures and who experiences time in a nonlinear fashion. According to the *Watchmen* story, it was because of Dr. Manhattan's unbeatable abilities that the United States won the Vietnam War, and he continues to work for the U.S. government, which uses his powers to maintain its status as the global superpower;

- Laurie Juspeczyk (Silk Spectre), once a teen superhero and now unhappily married to Dr. Manhattan;

- Adrian Veidt (Ozymandias), the smartest man in the world, who has become one of the world's richest men as head of a large corporation.

As Rorschach continues his investigation into the Comedian's death, other events begin to unfold. Laurie realizes how unhappy she is and leaves Dr. Manhattan. And people who have worked with Dr. Manhattan for years are diagnosed with cancer. Both of these events cause Dr. Manhattan to leave Earth, shifting the power balance in the world. The Soviet Union then threatens to invade Afghanistan, and the world comes to the brink of war. Death continues to loom—not only over the heads of the former Crimebusters, but also for the Minutemen. As the plot unfolds, Rorschach teams up with Dreiberg and Juspeczyk and begins to learn the truth. Someone has engineered these events in a drastic bid to bring peace to the world, even if it means destroying millions of lives in the process.

SUPERHEROES IN THE REAL WORLD
The heart of the series is Rorschach. A crazy conspiracy theorist

---

Believe it ore not: The average human body contains about 0.2 milligrams of gold.

who hates just about everyone, he still anchors the story with his insights into the minds of others and his intense thoughts, all conveyed through his journal.

In September 2007, England's BBC launched *Comics Britannica*, a series of interviews with *Watchmen*'s creators. In the interview, Moore revealed his motives behind creating the *Watchmen* story:

> Wouldn't these characters be somehow kind of sad and touching in the real world . . . You find that, yes, superheroes in the real world are kind of funny. They're also kind of scary, because actually a person dressing in a mask and going around beating up criminals is a vigilante psychopath. That's what Batman is, in essence. We came up with the character of Rorschach as a way of exploring what that Batman-type, driven, vengeance-fueled vigilante would be like in the real world. And the short answer is a nutcase.

BATTLE OF THE SUPERPOWERS

For a comic book about superheroes, *Watchmen* is noticeably short on abilities beyond those of mortal men. In fact, all of the masked adventurers, except Dr. Manhattan, fight with just their hearts, minds, and fists. The real superpowers, just as in the actual world, are the frontrunners in the arms race. The United States struggles to keep up with its main enemy, the Soviet Union, and the world deals with the issues of poverty, warfare, and nationalism as well as the social upheavals of civil rights, feminism, and gay culture.

COMIC OR SOMETHING MORE?

Watchmen asked what separated costumed heroes from ordinary people and showed that neither was far removed from the other. Even more, it tore down many of the traditions comics had been based on (like clear-cut battles between good guys and bad guys) and built something new in its place. It was unique in other ways, too:

- The majority of the series is drawn in a gridlike pattern, three panels by three panels, nine to a page, providing a framework for the story.

- No thought balloons were used throughout the series. The only look inside the minds of the characters comes from their writings, such as Rorschach's journals and sections of one character's autobiography.

- Similarly, no "motion lines" (two or three wavy lines drawn around a character or object to convey movement) appear in the book.

- Each of the first 11 issues of *Watchmen* featured supplemental text, ranging from fictional book excerpts to magazine interviews with the characters to marketing concepts used for the promotion of action figures. Each one provided background, context, or irony (or all three) for the chapter that appeared before it.

- The year after its release, *Watchmen's* 12 issues were bound together and released as a graphic novel. It won a Hugo Award (given for best science fiction or fantasy works), four Kirby Awards (recognizing comic-book achievements), and four Eisner Awards (also for comic-book achievements). And it has been named to *Time* magazine's list of the "100 Best English Language Novels from 1923 to the Present."

Today, *Watchmen* remains current and important, despite its Cold War backdrop and dated technology (a long-out-of-date computer system provides the final clue to solving the murder mystery). It represented a change in the way comics were created and the kinds of stories they told and brought a whole new genre—the graphic novel—into the mainstream.

*　　*　　*

MORE GREAT GRAPHIC NOVELS

Maus by Art Spiegelman (1991)

Based on his father's stories, Spiegelman shows a harrowing and terrifying account of the Nazi invasion of Poland, the Warsaw Ghetto, and World War II concentration camps. But there's a twist: Jewish people are portrayed as mice, the Nazis as cats.

Jimmy Corrigan: The Smartest Kid on Earth by Chris Ware (2000)

Corrigan is neither a child nor a genius, but an overweight, depressed man who tracks down (and is ultimately disappointed by) his long-lost father. Along the way, he finds redemption and belonging when he meets a sister he never knew he had.

Leather doesn't have a smell—the scent comes from the chemicals used in the tanning process.

THE BIG BROTHER AWARD

Microchips

From pets to people, microchips are everywhere, and as the technology evolves, privacy issues get trickier. (Uncle John is watching you.)

IT'S A GOOD THING

When a pet goes missing, the worry is tough to take. Microchips offer a relief for that worry. According to the American Microchip Advisory Council for Animals, more than 11 million household pets and horses have been chipped in the United States. Chipping programs began in the early 1970s, when the chips were placed on tags clipped to the animal's ear. Microchipping started in the 1980s, when technological advancements produced chips small enough to implant in the animals.

Most people don't complain about this use of microchips and even find it a comfort to know that their lost pets can be easily found. When animal control or a shelter picks up a stray animal, the animal is scanned for a chip. When the scanner reads the chip, the pet is identified and reunited with its owner.

NEW CHIPS OFF THE OLD BLOCK

Unfortunately, microchips in pets are plagued by a few problems. Before 2003, one universal scanner could be used to read all pet microchips. But late that year, multiple microchip manufacturers began producing chips differently, and the updated technology was no longer readable by the same scanner. Companies started making their chips identifiable only by their own scanners, and animal shelters couldn't keep up with the number of new scanners needed to identify every brand of microchip. Pets that were chipped before 2003 remain fine, but those that came after have less-than-universal coverage.

Q: When making a peanut butter and jelly sandwich . . .

Problems with microchipping get even more complicated when they involve human beings. It's too big of an invasion of privacy for most, and it raises complex moral and ethical issues. Still, that doesn't mean it isn't already being done.

CHIPS AHOY

In 2007, controversy swirled around a Florida-based company that announced it was partnering with caretakers of Alzheimer's disease patients to implant microchips in people impaired by the disease. Critics responded that the plan violated privacy rights and the patients weren't of sound enough mind to know what was being put in their bodies. Some loved ones and caretakers of the patients, though, disagreed and thought it was for the best—the chips would help them track down a person who'd wandered off. That debate continues.

BIONIC PEOPLE

Putting a chip in is easy. It doesn't require any cutting, just a little anesthetic and a quick shot in the arm (or wherever in the body you want to put it). Microchips are usually about the size of a grain of rice.

The chips are usually referred to as RFID, meaning "radio frequency identification." Currently, the chips themselves don't contain much data, just a unique number. Nothing else is imprinted on the chip, and there isn't a way at this time to place any kind of global positioning system or the like on it.

The number is read by a scanner outside the body, which connects the number with a Web-based database, presumably behind a firewall or some security system. That's where all the information is. Once the chips are inside the body, they usually last about 15 years before wearing out, but they can't be removed easily. Getting them out requires surgery and a tracking device, because the chips can travel inside the body. So once the chips are in, most people leave them in, even after they've worn out.

CHIPPING AWAY

In July 2004, Mexican Attorney General Rafael Macedo de la Concha and 160 of his employees were microchipped as a security measure so they could access top-secret areas of government buildings. Other workers who need access to highly secure buildings also have had microchips implanted in them.

The Department of Defense announced in 2007 that it was looking at microchips as a way to gain important health information about soldiers wounded in the field. However, the idea that the chips were going to be used to save lives didn't win over people who were worried that soldiers' privacy would be compromised. A spokesman for the Veterans of Foreign Wars was quoted as saying, "Even though you shelve some of your rights as a citizen [in the military], you don't shelve them all."

Many people flinch at the idea of putting a microchip inside their bodies, but most don't seem to mind carrying one around on the outside. Microchip technology has been used for years in automobiles, credit cards, and security systems. Smart card readers, like the ones used by employees to access the buildings they work in or by consumers who want to pay for gas by flashing a card by a reader, all use microchip technology.

In 2005, the U.S. government began including microchips in passport covers. Privacy-rights activists immediately challenged the move, but the State Department replied that the chips were not a privacy concern since a scanner had to be four inches away or closer to read them. Privacy advocates weren't convinced, and the debate continues.

In 2007, a school in South Yorkshire, United Kingdom, put microchips in students' uniforms so teachers could determine their whereabouts at any time. And retailers have begun looking into placing microchips in inventory to ward off theft.

HERE TO STAY

For many, another big concern about microchips is "swiping"—the process of thieves taking information from the microchip by intercepting the radio signal. As things stand today, that concern is more for chips outside the body because they are the ones that currently hold access to sensitive data. But any of that can change as the technology continues to develop.

So, microchips will likely continue to be a major cultural concern of the 21st century. But hopefully people won't always have to choose between their privacy and their health and safety.

THE TIP OF YOUR TONGUE AWARD

Words of the Year

Uncle John makes his living with words, so he loves them all . . . and wants to honor some of the words that seem to define the last two decades.

WORDPLAY

In 2007, the word "locavore" (a person who eats only food that has been grown or produced locally) sprang up in numerous magazines, newspapers, and blogs. Locavore was used so much that it became the *New Oxford American Dictionary* "Word of the Year."

WORD UP

The American Dialect Society (ADS), a group that studies the English language, began picking a word of the year in 1990. They assembled a board of linguists, lexicographers, etymologists, grammarians, historians, researchers, writers, and scholars to select and publish a list of words that had made the most impact on the language during the past year. The ADS says its purpose in making the list each year is to show that "language change is normal, ongoing, and entertaining." They also pick other categories, like "Most Useful" and "Most Unnecessary"—it's surprising that many of the words of the year did not fall into the latter category.

Here's a look back and a comprehensive list of the ADS words of the year:

2007: subprime—a risky loan or investment.

---

word "aftermath" was originally *aftermowth*, referring to the new growth of grass after mowing.

2006: Plutoed—to be devalued, as Pluto was when it was delisted from being a planet.

2005: truthiness—a word invented by television personality Stephen Colbert to signify something that one wants to be true, regardless of any facts that might get in the way.

2004: red/blue/purple states—based on the political maps prevalent during the year's election.

2003: metrosexual—a straight man who adopts some of the grooming and fashion habits of a gay man.

2002: WMD/weapons of mass destruction—the phrase used as justification for the war in Iraq.

2001: 9/11—the most important event of the year could also be spelled out or written "9-11."

2000: Chad—the famous "hanging chads" of the 2000 presidential election—pieces of paper punched out of ballots in the contested race—put this word to much use.

1999: Y2K—the unrealized fears surrounding the year 2000 led to this becoming one of the few obsolete words on this list; for another problem, see 1997.

1998: E-—meaning the letter that could be put in front of just about any word in the digital age: E-mail, E-money, E-commerce.

1997: millennium bug—this was reported to be the cause of the world's Y2K problems.

1996: mom—mom was chosen because of her part in the term "soccer mom."

1995: tie—World Wide Web and newt. The World Wide Web is the Internet; newt—the verb, not the amphibian—means to make a lot of changes despite being a newcomer. It's from Newt Gingrich, who became Speaker of the House in 1995.

1994: tie—Cyber and morph. Both words came about as part of the world's growing fixation with computer technology.

1993: information superhighway—the communications connections formed among various media.

1992: not!—from the Wayne and Garth *Saturday Night Live*

One acre of wheat can produce enough bread to feed a family of four for about ten years.

skits, "Not!" is a way to say that the sentence that preceded it is not true.

1991: mother of all—when Saddam Hussein invaded Kuwait in 1991, he warned that any international challenge to his country would lead to the "mother of all wars"; the phrase gained a life of its own as a result.

1990: Bushlips—a mash-up of Bush, the president, and lips, based on his "Read my lips" quote; it meant empty rhetoric on the political trail.

GLM'S GLUM CHOICES
Somewhat similar to the ADS, the Global Language Monitor (GLM) is also made up of people who study language—they analyze trends to see how words are being introduced and used. They started picking their words of the year in 2000, when the company was known as yourdictionary.com (it became GLM in 2004):

2007: hybrid

2006: sustainable

2005: refugee

2004: incivility

2003: embedded

2002: misunderestimate

2001: Ground Zero

2000: Chad

WEBSTER'S WEIGHS IN
Not to be outdone, Merriam-Webster began choosing Words of the Year in 2003. First, the dictionary ranked them according to searches users did on its Web site, and later, in 2006, the company allowed people to vote. Think of this list as the popular vote (or the People's Choice) when it comes to words of the year. In addition, Webster's system allows words (like "insurgent," for example) to get picked in more than one year:

2007
Winner: w00t—a celebratory term, pronounced "Woot!" Signifies

a victory; mostly used in online gaming activities, which is why it uses zeroes instead of "O"s.

Runners-up: Facebook, conundrum, quixotic, blamestorm (how a group will start pointing fingers at each other for something going wrong, especially in an office setting), Sardoodledom (an unrealistic and contrived story line in a work of fiction; it comes from French playwright Victorien Sardou's name), apathetic, Pecksniffian (having sleazy characteristics; from a character in a Charles Dickens story), hypocrite, charlatan

2006
Winner: truthiness
Runners-up: google, decider, war, insurgent, terrorism, vendetta, sectarian, quagmire, corruption

2005
Winner: integrity
Runners-up: refugee, contempt, filibuster, insipid, tsunami, pandemic, conclave, levee, inept

2004
Winner: blog
Runners-up: incumbent, electoral, insurgent, hurricane, cicada, peloton (a group of bicycle riders in a race), partisan, sovereignty, defenestration

2003
Winner: democracy
Runners-up: quagmire, quarantine, matrix, marriage, slog, gubernatorial, plagiarism, outage, batten
(Other dictionaries have gotten in on the act, too. We've already mentioned the *New Oxford American Dictionary* and its 2007 choice, "locavore." In 2006, the folks at *New Oxford American* chose "carbon neutral." The year before that, "podcast.")

THEM'S FIGHTIN' WORDS
Words of the year often get a great deal of criticism—sometimes from members of competing groups. When Merriam-Webster announced its selection of "w00t," the ADS Executive Secretary Allan Metcalf complained that it was "limited to a small commu-

nity and unlikely to spread and unlikely to last." And Michelle Malkin, a reporter, writer, and blogger, criticized "locavore" this way: "Shouldn't the word of the year be a word that more than four people have actually heard of?"

Of course, not everyone will agree on which word deserves "word of the year" honors. Sometimes, a word's ability to sum up the culture and mental state of the year trumps its staying power. In 2005, "refugee" took on new meaning because of Hurricane Katrina. And what else but "9/11" could have come out of 2001? We may not talk about "Bushlips" much anymore, but as a gauge of society, the word of the year is like a time capsule back to a particular year's state of mind.

* * *

A WORD BY ANY OTHER GUY

William Shakespeare introduced dozens of words and phrases into our language. It's difficult to say exactly how many, and it's also difficult to prove he was the first one to use them. Since written records from his lifetime are spotty, no one knows if Shakespeare was the first to use these or if they were common in his time and he just wrote them down. But the fact that there are so many speaks highly of Shakespeare and is at least circumstantial evidence that he was the first to use them. Here are some words and phrases we can credit Shakespeare with:

Fashionable	Pander
Sanctimonious	Outbreak
Arch-villain	Vulnerable
Method to the madness	Full circle
Bedazzle	Neither rhyme nor reason
Dauntless	One fell swoop
Go-between	A sorry sight
Lustrous	Strange bedfellows

In Canada, a southpaw is known as a "silly-sider."

THE MUD BATH AWARD

Weird Spa Treatments

*Jump on in . . . the water, beer, wine,
or chocolate—they all feel fine.*

AHHHH . . .
Spas are more popular than ever; there are currently about 14,000 of them in the United States alone, and the yearly growth rate for new spas is around 16 percent—150 million people visited spas in 2007.

The two main purposes for those visits are relaxation and beautification, so atmosphere and treatments have tended toward soft and soothing: lots of white towels, quiet New Age music, and gentle pats and pulls. In the past few years, though, spas and their treatment menus have taken a turn for the stimulating.

TWIST AND SHOUT: WATSU

Shiatsu is an ancient form of massage that involves isolating pressure points on the body and making their release relax other muscles. In 1980, Harold Dull, a Shiatsu practitioner, considered how the technique might work if it were conducted in the water. "Watsu," or "water shiatsu," was born.

In a watsu treatment, you arrive at a small, round pool in your bathing suit and meet a suited-up massage therapist who uses your body (if you don't float easily, you can attach small floats to your wrists and ankles) to manipulate your muscles through a series of balletic movements. It's not for the shy!

EGGSTRAVAGANZA: CAVIAR FACIAL

Biting into a fresh blintz topped with beluga or osetra is a pleasure for many. Having your face covered with a paste of fresh caviar might not be as great a pleasure (really, it's just a paste, and it doesn't smell), but it is food for the skin: the anti-aging properties of fish eggs make this the "Cadillac of facials." Make that the QE2 of facials . . .

SINUOUS TREATMENT: SNAKE MASSAGE

It's not an urban legend: Israeli massage therapist Ada Barak really does offer "snake massage," allowing her six nonvenomous snakes to slither across clients' backs to untangle their knotted muscles. Barak uses the California and Florida king, milk, and corn snakes because she believes that people find contact with living creatures soothing.

COLD COMFORT: SNOW AND ICE THERAPIES

The Qua Spa in Las Vegas has something a little different: a "cold room" complete with artificial snow. For anyone who's ever experienced a real Nordic sauna, this won't seem like too much of a shock: cooling down rapidly after a sauna or hot tub soak can be invigorating. With mint-scented air, snow drifting from the ceiling, and an ice fountain, this spa feature has a certain . . . je ne sais "Qua."

CHOCOLICIOUS: CHOCOLATE FONDUE WRAP

It might smell and feel as if you're being coated in thick, rich chocolate, but the Chocolate Fondue Wrap at Spa Hershey in Hershey, Pennsylvania, is actually a mixture of skin-renewing "moor mud" (the mud of European moors) and cocoa essence. Chocolate spa treatments have become so popular that chocolate-scented lotions, gels, powders, and candles are available in most bath and beauty stores. Just don't try nibbling on the candy bar-shaped soaps.

BEAUTY ON TAP: BEER BATHS

Many a man might believe a beer bath to be the height of happiness, but the Bodvar Brewery Spa in the Czech Republic doesn't offer beer baths so the bather can get a buzz from the fumes. It's so he or she can enjoy circulatory and exfoliant benefits for the skin. (Anyone who wants a buzz at Bodvar can access a tub-side bar, ready to dispense a pint of the cold stuff to enhance the warm bath.)

There are 6 universal facial expressions: Happiness, sadness, disgust, fear, anger, and surprise.

CONE HEAD: EAR CANDLING

Ear candling has been around for centuries, but in the last couple of decades it's become a "hot" spa treatment. A therapist at the spa inserts a narrow cone of waxed muslin into the spa-goer's ear and then lights the other end. The gentle suction supposedly draws out earwax and debris. Medical professionals have their doubts about whether or not ear candling is effective, but they believe when done by a spa or medical professional it's harmless.

FIRED UP: CUPPING

Cupping is a form of acupressure in which a flame is used to create a vacuum between a small glass cup and a person's skin. It can leave large, red, circular welts, but its fans swear by the treatment, saying it raises their energy levels and reduces musculoskeletal pain. Many spas now offer cupping treatments, and there are various methods. One that should never be considered in a spa setting is the old practice of "wet cupping," in which a small slit is cut in the skin, first. That can cause infection. So if you see your aesthetician with a scalpel, run the other way.

VINTAGE SOAK: WINE BATH

We've all heard about the benefits of tannins for the inside of the body, but now we can experience them on the outside. Cleopatra supposedly bathed in red wine, and the Hakone Yunessun Spa west of Tokyo, Japan, allows visitors to bathe in a pool that mixes water with Beaujolais Nouveau. The pool is replenished several times a day. The rest of the day, a 3.6 meter faux wine bottle "pours" and aerates the spa waters. Visitors can also drink glasses of the red wine while they soak.

FEET FIRST: "DR. FISH" FOOT BATHS

Got eczema? Psoriasis? The fish are ready to see you . . . the *garra rufa* or "doctor fish" footbath has become popular at many Asian spas. Soak your feet in shallow water while dozens of tiny doctor fish nibble away at the dead skin. According to one spa's Web site, the doctor fish cleaning "is not painful, because fishes have no teeth."

THE "CALL ME ISHMAEL" AWARD

Great Opening Lines from Novels

Sometimes the first sentence is all you need to keep reading.

LITERATURE'S OPENING GAMBITS

The first line of a book can tell you a lot about the rest of story. For example, when you read the opening line of *Pride and Prejudice* by Jane Austen, "It is a truth universally acknowledged, that a single man in possession of a good fortune, must be in want of a wife," you know that you're in for a comedy of manners that will include discussions of marriage.

Other times, the first line of a book tells you almost nothing, but is so intriguing and seductive that you want to keep reading to find out more. For example, Toni Morrison's opening line for *Beloved*—"124 was spiteful" leaves you wondering . . . Who or what is 124? Why was 124 spiteful? What has been done to 124? You're hooked.

Getting hooked is the universal truth about great first lines. When you read one, you know you're in the hands of a great writer.

READER, SHE MARRIES HIM

The opening line mentioned above from *Pride and Prejudice* says many things with just one sentence: Austen declared her subject to be courtship and marriage, established an ironic tone, and set the scene for a "chase" between men and women. We may already know that Elizabeth Bennet marries Mr. Darcy—but this line makes us eager to know how that ending came to be.

TRAIN OF THOUGHT

"Happy families are all alike; every unhappy family is unhappy

---

Snakes were once called "nadders," until a misspelling turned them into "adders."

in its own way." How did Leo Tolstoy know there would be so many memoirs written in the 21st century? This first line of his great work *Anna Karenina* is meant to ground the Karenin family in its own particular torment, but its psychological truth is so powerful that it is quoted by people who have never even read the novel.

FIGHTING WORDS

First doesn't always mean brief:

> It was the best of times, it was the worst of times, it was the age of wisdom, it was the age of foolishness, it was the epoch of belief, it was the epoch of incredulity, it was the season of Light, it was the season of Darkness, it was the spring of hope, it was the winter of despair . . .

Thus begins Charles Dickens's 1859 *A Tale of Two Cities*, about the French Revolution. Even without its famous twin closing line ("It is a far, far better thing to do than I have ever done; it is a far, far better rest that I go to than I have ever known"), this line sets the tone perfectly for a story of all these things battling within two lookalike but very different men: Charles Darnay and Sydney Carton.

LUST FOR LIFE

There's no doubt about what is driving the narrator of Vladimir Nabokov's book: "Lolita, light of my life, fire of my loins." Sounds like a steamy romance, says the reader—and then he discovers that the fire of Humbert Humbert's loins is all of 12 years old. Cue the "ew" factor, but by this time, you're less focused on Lolita's youth and more fascinated by Humbert's reckless, life-shattering compulsion.

ANOTHER COUNTRY

Sometimes an opening line gains status as a saying stripped of its original context. "The past is a foreign country; they do things differently there," wrote L. P. Hartley in his 1953 novel *The Go-Between* (adapted into a 1971 movie by playwright Harold Pinter). Does anyone read Hartley any more, except for a students of Modern British Literature? But Hartley's opening line captures an essential human truth, especially for the English. Disillusioned by

World War I, exhausted by World War II, and tired from still-imposed rationing, to them the past was vanished.

TEEN ANGST

Meanwhile, on the other side of the Atlantic, Holden Caulfield, the 20th century's most famous teenager, began his story:

> If you really want to hear about it, the first thing you'll probably want to know is where I was born, and what my lousy childhood was like, and how my parents were occupied and all before they had me, and all that David Copperfield kind of crap, but I don't feel like going into it, if you want to know the truth.

You're hooked and want to know what Mr. Caulfield will tell you.

TURNING UP THE HEAT

"It was a pleasure to burn," begins Ray Bradbury's science-fiction classic *Fahrenheit 451*. His protagonist, Fireman Guy Montag, is talking about burning books. However, Bradbury wasn't talking about the kind of book burning the Nazis did, or about censorship. He said famously that his book was about what happens when people come to rely more on television for their information and forget about facts. In that case, Bradbury implied, you might as well burn all the books because they take up space and getting rid of them becomes a productive task . . . like mowing the lawn or filing papers.

MORE OR LESS

When Kurt Vonnegut opened his groundbreaking *Slaughterhouse-Five* with the sentence "All this is true, more or less," he wasn't yet speaking in the voice of the novel's protagonist, Billy Pilgrim, but in his own. One of the things that make this sci-fi modernist novel so important is that it's also the story of the author trying to come to terms with his participation as a young soldier in the fire-bombing of Dresden during World War II and his incarceration in a German prisoner-of-war camp. What was true? What was false? Even the narrator wasn't sure.

SOUTHERN GOTHIC

"In the town, there were two mutes, and they were always together," begins *The Heart Is A Lonely Hunter*, Carson McCullers's 1940 novel. Although the book has three distinct parts, this sentence gives us the place, its oddness, and its sense of community. The two deaf men, Spiros and John, are true outcasts: one is an immigrant and mentally unstable; the other is a possible Jew, and a possible homosexual. McCullers was an early bard of the underdog, and this memorable first line emphasizes her quiet compassion.

PURPLE PROSE

Alice Walker's 1982 *The Color Purple* was a literary landmark for several reasons: its attention to individual fates of African Americans, its sensitivity to different kinds of sexuality, and in large part because of its masterful use of dialect. The opening line is "You better not never tell nobody but God." The double negative, the urgency, and the reference to a divinity all indicate a novel concerned with authenticity rather than style.

POSTMODERN POSTER BOY

"Once upon a time and a very good time it was there was a moocow coming down along the road and this moocow that was coming down along the road met a nicens little boy named baby tuckoo." No, it's not a line from Dr. Seuss; it's the opening of *Portrait of the Artist As a Young Man* by James Joyce, published in 1916. Readers know immediately that this is a book unlike any other, and that's the point: you either keep reading or you don't. Joyce has no need to pander or seduce—he's truly the artist, all grown up.

BELLY OF THE BEAST

"Call me Ishmael," wrote Herman Melville in 1851 as the beginning to *Moby Dick*, his epic story of man versus whale. But why has this simple declaration remained so famous and so compelling? By telling us immediately that he is adopting the name of a Biblical orphan, the narrator indicates he's an outsider and may not view events in the same way as the other characters.

IT PRINTS THE WORST OF LINES

Given that opening lines are so often memorable, it was inevitable that someone would start lampooning them. The Bulwer-Lytton Fiction Contest can be found online at www.bulwer-lytton.com, "Where WWW means 'Wretched Writers Welcome.'"

Why Bulwer-Lytton? You may not recognize the name, but you'll certainly recognize the opening line, from Edgar Bulwer-Lytton's (justly) forgotten 1830 novel *Paul Clifford*:

> It was a dark and stormy night; the rain fell in torrents— except at occasional intervals, when it was checked by a violent gust of wind which swept up the streets (for it is in London that our scene lies), rattling along the housetops, and fiercely agitating the scanty flame of the lamps that struggled against the darkness.

Such extravagant prose, so many digressions, and so little information apart from the fact that a) it's raining and b) we're in London. No wonder San Jose State University professor Scott Rice chose Bulwer-Lytton as the figurehead for his bad-writing contest, held annually since 1982.

* * *

A GOLDEN PLUNGER TO ANYONE WHO DOESN'T GIVE A BORING ACCEPTANCE SPEECH

"I'm not going to thank anybody; I'm just going to say I damn well deserve it."

—Humphrey Bogart, 1952, after winning for
The African Queen

"I can't deny the fact that you like me, right now, you like me! You really like me!"

—Sally Field, 1985, after winning for
Places in the Heart

"I just want to thank everybody I've ever met in my entire life."

—Kim Basinger, 1998, after winning for
L.A. Confidential

THE TROJAN HORSE AWARD

Allspice

Contrary to what its name suggests, allspice is not a mixture of different spices. Its unique flavor comes from dried fruit, and it gets an award for being the sneakiest of spices.

TAKE A WHIFF

Allspice's spicy aroma hints of nutmeg, pepper, ginger, juniper, cloves, and cinnamon—all spices. As a result, people assume that it's a spice blend when it really comes from a berry. Cooks use it as both a sweet and savory seasoning, but allspice is worthy of distinction for its strong flavor and its rich history.

A SPICY STORY

Spanish explorers in the West Indies discovered the evergreen tree *Pimenta dioica* in the early 16th century. The tree's white flowers develop berries that are picked and dried in the sun to give us allspice. It takes four to five years for a Pimenta tree to bear fruit, and the berries have to be picked at just the right time, before they ripen, because the fruit's flavor exists mostly in the rind of the unripe berries. When the berries do ripen, they lose a lot of their aromatic properties. The tree grows wild only in the Western hemisphere and is produced (for commercial use) primarily in Jamaica, Guatemala, Honduras, and Mexico.

South Americans have used allspice for centuries as a meat curative and as a flavoring for chocolate. The spice came to Europe in the early 17th century, and soon it was called "English spice" because the English were its largest distributor (having colonized Jamaica in 1655). In 1693, Europeans started calling it allspice—a name chosen to convey the multiple spices it seemed to contain—and the popular misnomer stuck.

The three biggest party days in the U.S.: New Year's Eve, Super Bowl Sunday, and Halloween

Over the years, different cultures have adapted allspice to particular uses. It remains most popular in the Caribbean, where it flavors jerk dishes, but it's also used to flavor sausage in Germany, stews in the Middle East, and cakes in England. In Scandinavian countries, it's used to marinate herring.

ALTERNATIVE MEDICINE

Some also swear by allspice's medicinal properties. It has a mild anesthetic quality, sometimes relieves arthritis pain, and has been used as an aphrodisiac. People also add it to hot tea to eliminate gas pains and other digestive problems.

For more than 400 years, French monks of the Order of Chartreuse have made their namesake elixir, and allspice has been cited as a secret ingredient. Legend says that a French diplomat named François Annibal d'Estrées gave them the recipe in 1605. It includes 130 plants, herbs, roots, and leaves in a brandy base. Rumored to deliver long life, the elixir definitely delivers a strong punch—it's 142 proof, or 71 percent alcohol by volume. It quickly became popular among locals. A less-potent version, green chartreuse—a mere 55 proof—was made available to those who wanted it for its medicinal effect. It's still available today, as is yellow chartreuse, a slightly stronger version (80 proof). The monks continue to sell the liqueur to finance their monastery.

Allspice can also be found in another herbal liqueur: Benedictine, a cognac-based beverage with herbs and roots. It was first developed in the 16th century for Benedictine monks and is still around. On the bottle is the phrase *Deo Optimo Maximo* ("to God, most good, most great"). A lovely sentiment for allspice too.

PUNGENT PARTICULARS

• During the Napoleonic wars, Russian soldiers put allspice in their boots to keep their feet warm. The spice made their feet smell better too, and allspice got a reputation for being a men's toiletry item. Today, its oil still turns up in colognes, aftershaves, and other things with "spice" in the title.

• The Mayans used allspice to embalm corpses.

THE BETTER BUSINESS AWARD

Newman's Own

It began as a mix of oil and vinegar in Butch Cassidy's bathtub.
It ended as a way to raise millions of dollars for
children's camps and other charities.

SHARP DRESSER

In December 1980, Paul Newman made a batch of home-made salad dressing (a mustardy vinegarette) in a bathtub in the basement of his Westport, Connecticut, home. He called his friend, writer A. E. Hotchner, and asked him to help fill old wine bottles with the dressing, which he intended to give to his neighbors as Christmas gifts.

Newman had been making his own salad dressing for years. He was never happy with store brands (too many chemicals, sweeteners, and artificial products), and in restaurants he'd often go into the kitchen and mix up his own.

After filling up a few dozen bottles, Newman and Hotchner found themselves with half of a bathtub of dressing left over. Newman figured he could bottle the rest, sell them to a local upscale grocery store, and pocket some cash. It never happened. Newman and Hotchner got sidetracked with the holidays, and Newman spent most of the next year filming *Absence of Malice*.

THE VERDICT

Newman still thought his dressing was good enough to sell commercially. In 1982, he approached several food companies and bottling plants, but none were interested. So Newman and Hotchner decided to do it themselves. Newman put up $40,000 in seed money, leaving now and again to go film *The Verdict*, while Hotchner tried to get the company off the ground.

Deciding that they should probably taste-test their dressing before they spent a lot of time and money marketing it, Newman and Hotchner arranged a test against bestselling dressings at the kitchen of a Connecticut caterer named Martha Stewart (yes, that Martha Stewart). Of about two dozens ballots, Newman's was judged the best on all but two—not bad for a homemade dressing. Newman left the tasting ecstatic, declaring himself "the salad king of New England." Hotchner and Newman decided that Salad King would be the name of the business, and the next day they formed Salad King Inc.

SOMETHING STEWING

A friend put Newman in touch with Stew Leonard, owner and manager of Stew Leonard's, the biggest supermarket in Norwalk, a town near Newman's home of Westport. He told Newman that he liked the dressing and it was good enough to sell, but there was one problem: It would flop if he called it Salad King. And he said, in order for the dressing to sell, Newman's face would have to be on the bottle. Newman's response: "Not a chance in hell."

Stew Leonard was the nation's top seller of Ken's Steakhouse salad dressing. He told Newman and Hotchner that if Newman put his face on the bottle, he'd get the Ken's bottler to package 2,000 test cases and he'd sell it at his store with a huge promotion. Newman remained uninterested.

THE HUSTLER

A few days later, Newman and Hotchner were fishing on Newman's boat, the *Caca de Toro*. They were at an impasse. Newman didn't want to plaster his face on the bottle. He thought it was crass, and similar to appearing on TV talk shows to promote his movies. He just wanted to make his all-natural dressing, call it Salad King, and put it in stores without calling attention to the fact that it was created by one of the world's biggest movie stars. Hotchner suggested they just forget the whole thing. Newman had another idea: he'd put himself on the bottle, but give the proceeds to charity. Hotchner agreed.

The pair devised a Napoleonic "N" logo for the bottle, accompanying a picture of Newman wearing a laurel wreath. They also

tween 1520–1630, some 30,000 people were reported to French authorities for being werewolves.

created a slogan: "Fine Foods Since February." And the name of the dressing was officially changed from Salad King to "Newman's Own."

Stew Leonard held up his end of the deal. He got Ken's to produce 2,000 cases of dressing and held a promotion at his store in May 1982. He put a sign in front that said "Welcome Paul Newman." Hundreds packed the store. And in two weeks, Stew Leonard's had sold 10,000 bottles of Newman's Own dressing.

What began as a lark quickly became a real business. Newman's Own rented an office above a bank in Westport and furnished it with the actor's patio furniture. In late 1982, the brand expanded with the introduction of a pasta sauce. In 1983, its first full year of business, Newman's Own recorded sales of $3.2 million, with a profit of $397,000.

THE TOP TOMATO

Over the past 25 years, Newman's Own has grown into one of the bestselling salad dressing lines, but also one of the first companies to offer nationally available all-natural—and even organic—products. In addition to dressing and pasta sauce, Newman's Own makes salsa, popcorn, juice, cookies, cereal, coffee, mints, and pet food.

All of those products have raised more than $200 million in profits. Newman had no idea that the proceeds he'd pledged to charity would amount to so much. True to his word, he (and Hotchner) have given away every penny. While the company is secretive about which charities it funds, it is very vocal about its complete financial support of the Hole in the Wall Gang Camps, summer camps for children with life-threatening illnesses. There are five in the U.S. and two in Europe and it costs nothing for the 13,000 campers who annually attend.

*   *   *

"The embarrassing thing is that the salad dressing is outgrossing my films."

—Paul Newman

THE RUN FOR THE ROSES AWARD

Empress Josephine

Even in wartime, Napoleon promised her a rose garden.

A ROSE BY ANY OTHER NAME

Marie-Joseph-Rose de Tascher de la Pagerie—also known as Rose—was born in 1763 on her family's Martinique sugar plantation, where she acquired her love for gardening. At 14, she was married off to a rich young army officer, the Vicomte Alexandre de Beauharnais, and they moved to Paris. She bore him two children, but he was ashamed of her provincial ways and was so indifferent to her that she eventually obtained a separation. After lingering three more years in Paris, she returned home in 1788, where she remained until until a 1790 slave uprising forced her to return to Paris, now in the throes of the French Revolution.

In spite of their estrangement, her life was endangered when her husband, who'd been serving in the Revolutionary army, fell out of favor and was guillotined in 1794. Joséphine herself was imprisoned, and then released.

ROSES RULE

No longer unsophisticated, Joséphine caught the eye of Napoleon Bonaparte, then a rising young army officer, and they married in 1796. When Josephine paid 325,000 francs for a run-down country house outside of Paris, appropriately named Malmaison or "bad house," Napoleon was furious. Josephine's extravagances would continue to put a strain on their marriage as time went on.

Meanwhile, Josephine was tending her garden and filling it with her namesake—roses. Her passion for roses left a floral legacy that lives on in one of the most important rose books ever published and, more importantly, in gardens worldwide.

. . . In 2006 William Shatner's kidney stone sold for $25,000.

ROSE RENAISSANCE

Empress Josephine's passion for gardening was new and unfashionable when she began the garden in 1798. But she was determined to make her gardens both unforgettable and meaningful, and in the 16 years she kept them, she created a kind of "rose renaissance."

Josephine was growing as many species of plants as she could. She introduced 200 plant species to France including jasmine, camellia, and phlox, as well as dahlias, tree peonies, and magnolias. She ordered plants from the best suppliers and spent as much money as she wanted on them (and was always in debt; when she died, her debts amounted to 2½ million francs). Even while France was at war with England and the continent was under continuous blockade, Josephine bought her plants from the London nursery Kennedy & Lee, persuading Napoleon to issue Mr. Kennedy a passport and papers of safe conduct. The Emperor was so obliging, in fact, that he often brought seeds and plants captured from British ships back home for her, including some new ones discovered by Captain James Cook in Australia.

Mr. Kennedy also assisted the Empress in the plan and layout of her gardens. Josephine's goal was to bring every rose in existence to the chateau's garden.

CULTIVATED TASTES

Josephine didn't simply collect roses; she cultivated them, too. Previously, roses had been grown as an aromatic and medicinal plant; Josephine created interest in growing them for their beauty. Her garden's reputation ignited an interest in rose growing so strong that by 1815, France had become a leading grower and exporter of roses, and by 1830, there were over 2,500 varieties.

As rose enthusiasts know, the increase in the number of species comes from cross-pollination and seed production. Josephine's gardener, Monsieur Dupont, gets as much credit as his flower-hungry employer in the craze for rose propagation. Dupont was one of the earliest cultivators of roses from seed, which helped to strengthen certain cultivars.

During Josephine's residence at Malmaison, Dupont amassed

nearly 260 rose species and cultivars. Dupont passed on this legacy to Alexandre Hardy, who took over the Luxembourg Garden in Paris and raised many roses we still grow today, including 'Mme. Hardy' and 'Safrano.'

THE REDOUBTABLE REDOUTÉ

Another of Josephine's legacies was commissioning Pierre-Joseph Redouté to paint the roses in her collection and hiring leading botanists to describe the plants in accompanying texts. Redouté had been the court painter to Queen Marie-Antoinette, but despite the Revolution, survived to become Josephine's rose painter. The Empress paid him 180,000 francs per year to catalog her living collection.

Redouté's work, *Les Roses*, was completed after Josephine's death. The three volumes, issued between 1817 and 1824, are among the most important rose books ever published. (Some consider Redouté's "Blush Noisette" to be the masterpiece of botanical illustration.) It is still used to identify older varieties of roses, and many of the included species can still be found in today's gardens.

A ROSE IS A ROSE, TO A "ROSE"

By all accounts, Napoleon adored Josephine, but her flirtations, her extravagance, and her inability to bear Napoleon a son strained their marriage, which Napoleon had annulled in 1810.

Joséphine retreated to her private residence at Malmaison. She continued to entertain lavishly, with the emperor paying the bills. After Napoleon's abdication she won the protection of the Russian emperor Alexander I, but she died soon after.

Napoleon died in exile on Elba in 1812, and Josephine died in 1814, but both they and her children from her first marriage live on in roses that exist in great part due to the Malmaison gardens.

Two roses named "Josephine de Beauharnais" and one named "Empress Josephine" exist, all of which have light pink blossoms and originated in France. "Madness at Corsica/Napoleon" is pink. "Hortense de Beauharnais," named after Josephine's daughter, is pink, while "Eugene de Beauharnaise," after her son, is a mauve-colored climbing rose.

THE COMEBACK AWARD

Cryogenics

The quest for mastering lower temperatures led to some amazing discoveries—and some people see them as a way to bring life back after death.

CRYOGENICS IN THE OLD DAYS

As early as 1823, scientists were looking at ways to create extreme low temperatures with gases. Two British chemists, Sir Humphry Davy and, later, his assistant Michael Faraday, spent more than two decades—between 1823 and 1845—whipping up a cold concoction involving carbon dioxide, ether, and test tubes.

It's a complex process to make gases so cold that they liquefy, but they did it, and they managed to get the carbon dioxide to drop down to a temperature of -166°F. In 1877, two French physicists improved on Davy and Faraday's work—the Frenchmen were able to get oxygen to liquefy. From then on, scientists from European countries spent several decades experimenting with more and more gases, like hydrogen and helium. Today, cryogenics deals with temperatures ranging between -238°F and -459.67°F (absolute zero).

The pursuits of these early cryogenic scientists were not just for fun. It was serious business because many of them considered cryogenics to be the answer to humanity's greatest mystery—death. Cryogenics didn't hold all the answers to life after death, but it did, some contended, hold the ability to make death a temporary condition. This is still the prevailing theory of cryogenics: If you can use the technology to freeze a person, maybe you can bring him back later on.

A CHILL IN THE AIR

People commonly refer to cryogenics as a way to preserve a human

---

Q: When is the only time that a soldier is not required to salute? A: When he is a prisoner.

body after death, but the correct term when applied to people is "cryonics." And the real question a person considering cryonics faces is this: If you want to be frozen after death (and by law, you must wait until you have been officially pronounced dead) you must first make a choice—do you want to freeze just your head, or do you want to keep your whole body?

Usually, the deciding factor is money. Freezing just your head will cost about $80,000. Freezing your whole body costs more than $150,000. (There's also an annual fee for preservation and storage, so many patients set up a trust fund to keep payments up in perpetuity.) The folks who choose to go bodyless presume that when science has advanced enough to bring your head out of the cryonic soup, it will also be far enough along to regrow your missing body.

Those who opt for crynoics are also betting on a few more scientific outcomes: 1) a cure for whatever killed them in the first place; 2) a way to reverse the aging process so they're not right back in the freezer; and 3) the ability to undo the damage done by the cryonics.

In the least case, that damage could be substantial, so doctors try to stave it off by taking a few steps right after the person has died. The first step, as soon as possible after death has occurred, is for the cryonic scientists to artificially restart the breathing and blood circulation process. Then the cooling process begins. Chemicals called cryopectants are added to (theoretically) prevent the brain from freezing completely. Finally, the body (or head) is placed in a titanium steel vat of liquid nitrogen. From there, the remains are stored, and the next step is to wait . . . and wait.

Cryonics was first performed in 1967—the first person to undergo the procedure was a psychologist named Dr. James Bedford. Over the past four decades, about 100 more people have chosen it.

FAMOUS FACES IN CRYONICS
Companies that practice cryonics are committed to preserving anonymity, so rumors about which celebrities chose the procedure are rampant. But we got the frozen scoop on two of them:

- Walt Disney—the man behind the mouse died in 1966, and ever since then, stories have persisted that his body was cryonically frozen. Some say he's even lying in liquid nitrogen in the catacombs below Disneyland. Not so. He was cremated.

- Ted Williams—the baseball great died in 2002, and his son hired an Arizona cryonics firm to freeze Williams's head.

THE PRACTICAL SIDE OF CRYOGENICS

Cryogenics is not just a theoretical method to cheat death. It also has practical applications that humans use today. Here are a few:

- Cryosurgery—using extreme cold to treat disease, doctors are able to fight illness by selectively killing off harmful tissues and cells. It's been used as treatment for Parkinson's disease, brain tumors, and cervical cancer.

- Nuclear power—cryogenics is used to keep hydrogen and helium in liquid form, both of which are needed for nuclear fusion.

- Frozen foods—liquid nitrogen cools foods so quickly and completely that it's the safest way to freeze food immediately. It also keeps the foods frozen while they're transported to stores.

- Fertilizers—liquid nitrogen is a key ingredient for some fertilizers.

- Space travel—making oxygen a liquid can help to create a breathable atmosphere to be used in space shuttles.

*   *   *

SNOOPY'S SEVEN SIBLINGS

As Snoopy once said, he was born "one bright spring morning at the Daisy Hill Puppy Farm." There were seven other puppies born along with Snoopy that day. The most familiar was Spike, his fedora-wearing and mustached brother from Needles, California. Like pink-hued sister Belle (from Kansas City), Spike can play the violin. Marbles, the smartest of the litter, plays the banjo, and overweight Olaf wins an ugly-dog contest. Andy is the shaggiest; he and Olaf live together on a farm.

The last puppy pair, a boy and a girl, are never named in the strip. But they did get names when they appeared in the 1991 television cartoon, *Snoopy's Family Reunion*. Molly and Rover play the dobro and the mandolin.

THE "OUT OF MY CONTROL" AWARD

Bodily Functions

Ah, the body. What a strange and wonderful machine it is.
Sometimes, though, it's just baffling—or embarrassing.

HICCUPS

When the diaphragm muscle contracts involuntary, you've got the hiccups. The diaphragm is the muscle you use to breathe—it contracts to pull in air and expands to expel your exhalations. No one knows exactly why it spasms and contracts involuntarily. But when it does, it causes you to make an embarrassing noise that's caused by the quick closing of the opening between the vocal chords. In the vast majority of cases, hiccups last only a few minutes and aren't serious. But consider this: some hiccups cases can last for days, weeks, or even years and can be the result of serious afflictions, like pneumonia or kidney failure.

BRAIN FREEZE

It's hard to say no to a scoop of ice cream, but knowledgeable eaters know to fear the brain freeze—the quick headache that comes from eating cold food too fast. When something freezing cold touches the roof of the mouth, it sets off a chain reaction in the nerves of the head. The blood vessels immediately begin to contract to hold blood in, and then they swell, releasing a relatively large stampede of blood. And there you go . . . brain freeze. For most people, the brain freeze is gone within 60 seconds, but sometimes it can last up to five minutes. Ice cream and other cold treats may be worth the temporary pain, but still . . . slow down and chill—or drink something warm. That can help too.

SLEEPING FEET

Feet, don't fail me now . . . whoops, they already did. Sitting too

---

Pretzels that have no salt on them are called "baldies."

long in a way that cuts off circulation also cuts off communication between the nerves and the brain. The signals between the two get all jumbled, creating that all too familiar tingling feeling. Any part of the body, not just feet, can be affected by this, and the tingling sensation acts as a warning to switch positions to prevent doing any damage. Most people who move are back to normal within a few seconds (though it can take several moments for the nerves to return to normal and start sending out their regular messages). But beware of the condition known as Saturday Night Palsy: Intoxication (or some other condition) can put the body into a deep slumber, and people have been known to sleep right through the nerves' desperate messages to get up and move. In those rare case, it can takes days or even months to undo the damage. Something to think about when you're sitting for too long.

BELCHES
Ah, gas. The world would be a much duller place without it. And there's no getting around it, really. When you eat, you use the same mouth that you breathe with, and you can't help but take in air with your dinner. That air gets in the stomach and doesn't really have anywhere to go but back the way it came. It travels up through the esophagus and makes its rude little reentrance into the world. If burps really bother you, just be glad you don't have to hang around Brit Paul Hunn. He's in the *Guinness World Records* for having the loudest belch—118.1 decibels, about as loud as an airplane taking off.

FARTS
Ah, gas . . . oh, wait, we already said that. Well, it's still true. There's no shortage of gas in the body. The aforementioned oxygen that creeps into the stomach is one, and there are also blood gases and gases produced by bacteria inside the body. So much gas, in fact, that sometimes it just has to get out. And if it doesn't go out through the mouth, there's really only one other way it can go. The combination of gases produced are different depending on what you've eaten and what bacteria are inside your body, but the smell is usually from sulfur compounds. Oh, and beans may make you toot, but it turns out they're not very sulfuric, so discharges caused by them won't smell as bad. Something to chew on.

THE BATHROOM ACCESSORY AWARD

Rubber Ducky

On water or land, here's why a rubber duck is always welcome.

A TOY WITH STAYING POWER

No citation exists for the first rubber duck, but they've been around since at least the early 1800s, when they were hard and nonsqueaking rubber toys. Today, they're big business, and though they've retained the name "rubber ducks" since the 1950s, nowadays these bath-time playthings are made mostly of plastic.

Rubber ducks have always been fun toys, but since the 1970s, they've become an obsession for some. Ernie on *Sesame Street* was "awfully fond" of his, but some people take collecting to an extreme, amassing them by the hundreds and even thousands. Charlotte Lee of Santa Monica, California, holds the current world record in rubber duck collecting—she's amassed more than 2,600 of the little guys over the years. (That's a lot more than the few dozen that sit on our widowsills here at the BRI.)

ON YOUR MARK, GET SET . . . QUACK!

Every year, thousands of people participate in rubber duck races around the country. The largest, the Derby Duck Races, is held exclusively for charity. The first such race was in 1988, the brainchild of Eric Schechter, president of Great American Merchandising and Events (GAME). Since then, the races have raised over $140 million, and continue to raise more than $10 million per year. That's a lot of ducks—and bucks.

World's oldest working post office: Sanquer, Scotland (in continuous operation since 1712).

CREATIVE CANARDS

In 2007, an outdoor art exhibit in France called "Loire Estuary 2007" provided an opportunity for Dutch artist Florentijn Hofman to create one of the biggest rubber ducks on record—80 feet high! Hofman extolled the healing virtues of his "Canard de Bain," saying the giant mallard did not discriminate, did not have political views, and was basically just good for the soul to look at. The duck floated in the Loire River until the exhibit closed in September 2007.

Estonian sculptor Villu Jaanisoo created a giant rubber duck completely out of old tires in 2003. It's on display at the Retretti Art Center in Punkaharju, Finland, but unfortunately, it's a duck out of water—it rests on land.

* * *

TIME MAGAZINE'S PERSON OF THE YEAR

2007 Vladimir Putin

2006 You (Internet user-generated content)

2005 Good Samaritans (Bono, Bill and Melinda Gates)

2004 George W. Bush

2003 The American Soldier

2002 Corporate Whistleblowers

2001 Rudolph Giuliani

2000 George W. Bush

1999 Jeff Bezos of Amazon.com

1998 Bill Clinton and Kenneth Starr

1997 Andy Grove of Intel

1996 AIDS researcher David Ho

1995 Newt Gingrich

1994 Pope John Paul II

1993 Yasser Arafat, Yitzhak Rabin, Nelson Mandela, and F. W. de Klerk

1992 Bill Clinton

1991 Ted Turner

1990 George Bush

1989 Mikhail Gorbachev

1988 The Endangered Earth

1987 Mikhail Gorbachev

1986 Philippines president Corazon Aquino

1985 Chinese leader Deng Xiaoping

1984 Baseball commissioner Peter Ueberroth

1983 Ronald Reagan and Yuri Andropov

1982 The Computer

1981 Polish politician Lech Walesa

1980 Ronald Reagan

1979 Ayatollah Khomeini

Also available
from *Uncle John's
Bathroom Reader!*

THE LAST PAGE

FELLOW BATHROOM READERS:
The fight for good bathroom reading should never be taken loosely—we must do our duty and sit firmly for what we believe in, even while the rest of the world is taking potshots at us.

We'll be brief. Now that we've proven we're not simply a flush-in-the-pan, we invite you to take the plunge: Sit Down and Be Counted! Become a member of the Bathroom Readers' Institute. Log on to *www.bathroomreader.com*, or send a self-addressed, stamped, business-sized envelope to: BRI, PO Box 1117, Ashland, Oregon 97520. You'll receive your free membership card, get discounts when ordering directly through the BRI, and earn a permanent spot on the BRI honor roll!

If you like reading our books...
VISIT THE BRI'S WEB SITE!
www.bathroomreader.com

- Visit "The Throne Room"—a great place to read!
  - Receive our irregular newsletters via e-mail
    - Order additional *Bathroom Readers*
      - Become a BRI member

Keep on flushin'...

Well, we're out of space, and when you've gotta go, you've gotta go. Tanks for all your support. Hope to hear from you soon. Meanwhile, remember...

Go with the Flow!